KHMER AMERICAN

Identity and Moral Education
in a Diasporic Community

Nancy J. Smith-Hefner

University of California Press
Berkeley · *Los Angeles* · *London*

University of California Press
Berkeley and Los Angeles, California

University of California Press, Ltd.
London, England

© 1999 by the Regents of the University of California

Library of Congress Cataloging-in-Publication Data

Smith-Hefner, Nancy Joan.
    Khmer American : identity and moral education in a
diasporic community / Nancy J. Smith-Hefner.
      p. cm.
    Includes bibliographic references and index.
    ISBN 0-520-21348-3 (cloth : alk. paper)—
ISBN 0-520-21349-1 (pbk. : alk. paper)
    1. Cambodian Americans—Massachusetts—
Boston—Ethnic identity.   2. Cambodian Americans—
Massachusetts—Boston—Religion. 3. Boston (Mass.)—
Ethnic relations   I. Title.
F73.9.K45S65   1999
305.895'93074461—dc 21   97-51812

Printed in the United States of America

08 07 06 05
9 8 7 6 5 4 3

The paper used in this publication meets the minimum
requirements of ANSI / NISO Z39.48-1992 (R 1997)
(Permanence of Paper). ∞

KHMER AMERICAN

*For my parents,
Joan D. and William T. Smith*

Contents

Preface	ix
Acknowledgments	xvii
A Note on Transliteration	xix
1: Identity and Transition	1
2: To Be Khmer Is to Be Buddhist	21
3: Early Socialization: Observing the Child	64
4: Moral Education: The Child within the Family	94
5: Schooling in America	123
6: Sexuality and Marriage	151
7: The Search for the Middle Path	187
Notes	209
References	219
Index	231

Illustrations follow p. 122

Preface

On a warm Saturday morning in the summer of 1987, I attended the first of the many Khmer weddings I would witness in years to come. The bride's parents lived on the west side of Boston, in a part of town that looked like many other working-class neighborhoods in the city. There were the familiar rows of run-down brownstone apartments with crumbling cement steps; a small corner store with a sign in the window, *Se Habla Español*; and a busy laundromat. Cars parked bumper-to-bumper lined both sides of the streets, and mountains of garbage awaited pickup on the sidewalks. The scene was not that different or far from where I had lived when I first moved to Boston (in 1982) and began teaching at the University of Massachusetts.

As my Khmer companion and I continued down the street, sidestepping playing children and piles of garbage, I suddenly became aware of an incongruous sound that rose above the din of the scene around us. The sweetly high-pitched, slightly nasal melody of a Khmer wedding song came drifting from an open apartment window several stories above the street. A young man leaning against a shiny new car parked in front of the building greeted my friend politely in Khmer, "*Chŭmriep suo, bâng.*" Pressing his two hands together in front of his face and bowing slightly, he indicated that we had come to the right address. We rang the downstairs bell and followed the music up a steep stairway and through a dark hall. We knocked, and the door opened to a very different world. As we added our shoes to the mound of shoes accumulating outside the door and entered the wedding apartment, we left the streets of Boston behind and were embraced by the sights and smells of Southeast Asia.

The flat's cramped rooms were filled with the flowery fragrance of burning incense and a delicious aroma of curried meat stew. There was the medicinal, menthol smell of tiger balm and betel. Smoke from men's cigarettes, which were ubiquitous at Khmer gatherings, clouded the air. Pink crepe-paper streamers hung from the ceilings, and the doorways and windows had new red curtains with white lace ruffles tied back to allow a warm breeze in from the street. An ornate clock, its face decorated with red paper roses and a gold image of the Eiffel tower, chimed the Marseillaise on the half hour. On the same wall, blurry black-and-white enlargements of worn snapshots of elderly relatives hung prominently between framed grade-school attendance awards and advertising posters of pretty Asian models.

Most of the furniture had been removed from the apartment's main rooms, and the floors were covered with woven mats. Three saffron-robed monks sat cross-legged in front of the guests, eating an elaborate meal of meat dishes, vegetable stew, Khmer pickles, steamed rice, fruit, and orange Fanta. Shortly after our arrival, members of the bride's family knelt reverently before the monks, with their heads bowed and palms pressed together, and offered additional dishes of rice and sweets. Younger children from the host family were pushed forward, given plates heaped with food by their elders, and encouraged to bow and offer the plates to the monks, being careful to use the proper terms of address.

Nearest to the monks, chewing betel and spitting the red juice into plastic milk containers, sat *yeichi,* the "temple grandmothers." With shaved heads, white blouses, and beautiful white lace scarves that were arranged over one shoulder, they looked quite different from the other women in the apartment. Those female guests, many in traditional Khmer clothing, sat elbow to elbow along both sides of the room. Dressed in American-style suits, their husbands stood in an adjoining room and on the back steps, talking, smoking, and drinking beer.

At first, it seemed that no young children were present, other than the ones family members brought forward to make offerings to the monks and a few babies in mothers' arms. But I soon noticed small groups of school-aged children darting in and out of a back bedroom where a larger group of ten or twelve had gathered to eat sweet snacks and watch a Chinese kung fu video dubbed in Khmer. Another small group of younger children played noisily with a puppy on a front porch balcony and were repeatedly hushed by adult guests standing within earshot.

In the kitchen, adolescent girls and older women in their everyday clothes squatted on the floor, chopping enormous mounds of vegetables for Cambodian sour soup *(s'lăh mchou);* all the while, they joked and chatted among themselves. With fashionable outfits and carefully coiffed hair, adolescent boys stood at the edges of the scene, available to run errands—go to the store, pick up an elderly relative, or deliver food to a friend or family member who might be too ill to attend the celebration. Several stationed themselves at the kitchen door, openly flirting with the young women busy preparing food.

After their meal, the monks were escorted home, and the male *achaa* (a ritual specialist) went to work carefully arranging ritual offerings and implements. Among them were pink satin pillows on which the bride and groom would lean during the marriage ceremony, a large sword in a silver scabbard, two decorated betel boxes, plates of food and glasses of alcohol for the ancestors, and numerous gifts for the bride's family. I was amazed to see items familiar to me from years earlier when I had lived in Southeast Asia: silver betel sets, green coconuts, areca flowers, mangoes, Chinese enameled metal trays, ceramic bowls and plates, even cans of coconut soda and the whole head of a roasted pig! One of the *yeichi* grandmothers, seeing that I was intrigued by the display of ceremonial goods, told me that the areca flowers *(pka sla)* came from California at fifty dollars a bunch. These flowers, she explained, are used to inform the ancestors of the couple's intention to marry, as well as in the central ceremony in which people pay respect to the parents of the bride and groom. (After the wedding ceremony, the dry areca seeds are thrown at the bride and groom for good luck.) Other items, cans of coconut milk and lychees, and various packages of Chinese sweets, were marked "Made in Thailand" and had been purchased in Boston's nearby Chinatown.

The scene was not what I had expected, and not just because of its incongruence with the New England streets outside. I teach in a graduate program in applied linguistics. Through my work with Boston area teachers, I had often heard that Cambodian children have "no culture" or, at best, are caught between two cultures, being neither American nor Khmer. Such pronouncements came not only from American teachers but also from the ethnic Khmer bilingual teachers with whom I worked. I had also read many popular accounts of Khmer refugees, most of which focused on their shattered past, the dehumanizing horrors of the Pol Pot genocide, and the trauma and grief of war, flight, and resettlement. In contrast to my expectations, however, events such as this wedding attested to a deliberate and dignified effort by Cambodian elders to re-create families, community, and a Khmer culture in the United States. Although the culture has been deeply affected, even haunted, by recent Khmer history, it remains richly elaborate and sophisticated; it is a culture being reconstructed even while inevitably undergoing change and reinterpretation in a very different social milieu.

As I considered the colorful, bustling wedding scene in front of me and thought of the teachers' comments, I wondered, Just what does it mean to "be Khmer" for young people growing up in the United States? What kind of person do Khmer parents and elders hope to produce through their efforts at socialization, and what aspirations do they hold for their children in the United States and in American schools? How have expectations and behaviors changed in response to changing circumstances, and how are families dealing with those changes? Finally, what are the implications of such change for patterns of Khmer adaptation? In the years following, I attempted to answer these and related questions. This book is the outcome of that investigation.

BACKGROUND TO THE RESEARCH

My interest in the Khmer community emerged from earlier ethnographic and sociolinguistic work that I conducted in Indonesia (1978–80 and 1985) and through contacts with Cambodian students in my linguistics and anthropology classes. I was intrigued by the similarities and differences I perceived between my Khmer students and the Javanese with whom I am so familiar. In 1987, I received a faculty development grant from the University of Massachusetts for Khmer language study. In the years following, with support from the Spencer Foundation and from the Institute for the Study of Economic Culture at Boston University, I conducted more than 175 interviews with Khmer immigrants concerning Khmer socialization, religious training, and education. I also collected detailed life histories of community members, documenting their cultural backgrounds and often horrific prearrival experiences.

I conducted interviews in either Khmer or English, depending on the interviewee's preference; most preferred Khmer. A Cambodian counterpart assisted me by arranging meetings and discussing with me the complex cultural and ethical issues that came up in the course of the research. Each formal interview lasted between two and four hours and was tape-recorded with the participant's consent. Interviewees included Khmer elders and youths, bilingual teachers, ritual specialists, and community and religious leaders. I also carried out informal discussions and ethnographic observation in Khmer homes, neighborhoods, and schools, and I participated in life-cycle celebrations and community gatherings. All field material and interviews were transcribed, translated, and annotated on computer disk, resulting in some fifteen hundred pages of single-spaced text.

I began my investigation in the Boston neighborhoods of Allston, Brighton, and East Boston. As Khmer moved from these areas into the neighboring cities of Lynn, Revere, Chelsea, and Lowell, however, I followed them into their new communities. A single contact typically led to a surprising number of others as people kindly introduced me and my assistant to family members and friends.

Community members were consistently helpful and enthusiastic about our project. Nevertheless, conducting research among urban refugees can be challenging. Southeast Asian refugees tend to be extremely busy—or, to be more exact, socially overextended—in their struggle to adjust to life in the United States and make ends meet. Parents, for example, must accompany young children to school or to the bus stop in the mornings, typically passing through tough urban neighborhoods, and then retrieve them in the afternoons. Older children who are unable to drive are also escorted to community colleges or part-time jobs. Often, each child is on a different schedule and attends a different school, each at some distance from the others, because not all schools within the school district have bilingual or English as a Second Language (ESL) programs for various grade levels.

Many parents work several low-paying jobs or multiple shifts, including overtime, to support their families and save for a down payment on a house or car or to make mortgage payments. Often, one parent works the graveyard shift, arriving home in the early morning just in time to get the children off to school and freeing the other parent to leave for work.

Parents who did not work and who received some form of public assistance were the most available for interviews. Several of these individuals were too ill to sit or concentrate for long periods, however, and others had English lessons or job training classes to attend. Older people often spent much of their time participating in temple or church activities or helping their adult children with child care.

Community leaders and social service providers were the most overextended of all, because community members placed enormous demands on their time. Community leaders and social service providers often had to cancel several appointments with me before a meeting actually took place.

Because of these constraints, the more relaxed methods of participant observation I had used during three years of research in Indonesia proved entirely unworkable. Sitting around hearth fires for long hours, dropping in unannounced on neighbors for an informal chat, and just observing the daily course of village life—none of that applied in the hectic urban world of Khmer immigrants. I had to schedule interviews around the commitments and rhythms of busy working lives. Because virtually all these interviews were conducted at interviewees' homes, however, the setting still allowed me to speak informally with others present, observe family interactions, and note more "natural" speech and behavioral patterns.[1]

Scheduling difficulties aside, Khmer community members were unfailingly hospitable to me and generous beyond their means. They typically served my assistant and me tea and a snack during our visits and often invited us to stay for a meal. We were also invited to attend numerous religious ceremonies, family celebrations, weddings, and birthday parties. On such occasions, we had the opportunity to observe and record the behavior of community members in a variety of formal and informal settings.

This is not to say that our presence did not have any effect on the information we collected or the behaviors we observed. In fact, in good "reflexive" ethnographic fashion, we were not infrequently called upon as "experts" to address various family concerns, as well as current social and political issues facing the community. We also willingly wrote letters to schools and landlords, social service agencies, and utility companies when asked to do so.

Despite our status as guests and outside experts, I was consistently surprised by the candor and directness with which community members interacted with me. Although in a very few cases interviewees were concerned about our possible connection to government agencies, participants were open and animated once interviews commenced. This was in large part, I suspect, due to my assistant's much respected role in the community as an ethnic Khmer bilingual teacher and community leader. I also attribute the warm reception to our regular appearance in Khmer homes, classrooms, and community events over the several years of the study.

There was one other reason for people's openness to me and this project. Parents and elders were eager to tell me their stories so that I would record and preserve them for their children; indeed, many explicitly and repeatedly asked that I do so. Charged with this responsibility, I have tried in this book to present their words as authentically and completely as possible. Throughout the book, I quote from interviews and conversations more or less verbatim. I have changed or edited specific details and collapsed accounts together only where necessary in order to protect the identity of individual community members. All the names of individuals cited in the book are pseudonyms; when not critical to the account, place-names in Cambodia and Massachusetts have also been altered.

This account is told largely from the perspective of the parental generation of Khmer refugees. They are unique, in that they have experienced firsthand life in Cambodia before the war, the horrors of Pol Pot, and the struggle to escape and resettle in a new land. The experiences of Khmer adults, their upbringing in Cambodia, their lives before the war, their flight, and the inevitable comparisons between the past and their present situation in the United States have all shaped the community I describe.

These previous life experiences in Cambodia continue to inform parents' behavior and attitudes toward their own children's socialization and education in the United States. Many Khmer adults are confused by what they see happening to their children, largely because their experience and understanding of the world are so very different.

This emphasis on the prearrival culture and experience does not mean that the behavioral patterns and attitudes of Khmer refugees have not undergone important changes. Rather, this book attempts to view the changes that have occurred against the backdrop of earlier cultural patterns in order to respect the depth and direction of that adjustment. The possibility of telling such a story is fleeting, because the older generation is quickly being pushed aside by a new generation of younger and better-educated Khmer Americans who do not share the parental generation's prewar experiences and—most important— do not understand the meaning of many of their beliefs and practices.

In examining Khmer socialization, moral education, and conceptions of self and intelligence, I intend for this book to enhance our understanding of one of the least studied, and most troubled, recent immigrant groups in the United States. As the first in-depth ethnographic account of Khmer adaptation viewed through the optic of childhood socialization, it is also intended to contribute to our understanding of home culture and values in minority educational experience.[2] In addition, the book sheds light on important aspects of Khmer Buddhism—both its survival and its change—especially in relation to the meanings and morality of family, gender, and social identity. Most generally, the book is an attempt to document how first-generation Khmer are adapting to life in their new American homeland while preserving important aspects of their identity as Khmer.

My hope, then, is that this work can speak to the growing number of people interested in the Asian American experience, an experience vital to the contemporary reconfiguration of American culture itself. More particularly, I hope that this book will be of value to the next generation of Khmer Americans. Some among that generation may already find the voices and experiences of their elders strangely distant. But most, I know, also sense that these voices and their stories somehow speak to who they are and who they should become.

Acknowledgments

This work would not have been possible without the support of the Spencer Foundation, which generously provided grants during the ten years in which I have been involved with the Khmer community. I wish to express my gratitude to them and my hope that in some way this work provides a small return for their kindness. I also wish to express my gratitude to Peter L. Berger and the Institute for the Study of Economic Culture at Boston University. Early in my study, the Institute provided me with support that allowed me to take a semester's leave from my teaching duties at the University of Massachusetts. Finally, I wish to thank the National Endowment for the Humanities for providing a fellowship that allowed me to finish writing this book.

During the course of my research, many Cambodians offered me invaluable assistance and enthusiasm. Most prominent is my good friend and research associate Kim Nay Biv, a Khmer bilingual teacher and recognized leader in the Boston area's Khmer community. Kim not only made interviews possible through her extensive network of community connections but also worked closely with me as both social interpreter and intermediary. She offered me her friendship as well as her keen cultural insight. For all of these reasons, I am forever indebted to her. Also invaluable to my research was Saren Eo, my first Khmer-language teacher, who so patiently revealed the intricacies of her language while supplying me with richly detailed examples of its cultural context. Both Kim and Saren worked closely with me on the final form of the Khmer transcription used in the book, although, of course, responsibility for any transcription or translation errors is my own.

There is not enough room to thank each of the community members who were so gracious and hospitable in allowing us to come into their homes and ask the most personal questions. I do, however, want to single out Ely Phlek, who actually came into *my* home, initially to care for my infant daughter. As a young woman who left her country as an orphan and who was—at the time of my research—struggling to complete her college education, Ely asked the questions and expressed the anxious concerns about life in the United States that first prompted me to consider many of the issues discussed in this book.

I also want to thank Sheila Levine and Laura Driussi at the University of California Press for their fine editorial work and enthusiasm for my project. Kate Frieson and an anonymous reader carefully reviewed the manuscript for the Press and offered valuable suggestions for final revisions. I owe an especially large intellectual debt to May Ebihara, whose ethnographic study of a Cambodian village from 1959 to 1960 provides much of the background to my own study. She has consistently encouraged those of us who attempt to follow in her footsteps. I owe a similar debt to Hildred Geertz. She has shown a kind and unflagging interest in my work since my earliest research in Java in the late 1970s and has remained a wise and generous counsel for my research among Khmer in the United States. Her work on the Javanese family continues to be an inspiration and resource for my own studies, including the one I attempt here.

Finally, I want to thank my own family, without whose support and encouragement this book would never have been completed. My husband, Robert Hefner, patiently read (and reread) numerous drafts of chapters, offering his invaluable insight as an anthropologist of Southeast Asia. This book owes much to the years we worked together in Indonesia and, more recently, to his endless enthusiasm for my project and his insistence that it was well worth the considerable time and energy I spent away from our family. My special thanks also go to my daughter, Claire-Marie, who accompanied me enthusiastically to so many Khmer homes and cultural events. Not only did she serve as a catalyst for interesting comments and cultural comparisons on the upbringing and behavior of children but she also amazed all those present with her tremendous appetite for Cambodian food! Last but not least is my newly adopted son, William Francisco, whose energetic presence continues to be a joyful reminder of the wonder of parenthood and cultural socialization.

A Note on Transliteration

There is no universally accepted system for the transliteration of written Khmer into Roman script, and there is even less agreement about the transcription of spoken Khmer (see Huffman 1970a and 1970b).[1] For my fieldwork I relied on a simplified phonetic transcription system that allowed me to note spoken Khmer rapidly. It also streamlined the transcription of taped interviews that typically used both Khmer and English. I was thus able to transcribe interviews and field material directly onto a computer disk in a single script.

A phonetic transcription of spoken Khmer would be accessible neither to most Khmer—even educated ones—nor to the vast majority of non-Khmer scholars, however. I have therefore adopted a transcription system based on that which Franklin E. Huffman developed for written Khmer in 1983. Huffman's system seems to be familiar to at least some educated Khmer and is used by many Western scholars (see Ebihara, Mortland, and Ledgerwood 1994). Its limitation, for my purposes, is that it is based on written, not spoken, Khmer. To retain some of the flavor of Khmer speech, I have left off unpronounced final consonant sounds and dropped elided syllables, while always retaining enough of the written form features to render the term identifiable.

Huffman's scheme is similar to that used in many French-language works on Cambodia, but it adds diacritics to distinguish all the vowel sounds. Note that in spoken Khmer, words beginning with a vowel are preceded by a glottal stop. Word-final consonant sounds are typically unreleased. A word-final *s* in the standard dialect of Khmer is pronounced as aspiration, [h]; when dropped, a word-final *r* causes the preceding vowel to be lengthened. In the transcription, a single tick (') is used to denote an elided syllable or a portion thereof and an epenthetic glottal (*sǎmlǎh—s'lǎh*, "soup"; *niyeay—ni'yeay*, "to speak"). Finally, the Khmer *v* is pronounced very much like the English *w*, whereas the Khmer *nh* is typically pronounced [ny].

xix

Table 1 Franco-Khmer Transcription

Consonants 1st	Consonants 2nd	Transcription	Vowels	Transcription 1st	Transcription 2nd
ñ	ñ	k	- -	â	o
ə	ឈ	kh	-៎-	ǎ	ŭa
	ង	ng	-ា-	a	ea
ច	ជ	ch	-ិ-	ă	ŏa/ĕa[d]
ឆ	ឈ	chh/ch[a]	-ី-	ĕ	ĭ
	ញ	nh	-ឹ-	ey	i
ដ	ឌ	d	-ឺ-	ŏe	ĕu
ឋ	ឍ	th	-ុ-	oeu	eu
ណ		n	-ូ-	ŏ	ŭ
ត	ទ	t	-ួ-	au	ou
ថ	ធ	th	-ើ-	uo	uo
	ន	n	-ឿ-	aoe	oe
ប		b[b]	េ-ៀ	eua	eua
ផ	ព	p	េ-ៀ	ie	ie
ផ	ភ	ph	េ-	e	é
	ម	m	ែ-	ae	ĕ
	យ	y	ៃ-	ai	ei
	រ	r	ោ-	ao	ŏ
	ល	l	ៅ-	av	ŏv
	វ	v	-ុំ	ŏm	ŭm
ស		ṣ	-ំ	ăm	ŭm
ហ		h	-ាំ	ăm	ŏam
ឡ		l	-ាំង	ăng	ĕang
អ		Ø/'[c]	-ះ	ăh	ĕah

[a] When followed by another consonant, as in chnăm [year].
[b] Final ប is written p.
[c] When subscript to another consonant, as in s'at [clean].
[d] Before a velar final, as in nĕak [person].

SOURCE: May M. Ebihara, Carol A. Mortland, and Judy L. Ledgerwood, eds. *Cambodian Culture Since 1975: Homeland and Exile* (Ithaca, N.Y.: Cornell University Press, 1994). Used with permission.

1

Identity and Transition

CREATING THE REFUGEE FLOW

In April 1975, after six months of intensive air bombardment by the United States Air Force and a prolonged, bitter battle with the American-backed Lon Nol government, the Communist Khmer Rouge, led by Pol Pot, defeated its rival and triumphantly entered Phnom Penh, Cambodia's capital. In the following weeks, all those living in the city and in Khmer provincial centers were forced from their homes (Shawcross 1979:365–67). Black-clad soldiers brandishing revolvers and AK-47s ordered the city's inhabitants to pack their belongings and leave for the countryside, saying they would be allowed to return in several weeks. Families bundled up clothing, cookware, medicine, and sacks of rice. They hastily hid gold, jewelry, family heirlooms, and other valuables. Although there was much speculation, no one knew for certain why they were being evacuated.

Initially, some Khmer welcomed the arrival of the Khmer Rouge, hoping that the new government would avoid the excesses of the former regime (Chandler 1991:250). It soon became clear, however, that anyone even distantly associated with the American-backed Lon Nol government or identified as a member of the Khmer intelligentsia was in extreme danger. Many were executed, often after enduring horrific brutality. Some families decided to split up to increase their individual chances of survival. Others were forced apart in the chaos of the evacuation.

> [Female, age 42] At that time, I was twenty-two or twenty-three. I was a student at the University of Science in Phnom Penh. My family lived in the south of Phnom Penh in Toul Tumpoung. So I lived with my sister and her husband near Tŏek Laâk, because it was closer to my school. When the Khmer Rouge took over the city in 1975, I had to go with my sister's family to leave the city. We didn't know where the rest of the family had gone. My sister's husband had been a police officer under Lon Nol, so he decided to separate from us because

he said, "If I stay with you, a lot of people know me and they will kill all of us."

So during the Communist regime, I only had my sister. We went first to Takeo, and then later the Khmer Rouge sent us to Battambang [in the northwest]. In Battambang, they were killing all the intellectuals and *něak mean* (middle-class), so we pretended we could not read or write. We were lucky because we knew how to sew. We survived because we sewed the uniforms for the soldiers.

In the new "Democratic" Kampuchea, all means of production were to be collectivized and class distinctions eliminated. In fact, however, the Khmer Rouge replaced traditional categories of class and status with a plethora of new, equally value-laden sociopolitical distinctions. The most basic of these was the opposition between "base people," who were poor and lower-middle-class peasants, and "new people," who were individuals (most of them urban) "liberated as of 1975" (Ebihara 1987:25). Under the Khmer Rouge, base people generally received better treatment. New people had far fewer rights.

Pol Pot reportedly boasted at one point that his goal was to make Cambodia "one big work camp" (Ablin and Hood 1987:xxxv). Consistent with this vision, the new government moved quickly to establish labor camps throughout the countryside. Cadres organized families into "production teams" and larger cooperatives. Adolescents were assigned to single-sex work teams. Even little children and old people were put to work.

Young people were separated from their parents in an effort to supplant familial bonds with allegiance to the revolutionary state. Work teams lived and slept together, and meals were eaten communally. Schools were closed, and religion was suppressed. Perhaps most horrifying to Khmer elders, children were indoctrinated with revolutionary rhetoric and encouraged to turn in family members to the "organization" *(ângkăă)* if they exhibited antirevolutionary attitudes.

Even language was made to conform to the new revolutionary ideology. Traditional terms of deference to elders or those of higher status were replaced with status-neutral terms. Terms for mother *(mae)* and father *(ŏv)* were to be preceded by or replaced with the term for friend *(mĭt)*.

Those who resisted the new order and those who were suspected of harboring antirevolutionary sentiments were imprisoned, tortured, or executed.

> [Female, age 33] During Pol Pot time, I had no family with me, and I lived with a woman from the city. She was the head of our group, and I was like her younger sister. I washed her clothes and helped her when she was pregnant. Then, they took her away to kill her. The Khmer Rouge accused her of being a CIA spy. They took me, too, and locked me in a room. I just prayed and prayed. And then one Khmer Rouge came in and said, "You are lucky. They won't kill you."

Within the Khmer Rouge, particularly in the first months of the revolutionary government, there were, in fact, a number of factions.[1] Conditions varied widely among different regions in the countryside, depending on which faction was dominant. In 1977, in the eastern province of Prey Veng, a coup was attempted against Pol Pot, who was euphemistically referred to as "Brother Number One." This uprising was followed in 1978 by another in the Eastern Zone adjacent to Vietnam, led by old-guard Communists opposed to the draconian policies of the revolutionary regime. Despite bitter resistance, however, Pol Pot emerged from both rebellions as the victor and moved swiftly and ruthlessly to eliminate his rivals and consolidate his power (Ablin and Hood 1987:xxxv; see also Kiernan 1986). During the same two-year period, the party and the country as a whole were ravaged by purges, torture, and mass executions. Few escaped the violence.

> [Male, age 45] From the beginning, the Khmer Rouge suspected me of being a Lon Nol soldier. But they had no proof, and I had no family they could use to turn against me. They were watching me closely for a long time. In the spring of 1978, they took me and held me in a group of prisoners for about one month. I wasn't really in a jail at that time. They even fed me rice every day. The soldiers joked with me and called me by my name.
> But after one month, late one night at like 12:00 midnight, a jeep came to pick me up. They took me to K'dal [southwest of Phnom Penh] and asked me again, "Were you a soldier with Lon Nol? Don't lie to me, or I will kill you!" I told them, "Never. I worked at an import-export company. I was just a regular worker, carrying, unloading. If I was a soldier for Lon Nol, I would kill myself!" I just said it like that. They took two chains and said, "Kneel down with your hands behind your back!" and they chained my hands. They

put another chain around my neck and attached the two. The leader of the Khmer Rouge put my head between his feet and squeezed my neck against the chain, saying, "I will kill you if you don't tell me the truth!" He kept squeezing like that. I said, "I never worked for Lon Nol!"

Finally, they put me in a truck and took me to Wat Ay Phnom [a large Buddhist temple that had been converted into a torture center and jail]. They chained me to about twenty people. I lived six months like that. And every day I saw them kill maybe ten or twenty people. Before they kill you, they torture you and keep asking, "Were you a soldier or a professor before? What did you do?" Before they kill you, they make you run across a bridge, and when you get to the other side, they kill you. They just say, "Run!" and on the other side there are soldiers and they hit you with an ax and you fall into a ditch. I saw one man who was hit, and he fell into that hole, and they started to fill the hole with dirt even though the man was still alive and trying to climb out. I saw that because they made me collect firewood in that area. They wanted me to see that killing so I would be afraid and confess.

Finally, in December 1978, in response to continued border skirmishes with the Khmer Rouge, the Vietnamese invaded Cambodia. As the Vietnamese advanced, conditions in the work camps worsened (Chandler 1991:311). Camp cadres feared that, once freed from bondage, their charges would turn against them. Killings in the camps increased, with prisoners being executed for the smallest infraction. Anticipating the arrival of the Vietnamese, the captors forced starving workers to stockpile huge supplies of rice and water in mountain hideouts while their own daily rations were reduced to watery rice gruel or a handful of parched corn (Szymusiak 1986:177–210; Martin 1994:189).

In the prisons, as in the work camps, already unbearable conditions took a turn for the worse.

[Male, age 51] When I first went into prison, I saw there were maybe three hundred people in that place. The guards would kill only two or three people a day; the others, they tortured so that they wanted to die. Those people would scream, "Just kill me, I want to die!" They tortured me like that, too—every week, the same method. They would tie a plastic bag around my neck until I passed out. It was so terrible, it felt like my head was bursting, like I was dying. I would lose consciousness and fall onto the floor. Then they would revive me by throwing water in my face! It was like that for more than two years.

> By that time, there were only maybe ten or twenty of us left. I was sure that I would be the next one to die. I was so thin, so very thin. I didn't care anymore; I wanted to die. They gave us only rice soup one time a day. Watery *bâbââ*. Once a day, one small bowl with a few grains of rice. I was so weak, I couldn't walk. I couldn't even lift my chains up to go to the bathroom. I just lay there in that filth. I was too weak to do anything.

Although Cambodians have historically viewed Vietnamese with considerable antipathy, those in the labor camps and prisons understandably welcomed the Vietnamese advance. By January 1979, Vietnamese troops had "liberated" major areas of the countryside (Chandler 1991:310).

> I remember sometime after New Year's Day 1979, I heard noises like gunfire and the guards yelling, "We have to run! It's the Vietnamese!" After that, I heard a lot of gunfire. I had a friend in prison with me, a Chinese man. He told me to get up, maybe the Vietnamese will rescue us. We both tried to stand up, but we were so weak, we kept falling down. Then I heard a noise, someone banging through the door, through the wall, and suddenly I saw a lot of Vietnamese soldiers, maybe thirty. They had machine guns and they were shooting at all of the guards and the guards were trying to get away. The Vietnamese had a lot of keys, and they used them to take off our handcuffs. And the Vietnamese doctor gave us injections, all six of us. They gave us coconut milk, too, but we were still too weak to walk. They had to carry us in cots to the hospital in downtown Battambang. By that time, there were only six of us left out of three hundred.

Some estimate that under the Khmer Rouge, more than one million people died (Banister and Johnson 1993:67). Others place the number significantly higher (see Knoll 1982; Kiernan 1990). Those who were not killed outright were slowly starved or worked to death. Others died from disease and a lack of medical care. Many others simply "disappeared" into the forest and were never seen again.

The survivors, once freed from the Khmer Rouge, were anxious to locate family and friends, so they returned to their homes in large numbers. During the chaotic months of fighting between various rebel factions and the Vietnamese-backed government forces and during the ensuing population movement, no crops were planted. Severe food shortages occurred throughout Cambodia in the spring and summer (Chandler 1991:313; Banister and Johnson 1993:74).

In the months following the Vietnamese invasion, some six hundred thousand Cambodians fled to the Thai border (Ebihara 1985:133–34). They left their country for a variety of reasons. Many were starving and had returned to their homes and fields only to find everything in ruins. Others hoped to escape the continued fighting. Many strongly distrusted the new People's Republic of Kampuchea supported by the Vietnamese. Although large numbers succeeded in fleeing to Thailand, the journey was not easy. Typically, they escaped only by walking over mountains, passing through jungles and minefields with very little to eat or drink.

> [Male, age 57] When the Vietnamese entered my country, I was living in Battambang province and I was very sick. I couldn't walk at all, my legs were so swollen—big like this. If I walked even two meters, I got very tired. I said to myself, I have to go west to Thailand, to escape, but my energy, my strength, I had none. Suddenly, I don't know where it came from—it was like a miracle. I could walk like five miles and not get tired! I faced many obstacles. I was stopped by a soldier, and he told me I had to go back. But I just kept walking. That soldier shot at me, at my back, but I started running and running and his bullets didn't hit me. I was very afraid, but I kept running. Finally, after days and days of walking, I made it to the border of Thailand.

The Thai, however, were reluctant to accept massive numbers of destitute Khmer. In a gesture that horrified Western observers, in the spring of 1979, Thai soldiers forced forty thousand refugees back into Cambodia by pushing them down into a remote ravine filled with land mines (Ebihara 1985:134; Ablin and Hood 1987:xliv). Those not killed by the mines or shot by Vietnamese soldiers faced starvation. Only after a number of Western countries, notably the United States, France, and Australia, agreed to ensure that Thailand would not be left with a permanent refugee population did Thailand relent and announce that it would not forcibly repatriate any more Khmer.

In the fall of 1979, refugee camps for the Cambodians were set up on the border under the auspices of the United Nations High Commission for Refugees (Ablin and Hood 1987:xliv). Although the situation gradually improved, life on the Thai border was still desperate and uncertain. Border settlements could not escape the continuing Khmer civil war; they were the repeated targets of raids and bombing attacks. Lacking established social order, some of the settlements came to be run by paramilitary thugs; residents were routinely subjected to rape, robbery, and extortion (French 1994:24–25). Refugees waited in these uncertain conditions for months, even years, hoping to eventually be resettled in a "third country."

These experiences have exacted a high toll on individual Khmer. As a result of their years under the Khmer Rouge, the horrors of their escape, and the desperation of their lives on the Thai border, many still struggle with serious depression and physical disabilities. The vast majority lost friends and family members to starvation, illness, or murder. Many personally witnessed torture, rape, and killings.

Years later, a young Khmer American woman linked such events to her mother's reticence to venture out of her East Boston apartment and her inability to "concentrate" enough to study English:

> [Female, age 23] When my mother saw my father killed by the Khmer Rouge, when she saw him taken away with his arms tied behind his back, she went crazy. At that time I was eleven. My little sister was only three days old. Somehow, my father knew he was going to be taken away. Someone must have told him, and he managed to come to the family about 12:00 one night to see us.
>
> We were all crying together, but I didn't really understand what was going on. He touched my head and said, "Ratha, you are the one who will have to take care of the family" (because, although you wouldn't believe it now, my older sister was very sick at that time and couldn't do anything). "Wherever you go in the future, after I am gone from this earth, get an education. Study hard for your future." I will always remember that, what he said to me that night.
>
> A few days later, when the Khmer Rouge took him and tied him up, I begged them, "Please don't kill my father. He didn't do anything wrong." The leader told me, "If you want to die, just go stand over there [with him]!" But another soldier led me away to my family.
>
> After they killed him, they cut his liver out and showed that to my mother. They said that was the "bad liver" (*prâmăt kmav*) and whoever cried for my father would be killed. But at night my mother cried and cried until her skin got really dark and her heart stopped. She still cries now, and she forgets a lot of things because of the shock of seeing that.

Many young Khmer like Ratha are burdened with the memories of death and stagger under the weight of responsibilities that loved ones conferred on them in their final moments. Strangers in a strange land, many Khmer live with haunting recollections of brutality and degradation and have no choice but to try to rebuild their worlds from shattered lives.

PATTERNS OF MIGRATION

Since 1979, an estimated 250,000 Cambodians have resettled abroad (Ablin and Hood 1987:xliv). Some 152,000 were accepted for resettlement by the United States (Banister and Johnson 1993:70). Refugees from Southeast Asia arrived in this country in what are commonly described in the literature as three "waves," or cohorts (Ebihara 1985:134).

Cambodians were underrepresented in the first and second migratory waves. In 1975, the year both Saigon and Phnom Penh fell to Communist forces, only 4,600 Cambodians came to the United States, as compared with 125,000 Vietnamese (Gordon 1987:156).[2] The number of Khmer refugees decreased significantly in the following two years. The second wave of Southeast Asians began to enter the country in late 1978 (Strand and Jones 1985:34). In this wave, many of the boat people of Vietnam, as well as Hmong, Mien, and Lao, began to arrive in the United States. For the first time, too, a significant number of Cambodians—perhaps 10,000 in all—joined the ranks of Southeast Asian refugees arriving in the United States.

Beginning in January 1980, the third wave of refugee migration brought the largest influx of Khmer to the United States. This final migratory wave was made possible by the passage of the Refugee Act of 1980. This legislation allowed for the resettlement of 50,000 refugees in the United States each year through 1983. It also gave the president power to increase that number after consulting with Congress. President Jimmy Carter exercised that prerogative in 1980 to allow some 166,700 Southeast Asian refugees to resettle in the United States; among them were 16,000 Khmer refugees and a larger number of Hmong (Knoll 1982:141; Gordon 1987:155–56). Between 1980 and 1982, more than 60,000 Khmer entered the United States (Ebihara 1985:135). Significant numbers of Khmer continued to enter the country over the next several years.

These varied cycles of Southeast Asian immigration correlate with what are, in fact, substantial differences of culture and socioeconomic standing among immigrant Vietnamese, Lao, Khmer, and Sino-Vietnamese. In general, the first refugees were more urban and better educated, whereas later arrivals tended to come from rural and less-educated backgrounds (Strand and Jones 1985:35; Kelly 1986:41). Indeed, many of the earliest arrivals were well educated even by American standards (Kelly 1986:43). Many of the Cambodians who came in this first, small group had worked for the U.S. government or had been otherwise involved in the Cambodian war effort (Ebihara 1985:135).

During these first years, the U.S. government's official resettlement policy was to disperse Southeast Asian refugees throughout the country. This was ostensibly done to avoid creating large, "unassimilable" enclaves. Under this policy, every state except Alaska received at least a hundred refugees; moreover, they were to be placed in small groups rather than in concentrated settlements across the fifty states (Baker and North 1984:55, cited in Gordon 1987:163). Ultimately, however, this policy was undermined by the large numbers of immigrants who simply decided on their own to move to communities of their choice. They fled in particularly large numbers from more isolated areas and uncomfortable climates and resettled in states such as California and Texas, where many had friends and family members. Schools and social services in these states were soon overburdened.

Later resettlement policies recognized living in concentrated ethnic communities would help refugees adapt socially and psychologically. In the face of the large influx of Khmer refugees in the early 1980s, the Office of Refugee Resettlement designated twelve "cluster communities" for Khmer resettlement. Groups of between 300 and 1,200 Khmer were placed in Atlanta, Boston, Chicago, Cincinnati, Columbus, Dallas, Houston, Jacksonville, New York City, Phoenix, Richmond, and Rochester (Refugee Resource Center 1981–82; Ebihara 1985:135; Gordon 1987:164). These communities were chosen because they had employment opportunities and available housing and were not already overburdened with large refugee populations. Boston had the added attraction of good public transportation and an established Chinatown with ethnic stores and services. The city also has a long history of accepting new immigrant populations.

By the late 1980s, Boston's Suffolk County had an estimated 5,362 Khmer (MORI 1988). In the 1988–89 school year, there were more than 450 Khmer-speaking children in the city's public school system (MDE 1988; Smith-Hefner 1990a:252). In the early 1990s, in the face of Boston's escalating rental and real estate prices, the Khmer population in Boston proper began to decrease as families began to look for less expensive housing in areas just outside the city. During this same period, the nearby cities of Lynn, Lowell, and Revere experienced a significant increase in the number of Khmer children in their schools. By 1990, the last of the Thai border camps were closing, and the number of new Khmer immigrants allowed into the United States had slowed to a trickle. However, continued *in-migration*, the movement of Cambodians from one place to another within the state, as well as *secondary migration*, the movement of refugees initially settled in one state to another, had resulted in a growing concentration of Khmer in the Merrimack Valley region of Massachusetts, just north of metropolitan Boston (MORI 1988).

Khmer were drawn to the Northeast initially because of employment opportunities in plants that assembled electronics, computers, and medical supplies. Others came to be united with friends and family. Although some Khmer left the state during the five-year economic downturn that shook the Northeast from 1987 to 1992, the sheer size and vitality of the Khmer community served as a magnet for continuing migration.

At its height in the late 1980s, the Khmer population in eastern Massachusetts reached somewhere between 18,000 and 25,000 individuals, according to newspaper accounts.[3] Today, the city of Lowell, one hour north of Boston, is said to have the second largest Khmer population in the United States after Long Beach, California. Lowell community leaders estimate that their city has between 12,000 and 15,000 Khmer. The 1990 U.S. census, however, only shows some 6,000 Cambodians living in Lowell (but this number is based on reported home language and does not include children under the age of five).[4] The actual number probably lies somewhere between these figures. Boston's Khmer population has stabilized at around 1,500, whereas Lynn's population is now closer to 2,500, with 1,000 Khmer in nearby Revere and another 500 in Chelsea.[5]

Boston Khmer benefit from the social contacts and services in these adjacent Khmer communities. Many, for example, attend the Cambodian Buddhist temple in nearby Lynn. At the same time, Khmer from Lynn, Chelsea, Revere, and even Lowell hold their weddings in Boston's Chinatown, and many patronize Chinatown businesses. There is thus considerable interaction among these communities.

KHMER IN GREATER METROPOLITAN BOSTON

As members of the third and most recent wave of Southeast Asian migrants to the United States, the great majority of Khmer in greater metropolitan Boston share a rural background. Many have received less than a primary school education; indeed, the majority of rural Khmer women over the age of forty in the Boston area were illiterate in their native language at the time of their arrival (Smith-Hefner 1990a:255). Compared with the Khmer who settled in other areas of the United States and in Western Europe, relatively few middle-class Khmer have settled in eastern Massachusetts. Most of the Khmer intelligentsia and business class were murdered by the Khmer Rouge. Those who survived have preferred to emigrate to France, California, New York, or Washington, D.C. (particularly the suburb of Silver Spring, Maryland), where they have family members or military and business contacts. As with Khmer populations elsewhere, however, the Boston area Khmer population includes a disproportionate number of widows and young children and relatively few elderly. The class composition of Boston area Khmer has had an important influence on community developments. These Khmer generally lack the social and financial resources that are available in some other Khmer American communities. Perhaps most important, they have suffered from a dearth of politically and economically successful role models in the early years of resettlement.

Although it is possible to find streets or apartment complexes that are completely inhabited by Khmer, Cambodians in eastern Massachusetts typically live in dispersed settlements among other immigrant or minority populations. Most Khmer spend a good deal of time in mainstream, working-class American society, where they work, shop, and attend school. The Khmer community's social relationships are thus best characterized as increasingly "centrifugal," or tending outward. This centrifugal nature of Khmer social life is especially characteristic of certain categories of Khmer, most notably school-aged youth, many of whom spend few of their daytime hours in integral Khmer communities. As a result, and perhaps not surprisingly, it is Khmer youth who experience the greatest challenges in the reestablishment and adaptation of Khmer culture to life in the United States.

Khmer parents came to the United States with values and expectations shaped by their experiences of growing up in their own country, or, in the case of young adults, by the values they learned from their parents. This is true even though most Khmer refugees led atypical lives for many years, first under Pol Pot and then in the refugee camps. These more recent experiences inevitably affected Khmer ideas and Khmer worldview; however, many older refugees make strenuous efforts to differentiate such experiences from what is "truly Khmer."

This process of sorting out and redefining what is authentic or valuable from the past and what can be set aside while re-creating an identity in an American context has been an important part of the experience of all American immigrant groups. For Khmer, of course, this process of accommodation is not simply a matter of choosing between timeless "tradition" and American "modernity." In fact, some of the changes Khmer Americans are undergoing are continuations of processes of modern social change begun in Southeast Asia.[6]

If those changes began in Cambodia, however, they have certainly intensified here (Caplan, Whitmore, and Choy 1989:20). Other such changes—most notably, the challenge of maintaining a distinct minority identity in a culturally dominant mainstream society—are new for Khmer. Whatever their source, these changes are the subject of endless and sometimes impassioned debate among Khmer Americans. Some of the most vexing debates involve issues of identity, morality, and the upbringing of children.

IDENTITY AND CULTURAL TRANSMISSION

Cultural and historical accounts of Khmer by May Ebihara (1968, 1985) and others (Leclère [1899] 1975; Porée and Maspero 1938; LeBar, Hickey, and Musgrave 1964; Keyes 1977; Mabbett and Chandler 1995) provide us with a clear sense of the characteristics that distinguish Khmer from other Southeast Asian groups. Unlike Vietnamese, Sino-Vietnamese, and Hmong (but similar to Lao), Khmer have sociocultural roots that show the stronger influence of Indian rather than Chinese civilization. (The only exception to this generalization is in commerce, in which Chinese cultural influence is extensive.) Unlike the Chinese or Vietnamese, Khmer lack any kind of unilineal descent groups. Instead, as in many other Southeast Asian (and, for that matter, Western European) cultures, family structure is loosely neolocal, cognatic ("bilateral"),[7] and focused on the nuclear family. By many accounts, too, Khmer are more individualistic than collective when compared with some of their neighbors, especially those influenced by Chinese tradition. Behavior among kin is less rigidly prescribed and more dependent on individual likes and dislikes.

The overwhelming majority of Khmer are Theravada Buddhists, and the Buddhist doctrine of karma *(kam)* is often cited as an influence on the relatively individualistic disposition noted in ethnographic studies of Khmer. According to karmic doctrine, everyone is responsible for the merit or demerit he or she accumulates in this world, which determines the position achieved in the next life (Keyes 1977:84; Tambiah 1970:53).

Although there has been a significant amount of research on the more doctrinal aspects of Khmer Buddhist tradition, far less attention has been devoted to "vernacular" or "practical" Buddhism. Even less research has been devoted to the processes by which elders transmit practical Buddhist and Khmer values to youth. Yet these processes lie at the heart of Khmer identity. If karmic doctrines or individualistic attitudes are indeed features of Khmer social life, at some point they must be inculcated in members of the Khmer community. That process of cultural transmission is a focus of this book.

Over the six years of my research among Khmer refugees living in the Boston area, I aimed to explore both the resilience and social transformation of Khmer identity in the United States. One of the central purposes of my research was to determine which aspects of Khmer Buddhist worldview and socialization are most directly involved in Khmer adjustment to American society. Grounded in the intensive examination of a particular community, the study builds on the growing interest among anthropologists and linguists in the transmission of culture and the processes of socialization (Schwartz 1978; Schieffelin and Ochs 1986; Peak 1991; Shweder 1991; Stafford 1995). Research on child socialization is seen as one important means of uncovering adult social norms. In also focusing on how the child acquires these norms, however, it is possible to document the attitudes and assumptions that form and inform their acquisition and transformation. Equally important, the focus on cultural acquisition provides an important optic for distinguishing idealized expressions of attitudes and norms from their practice in social life and their embodiment in the habits, perceptions, and attitudes of real people (Bourdieu 1977; Schwartz 1978; Bloch 1989).

Although it exercises a profound influence on the later acquisition of formal knowledge and discourse, this general socialization begins in the family even before the child can speak, when others may put appropriate words in her mouth and mold her body into appropriately deferential gestures. Patterns of respect and deference involving the child's kin relations are taught within the family and typically become models for later interactions with authority figures in the public sphere. At the same time, community and parental expectations about the child's cognitive abilities and hence social responsibility change in the course of the child's development. Different ethnocultural groups may hold quite distinctive theories about how that development should progress. Although these theories do not exhaustively determine actual socialization processes, they nonetheless play an important role in their outcome.

SOCIALIZATION AND MORAL EDUCATION

The concept of moral education with which I am concerned in this book has to do with the general social processes or patterns of socialization by which children are taught to identify with a whole way of life. This socialization especially includes the largely unspoken sensibilities about the nature of right and wrong, entitlements and responsibilities, individuality and the group. My methodology draws on and has common emphases with "character education" approaches under discussion in American education and public policy circles (see Glendon and Blankenhorn 1995). My approach differs, however, in its anthropological emphasis on the ways in which different peoples or cultures construe the nature of the moral. I draw on the work of such diverse authors as Arthur Kleinman (1988), Beatrice Whiting and Carolyn Pope Edwards (1988), and Richard Schweder (see Shweder, Mahapatra, and Miller 1987; and Shweder 1991). With this foundation, my approach shifts attention away from discussion of the virtues appropriate to a particular kind of modern society (such as, in most character education literature, a liberal society). Instead, I focus on the general processes by which children learn to identify with a particular reference or solidary group and, in so doing, open themselves to the assimilation of its culturally specific mores.

Central to this anthropological concern, then, is the process of moral identification. Even if a child is extensively exposed to the

Identity and Transition 15

moral ideas and feelings of a particular culture, this moral socialization will not take hold unless the child identifies affectively with that group. From a general, anthropological perspective, moral education is as much a matter of identification with a culture and social group as it is a simple transfer of moral knowledge from elders to youth. A critical variable in the process, therefore, is what sociologists and anthropologists call *reflexivity,* individuals' capacity to look at the content of their culture or society and to evaluate, embrace, or even reject it in light of their reflexive disposition (Giddens 1991; Beck, Giddens, and Lash 1994).

Reflexivity exists in all societies. Although public discussions of the concept sometimes depict culture as more or less uniformly distributed among a people, in even the smallest "traditional" society, there will be differing degrees of commitment to and engagement with local cultural mores. This reflexive engagement with culture becomes all the more important in modern, plural societies, in which people committed to very different customs and moral ideals may live together. In such circumstances, a child exposed to the moral socialization of elders may simultaneously be engaged with social or moral learning of a very different sort with others in the surrounding society.

At its most elementary level, this is the situation of Khmer Americans. They live in an extraordinarily plural and modern society. Moreover, the urban communities in which many Khmer Americans are concentrated are among the most diverse sectors of this multicultural society. They live, study, and work with Mexican Americans, Puerto Ricans, Irish Americans, African Americans, Salvadorans, and Italian Americans. In these circumstances, the moral values that Khmer parents convey are not necessarily reinforced by the myriad exchanges of everyday life. On the contrary, Khmer Americans daily find themselves in circumstances in which they ignore or outright deny the ethical values and interactional sensibilities of their elders.

Explicit moral instruction works best when it benefits from an ongoing, massive, implicit, contextual, and often unconscious reinforcement (Bourdieu 1977). As we shall see in this book, this multidimensional reinforcement of explicit moral teaching is exactly what Khmer moral education in the United States so often lacks. Nowhere is this tension more apparent than in the marked discontinuity between the moral messages conveyed in Khmer households and those to which children are exposed in mainstream American society.

This aspect of Khmer American socialization does not mean that the moral education of youth is destined to fail. It does mean, however, that the tried-and-true modes of cultural transmission and moral inspiration that may have worked in Cambodia are unlikely to be sufficient in the United States. Khmer parents grapple daily with this challenge. To preserve certain portions of their cultural and moral traditions, they must adjust and change others. Of course, over time, all cultural "reproduction" requires cultural adjustment and transformation (Hefner 1985, 1990; Lambeck 1993). This fact becomes a powerful and problematic imperative, however, for a small, diasporic community attempting to reconstitute itself after a holocaust.

CULTURE AND REFUGEE ADAPTATION

Studies of Southeast Asian refugees have generally concentrated on immigrants' economic and psychosocial adjustment and have paid surprisingly little attention to the role of culture or religion in that adjustment. Studies that do consider religious beliefs and cultural values treat this aspect briefly and, for the most part, superficially.[8] Moreover, the most sustained research has been conducted among Vietnamese, whereas, with a few fortunate exceptions, the Lao and Khmer have been "systematically ignored" (Indra 1987:12). Commenting on this lack of attention to religion and cultural beliefs, Penny Van Esterik writes, "It is not surprising that Theravada Buddhism, the religious tradition followed by the Lao and Khmer, is largely unknown or misunderstood in North America" (1992:34).

Despite the trauma of their passage and their extensive exposure to Christian culture in the resettlement process, most Khmer refugees continue to embrace Theravada Buddhism (Smith-Hefner 1994:24). Christianity has not had the far-reaching impact on Khmer that it has had on some other Southeast Asian immigrant groups, such as the Hmong. Khmer refugees commonly respond to questions about their religion with the statement "To be Khmer is to be Buddhist." Many view Khmer individuals who have converted not merely as having changed their personal "belief" but as having abandoned the very core of their ethnic identity. Khmer Buddhism is a distinctive blend of Buddhist, animist, and Brahman beliefs that makes it distinct in its flavor from Thai or Lao Buddhism and certainly very different from the forms of Buddhism embraced by some Americans.

In chapter 2, I discuss the basic beliefs and practices of Khmer Buddhism and document Khmer immigrants' efforts to reestablish their religion in their new homeland. It has not been possible, of course, to "rebuild the temple" without making considerable concessions to America's physical and cultural realities. With this in mind, I discuss what form Buddhism takes and the extent to which it continues to be a focus of identity among Cambodians in the United States.

Chapter 3 examines Khmer socialization practices. The discussion analyzes a curious and critical paradox in Khmer childrearing beliefs and behavior. On the one hand, Khmer parents express a strong belief in the individual's integrity and hesitate to interfere too much in their child's development. The resulting treatment of young children, often described as indulgent (Ebihara 1968:115; Wood 1983:10; Kelley 1991:53), is clearly informed by the Buddhist emphasis on the individual and by Khmer spirit beliefs that underscore the child's independence and autonomy. On the other hand, Khmer believe that the child is born into a family with a particular status and reputation within the community and plays a vital role in upholding that reputation. Hence, the parents must teach the child the behaviors and demeanor appropriate to the family's social standing and insist that the child uphold the "face" *(mŭk môt)* of the family (see also Ponchaud 1977a; Martin 1994).

I explore the moral education of children in greater detail in chapter 4. Generally speaking, Khmer parents consider the most critical ingredient in moral socialization to be a child's recognition of the moral debt owed to elders. Parents underscore this understanding in everyday interaction by emphasizing the vital importance of respectful address and polite demeanor. In addition, on reaching adolescence, a child is enjoined to acknowledge his or her filial obligation by offering ritual obeisance and performing acts of merit making for those who brought him or her into the world.

There is an important gender dimension to this aspect of Khmer socialization. Parents distinguish the rights and responsibilities of sons from those of daughters early on. Boys are afforded opportunities to act independently, especially outside the home, whereas girls are enjoined to stay close to home and avoid behaviors that might reflect badly on the family. This association of males with public independence and females with domestic space is, of course, an often-noted (if not universal) feature of societies around the world (Ortner 1974; Atkinson and Errington 1990; Peletz 1996).

This aspect of gender relations among Khmer has experienced severe strains, however, as Khmer Americans have adapted to U.S. life. Filial responsibilities and gender role expectations introduced within the family are often a source of intergenerational misunderstanding as children move away from the family and into mainstream American society. Parents not infrequently react with severe disciplinary measures. In chapter 4, I explore parents' attitudes toward physical discipline. In so doing, I attempt to explain the apparent contradiction between an indulgent and largely "nativist" view of child development and a relational, "sociocentric" view that requires sometimes severe physical punishment if children jeopardize the family's reputation.

Chapter 5 considers the cultural discontinuities that Khmer children face in American schools. To explain these discontinuities and the educational expectations of Khmer parents, I examine the educational experiences and attitudes of Khmer elders in some detail. Khmer refugees have markedly different attitudes toward education from those widely reported for Vietnamese, Sino-Vietnamese, and Hmong immigrants. For example, Khmer parents express a strong desire for their children to learn to read and write in Khmer; these hopes of Khmer literacy for their children lead to their consistently positive assessment of American bilingual education programs. Despite these evaluations, however, parents also emphasize that, whatever their own desires, educational achievement is ultimately up to the individual child. Again and again, parents stress that it is not possible to "push" one's child, that one must "look to the child to determine his future." Khmer parents may decide that the child who does not perform well in school is just not destined for that particular "path" (Smith-Hefner 1990a).

I take up issues of sexuality and marriage in chapter 6. In keeping with a deeply relational view of moral responsibility, which has parallels in other Indic-Asian cultures (Shweder, Mahapatra, and Miller 1987), Khmer parents are enjoined to control their children's actions whenever that behavior places the family's reputation and face in jeopardy. Not surprisingly, a young daughter's sexuality is among the most compelling concerns for Khmer families, because the unsanctioned loss of virginity severely damages a family's good name. That event may also affect the family's economic resources, as it may be obliged to forgo bride-wealth *(prak [banda]kăă)* where the prospective bride is not a virgin. In the face of these very real threats to family reputation and resources, Khmer parents often hastily arrange a marriage for a daughter at the first hint of sexual misconduct. At the same time, a perceived lack of "virtuous" brides and an increasing preoccupation with face and status have resulted in larger and more expensive bride-wealth payments.

There is a broader cultural logic at work here. Parents quite consciously and explicitly view lavish weddings as a form of social security. They hope children will reciprocate the time and money invested in weddings by caring for parents in their old age. This expectation has become even more critical in the United States, where there is not the extended family that would exist in Cambodia to provide such elder care.

Here again, however, tried-and-true principles of Khmer life in Cambodia encounter practical difficulty in the diasporic circumstances of the United States. As Khmer youth acquire American lifestyles and expectations, they resist the cultural values concerning sexuality and marriage that elders are trying to impose.

Chapter 7 examines the dual pattern of adaptation that has emerged among Khmer. It notes the increasing gap between, on the one hand, a small group of "haves" and, on the other hand, a much larger group of "have-nots." This final chapter considers some of the social and cultural concomitants of that pattern, hypothesizing that this gap will likely continue to widen for some time to come.

In detailing the shape of Khmer religion, childrearing, moral education, schooling, and sexuality and marriage, I seek to examine the social and cultural mechanisms for reconstructing a Khmer identity in the United States. All of these social processes reflect a cultural tension or ambivalence (Peletz 1996) in Khmer conceptions of person and self, an ambivalence that has become more pronounced in Khmer American life. Although this tension has been heightened in the United States, it has long been at the heart of Khmer social life. It is a tension between, on the one hand, the ideals of Khmer Buddhist doctrine and related religious beliefs that emphasize the individual's autonomy and integrity and, on the other hand, the more "embedded" or relational morality of community life, with its focus on face, status, and family reputation.

The failure to understand this conflict between Buddhist ideals and everyday practice has often resulted in a misunderstanding of Khmer notions of self and identity. In particular, Western scholars have sometimes overemphasized the individualistic nature of Khmer social relations to the exclusion of socially embedded or "communitarian" tendencies (but see Keyes 1990b; and Tambiah 1970 for a Thai illustration of a similar pattern). It is essential to recognize this tension in order to understand Khmer educational performance and, more generally, the challenge of Khmer adjustment to the social idioms and morality of life in the United States.

2

To Be Khmer Is to Be Buddhist

Theravada Buddhism was the official national religion of the Khmer Republic (Ebihara 1985:131). In prerevolutionary Cambodia, the Buddhist temple (*wat* in Pali, the holy language of Theravada Buddhism; *vat* in Khmer)[1] was a central fixture in Khmer villages, where it functioned not only as a religious shrine but also as a school, refuge, and social center. Buddhist holy days and life-cycle ceremonies punctuated the Khmer calendar and gave religious meaning to the stages of life. Buddhist norms of conduct were important guides for daily behavior.

Familiar figures in both urban and rural life, monks (*bhikkhu*, Pali; *lŏk sâng*, Khmer) were highly respected as both embodiments of Buddhist doctrine and important sources of merit. Although only a few individuals entered the monkhood for life, the majority of Khmer men became monks for at least a short period of time at some point in their lives (Steinberg 1959:65; Ebihara 1968:385). Because of their learning and moral character, former monks were considered desirable marriage partners and played an important role as liaisons between the temple and the lay community.

A series of developments in the late 1960s and early 1970s, however, removed Buddhism from its central role in Khmer life and eventually brought about the near annihilation of the monastic order (*sângha*, Pali; *sâng*, Khmer). In the late 1960s, educational reforms and the resulting expansion of state educational opportunities began to affect recruitment to monasteries in cities and provincial centers throughout Cambodia. Young men increasingly opted to pursue their education through state schools rather than through the monkhood (Kalab 1976:165). Rates of ordination dropped further as the Khmer civil war spread between 1970 and 1975. Not only did the war disrupt rural life, but large numbers of ordination-age men were also conscripted into the national army or drawn into opposition groups.[2]

The physical destruction of the *sângha* intensified with Khmer

Rouge atrocities and the U.S. bombing of eastern Cambodia in an effort to destroy North Vietnamese supply routes. Temple activities were disrupted almost everywhere, and in the eastern provinces, many temples were destroyed, dispersing or killing their monk inhabitants.

The war officially ended in 1975 when the Khmer Rouge seized Phnom Penh, but the revolutionary government's triumph only intensified the assault on the *sângha*. The Pol Pot regime of "Democratic" Kampuchea (D.K.) defined Buddhism as exploitative and feudalistic, because temples and monasteries were supported by the laity's donations (Hawk 1987:132). Monks were ridiculed as lazy and unproductive "leeches." Early in its reign, the D.K. government launched a campaign to supplant Buddhism with a revolutionary political ideology. The goal was to introduce values and behavioral codes consistent with the government's totalizing ideology (Ebihara 1985:22–23).

Inevitably, the physical and social toll on the *sângha* was enormous. Large numbers of Khmer temples were desecrated or destroyed, their religious images stolen or defaced. Because monasteries were among the most sacred and imposing architectural structures in much of the countryside, many were transformed into communal meeting halls where kinship ties were to be replaced by the bonds of universal revolutionary citizenship. Several monasteries eventually became the era's most notorious prisons and torture centers (Gyallay-Pap 1990:2).

The government's policies on monks were equally austere. Monks were defrocked and forced into "useful" labor in the fields. Those who refused to leave the order were subject to immediate execution, often after gruesome torture. A small number managed to flee to Thailand, where the Thai Sangha welcomed them. Others crossed into Vietnam. Still more monks returned to ordinary life for the revolutionary government's duration, marrying and fathering children; at the end of the war, few of these individuals returned to monastic life.

Statistics bear cold witness to the devastating effect of these developments. Whereas there were an estimated forty to sixty thousand *bhikkhu* before the war and before the new government, by 1984—even as the *sângha* was recovering—only some five thousand *bhikkhu* were left (Hawk 1987:132–33; Ebihara 1987:42).

Khmer who managed to reach the Thai border camps in 1979 found that many of the nongovernmental organizations (NGOs) that ministered to their needs and helped them resettle were affiliated with Christian churches.[3] The foreign governments supporting the camps and resettling refugees in conjunction with the United Nations High Commission for Refugees primarily attended to refugees' needs for food, shelter, and medical assistance; they did not provide for religious needs, much less for the establishment of Buddhist temples or meditation groups.

Contracted as service providers, NGOs were not supposed to proselytize—not even Christian ones. There were, nonetheless, reports that some missionary aid workers used food and medicine to induce Khmer refugees into undergoing baptism in Khao I Dang Camp (see also Gosling 1984:62, cited in Van Esterik 1992:21).

Most pressures to convert to Christianity, however, were less heavy-handed. In the words of one Boston-based cleric—a liberal evangelical who had worked in the camps for several years—the trauma of resettlement provided ample opportunity for "teaching God's message through Christian example" and "offering spiritual comfort to those in distress." The effects of this subtle pressure are clear in the stories of refugees who did convert to Christianity in the camps.

> [Widow, age 47] The missionaries in the camp saw that I was so sad and worried. They told me that if I am upset, I should pray to God for help, that Buddha cannot help me. In the camp, I felt a lot of suffering. I could not forget my dead husband, my parents, and my only daughter. They told me I had to pray to God to ask for peace. So I started to believe in Jesus, and slowly I could forget about the past, about my daughter and all of my suffering under Pol Pot and the Khmer Rouge. So I repented, and I entrusted my life to God.

In the wild uncertainty of camp life, in which exit from the camps depended on a foreign institution's sponsorship, many refugees believed that conversion to Christianity would guarantee resettlement in the most desired destination, an affluent Western country. According to the Khmer living in eastern Massachusetts today, many (perhaps most) refugees in the camps attended Christian services at some point. Christian missionaries who worked in the camps at that time confirmed that large numbers of refugees converted while awaiting resettlement. For a time, it seemed as if civil war and resettlement were combining to deal a death blow to Khmer Buddhism (Vickery 1984:12; Mortland 1994).

When Khmer began to arrive in the Boston area in the early 1980s, Christian agencies once again helped many to resettle. The most notable of these were the Catholic Charities Services, Lutheran Social Services, and Church World Service (Refugee Resource Center 1981–82). Many individual sponsors were also Christian; it was not uncommon, for example, for a whole congregation to sponsor one or more Khmer refugee families. Because of these circumstances, many Khmer refugees attended Christian services in the early resettlement period.

In addition to serving as sponsors, Christian churches provided a variety of social services unavailable from the state or local government. These included English classes, advice on negotiating the maze of social assistance offices through which refugees had to pass, and general programs on adjusting to U.S. life. Today, many Buddhist Khmer still feel deeply obligated to the churches and their sponsors for providing this support. It would have appeared ungrateful and disrespectful, they believe, not to have participated in their sponsors' religious services.

Even if some Khmer had wanted to attend a Buddhist religious service, they would have faced daunting physical obstacles to doing so in the early years of Khmer resettlement. Although Khmer refugees who arrived before 1975 had established a rudimentary Khmer Buddhist temple in Providence, Rhode Island (fifty miles southwest of Boston), it was located in a small, cramped, rented apartment. Moreover, in those early days of the Khmer diaspora, few Cambodians had cars or driver's licenses.

Since those early years, refugees have dedicated enormous energy and financial resources to creating Buddhist institutions and a Buddhist way of life in their new homeland. Peter Gyallay-Pap of the Khmer-Buddhist Educational Assistance Project in Amherst, Massachusetts, estimates that by 1990, there were some fifty Khmer temples and one hundred fifty monks in the United States (Gyallay-Pap 1990:17). Today there are seven Khmer Buddhist temples and thirty to forty Khmer monks in eastern Massachusetts alone.

In what follows, I document Khmer refugees' efforts to reestablish their religion in their new homeland. I outline the basic tenets of Khmer Buddhism and examine its role in the lives of Cambodians in the greater Boston area. I describe the Khmer temple, religious practitioners, and key Buddhist practices to show the degree to which Khmer Buddhism continues to be a force in Khmer American identity and the form that it has taken.

REBUILDING THE TEMPLE

In 1983, Boston area Khmer organized the Cambodian Buddhist Association of Massachusetts to support temple development and expand Buddhist social activities. At its founding, the association had more than one thousand members. The new organization was led by several Khmer businessmen and community leaders, at least one of whom was a former monk. At the time, there were no senior monks in eastern Massachusetts; whenever special services were held, monks had to be brought in from Rhode Island and Washington, D.C. They officiated at rituals and life-cycle celebrations in the cramped apartments of newly arrived refugees. Community leaders and ordinary people alike felt that Boston sorely needed a temple and monks of its own.

The new organization took a small step toward establishing a permanent temple when it rented a three-bedroom apartment in an Italian and Hispanic American neighborhood in Revere and created a makeshift temple. The fledgling temple was supported entirely by refugees' donations.

With the assistance of the Buddhist temple in Rhode Island, a smaller committee composed of local lay leaders and elders brought in two resident monks for the new temple. One of the monks had been recruited from the Thai border camps. He entered the country as a refugee, with the temple committee as his sponsor. The congregation paid the expense of his relocation. The second monk came from the Khmer Buddhist temple in Rhode Island, where he had been residing since 1981.

From the beginning, a controversy marred this otherwise successful initiative. Soon after the Rhode Island monk moved to Revere, questions arose about his background. Some Cambodians accused him of being a former Khmer Rouge member who entered the monkhood to cleanse himself of his past misdeeds. Such controversies have plagued similar Khmer American temple-building efforts. They often involve accusations against individuals, particularly those in leadership positions, and acquire a special intensity whenever the individual plays an important role in Khmer political or religious life. In this instance, temple committee members made repeated attempts to investigate the monk's background but were unable to confirm that he had belonged to the Khmer Rouge. Haunted by the accusations, the monk eventually left the temple and moved with family members to another state. Shortly thereafter, the temple committee arranged to sponsor the resettlement of another Khmer monk from Thailand.

After one year in Revere, the temple committee had collected thirty thousand dollars in contributions. This was enough for a down payment on a small building in Lynn, a town north of Boston. In 1984, the temple moved to a blue-collar neighborhood in Lynn, where it remains.

Not long after the move, one of the original monks moved to the Khmer temple in Washington, D.C., to be closer to his extended family.[4] Another monk was brought in from the Rhode Island temple to replace him. Although the number of monks living in the Lynn temple has fluctuated over the years, it has maintained a monastic staff of between three and eight individuals since this time. The numbers vary because, as in Cambodia, monasticism is rarely a lifelong commitment. Novices *(lŏk néan)* typically stay in the temple only for a few weeks or months; even monks of long-standing service occasionally move from one temple to another. Some of the fluctuation, however, also reflects the temple's fragility and its vulnerability to the tensions and factionalism within the Khmer community.

Temples have been developed in eastern Massachusetts wherever significant numbers of Khmer refugees have settled. Several years after the Lynn *wat* was established, a Khmer Buddhist temple was organized in Lowell to serve the large influx of Khmer immigrants to that area. As the Lowell population increased in the mid-1980s, a second temple was added in neighboring North Chelmsford. Around the same time, a makeshift temple with a single monk was established in a rented apartment in Amherst to serve that city's small but well-educated Khmer population; the Lynn and Lowell Buddhist communities helped in this endeavor. Shortly thereafter, another small temple was established in Fall River. More recently, construction on a new, permanent temple has begun in Amherst; a new one has also been established in Revere. Although Amherst's Khmer population remains quite small, it boasts an active lay meditation group.

The Amherst temple grounds also include a separate structure, in which the meditation group can meet without being interrupted by temple activities. Even more recently, a Khmer temple was founded in a rented apartment in North Attleborough.

REBUILDING THE SÂNGHA

The organizational life of a Khmer Buddhist congregation in the United States resembles that of congregationalist communities in Christianity. In particular, responsibility for establishing a temple and securing monks lies with the local religious organization rather than with a central ecclesiastical authority. The community members decide that they need a temple and then form a committee to raise the necessary funds. Monks are not assigned to a particular temple by a higher administrative authority but are recruited directly by temple committee members.

This pattern of organization resembles the way in which temple congregations were established in Cambodia. Local communities formed committees to raise funds for temple construction, and monks were recruited from nearby *wats*. In prewar Cambodia, however, the *sângha* also included an extensive ecclesiastical hierarchy. This consisted of village-level abbots, provincial heads or bishops, and a *sângha* head (the supreme patriarch, or *sǎmdach sâng*).[5] The entire structure paralleled that of the government and was technically under its jurisdiction.

Despite this hierarchy, individual monasteries, especially those in rural areas, remained relatively independent in their everyday decision making and administration (Yang 1987). Ecclesiastical councils *(kanak sâng)* made up of senior monks generally sanctioned decisions that local temple committees had already made and would intervene in temple business only when disputes could not be settled locally. As in Thailand, governing bodies in Cambodia had more to do with national projects, such as the revision of doctrinal texts, than with the administration of individual *wats* (see Tambiah 1970:79). Nonetheless, the *kanak sâng* councils wielded significant power in the Khmer capital. They fulfilled the important functions of ratifying religious titles and credentialing monks who passed annual religious exams at the Buddhist University in Phnom Penh.

With the Khmer civil war almost all of this religious administration was destroyed. The Vietnamese-backed People's Republic of Kampuchea (1979–89) reestablished a limited administrative structure for the *sângha* (Keyes 1990a). Many Khmer Americans, however, refused to acknowledge its legitimacy and instead sought contact with the Thai Sangha, which had welcomed Khmer monks during the Pol Pot period.

Shortly after the Vietnamese withdrew from Cambodia in 1989, Khmer Buddhism was again declared Cambodia's official religion, and the Buddhist religious hierarchy was reinstated. Many monks appointed by the Vietnamese-backed regime reportedly remained in place, though. Khmer Americans generally distrusted these religious authorities, regarding them as deficient in religious training and tainted by association with the Vietnamese-backed regime. The following comments from a Buddhist laywoman interviewed in the early 1990s reveal widespread sentiments in the community.

> [Female, age 44] Before the war, monks would be sent to India to learn Pali, Sanskrit, and everything about Buddhism. They had their degree from an Indian university. Some also went to Thailand or Laos. But those educated monks were all killed during Pol Pot time. The former head of the monks, Sǎmdach Choun Nath, had his degree from India. He knew lots of languages, including old Khmer. He could even talk to the birds and other animals!
>
> The new government in Cambodia has promoted their own people, those without any education. People here don't trust them. If the current *sǎmdach sâng* came now to Lynn, people would refuse to let him stay at the temple. They don't trust him.

Today, contact between Khmer American temples and the *sângha* in Cambodia is still somewhat limited. Nonetheless, American temple committees seeking young monks may approach highly placed, experienced *bhikkhu* at the Buddhist University in Phnom Penh *(Mohavichealay Preah Surammarith)* and ask them to help locate suitable and willing monk recruits. Reportedly, such assistance is easily obtained, as the Khmer Sangha is well aware of Khmer American economic support. In the United States, however, some monks and many Buddhist laypeople want to preserve their independent status. These individuals insist that there are enough monks in the United States to officiate at ordinations, consecrate temples, and oversee monastic developments, and that extensive contact with the Khmer Sangha is therefore unnecessary.

In recent years, a North American council of monks *(kanak sâng)* has been formed to offer guidance and counsel to Khmer American monastic communities. The advisory group includes a small number of senior monks who are well regarded by their peers and by the Khmer American community. The council, however, has minimal power to enforce its rulings, and its members are scattered across the United States and Canada. Assembling the council to consider proposals or complaints is time consuming and expensive and is thus usually limited to a general meeting once or twice a year or to phone calls. Most temple affairs in Khmer Buddhist *wat*s in the United States continue to be handled locally.[6]

THE LOSS OF CENTER

As the Khmer American community has made progress in reconstituting a rudimentary temple system, it has also allowed certain aspects of temple organization to change. Perhaps the most basic change, and for many Khmer the most disturbing one, concerns the *wat*'s role in community life.

Traditionally, the *wat* served as the center of social and religious life. It was not only a place of monastic residence, study, and meditation but also "a school, social center, medical dispensary, counseling center, home for the aged and destitute, news and information center, and social work and welfare agency for the larger society" (Lester 1973:6; see also Ebihara 1966:182). This quality of temple organization has been most severely undermined in the United States.

Unlike the typical *wat* in Cambodia, most *wat*s in Massachusetts suffer from severe space limitations. Moreover, their role as sacred and social community centers has been undercut by the dispersion of the Khmer American community and by work and school schedules that do not match the rhythms of the traditional religious calendar. As a result, both the temple and Buddhist religious activity have been compartmentalized and even marginalized.

The Lynn temple is typical in this regard and illustrates both the achievements and challenges of Khmer Buddhism in New England. Housed in what was formerly a Dominican Catholic church and located in a run-down, inner-city neighborhood, the temple is a two-story white clapboard structure with a single large turret. On the temple's main floor, a wide hall serves as the central sanctuary. Toward the back of this hall on a raised platform sit three life-size bronze statues of the Buddha decorated with fabric flowers, crepe paper, and colored lights. A group of laypeople bought the statues in Thailand, accruing great merit by donating them to the temple. Colorful paintings, copied from Cambodian originals and depicting events from the Buddha's life, decorate the walls on both sides of the hall. To the right of the altar is a large, impressive mural of the Buddha's struggles with the forces of evil. Another painting graphically portrays the Day of Judgment and the tortures of hell; individuals in chains await their sentences, sinners are boiled in hot oil, others have daggers in their arms and thighs, and still others have demons riding on their backs or sitting on their chests.

Next to the main sanctuary is a smaller room in which food offerings may be assembled and arranged during religious events. On Buddhist holidays, this room bustles with the activities of women, who assume primary responsibility for the food offerings, communal meals, and other social activities that occur after each temple ceremony. In the basement are a large meeting room, a kitchen, and bathrooms. On the upper floor are several bedrooms that were originally the monks' living quarters. In 1986, however, the monks moved across the street into a modest clapboard house that the temple committee bought to give the monks more comfortable accommodations.

Community members point out that the Lynn temple's size and location make it unsuitable for large social and educational events. Located in a semiresidential neighborhood and on the corner of two busy streets not far from downtown Lynn, the temple is next to an automotive repair shop. Parents fear that if their children play in the cramped, unfenced temple yard, they might run out into the street or be abducted by strangers. There is no direct public transportation to the temple, and parking is scarce.

Most Khmer live far from the *wat* and, at best, can visit the center only on special religious holidays. Even for those who live in the neighborhood, the *wat*'s practical and symbolic prominence is undercut by activities—school, shopping, and work—that draw Khmer away from the temple and into the surrounding non-Buddhist society. Many adult Khmer are deeply disturbed by this trend, but most have resigned themselves to it, given the new demands and opportunities of U.S. life.

Partly as a result of the *wat*'s social and physical displacement in community life, few Khmer are regularly active in their local temples. The Lynn temple, for example, claims to have at most only twenty to thirty members in regular attendance; most of these are female and middle-aged or elderly.

It would be misleading, however, to use temple attendance as a direct gauge of religiosity. Although Theravada Buddhists in some Southeast Asian urban centers (including Phnom Penh) have developed a more "Protestant," denominational style of worship (Gombrich and Obeyesekere 1988:202–40), popular Khmer Buddhism has no tradition of regular weekly temple services or structured religious education. In principle, *wats* in eastern Massachusetts are open at all times, and the monks are available for consultation. In practice, however, few people have the opportunity or inclination to visit the temple regularly.

When asked about their temple attendance, many Khmer respond that it is not necessary for Buddhists to go to the temple every week.[7] Buddhism emphasizes individual responsibility. Thus, Khmer say that in contrast to Christian belief, "In Buddhism you are responsible for yourself. Nobody else can save you." Khmer also consider it both normal and fitting that religious activity increases with age (Ebihara 1966:179). Younger people are expected to be preoccupied with marrying and establishing a family. Once they have achieved these goals, couples are expected to contribute money and time to the temple. Jobs may limit participation, particularly for men, but older Khmer, particularly women whose children have married and left home, have more time and are expected to dedicate themselves to religious activities. Some elderly Khmer erect elaborate Buddhist altars *(sakkarăk)* in their homes, where they make offerings and pray. Others practice meditation *(samatĕk)*, often under the supervision of a lay leader (an *achaa*), who is usually a former monk.

In contrast to ordinary days, when there are few worshipers, the temple comes alive on Buddhist holidays. Temple activity is particularly intense on the Khmer Buddhist New Year *(Chaul Chnăm)* and Souls' Day *(Phchŭm Bĕn)*. On these occasions, people of all ages stream into the temple for several days. Older and more devout community members come early, sitting near the monks so they can follow the prayers and sermon. Married women organize food offerings in the kitchen, while husbands smoke cigarettes on the front steps. Small children cling shyly to their grandmothers' skirts; others run up and down the temple stairs. Younger men and women, dressed in their best, size each other up discreetly. During the communal meal after the religious ceremonies, adults catch up on the latest news about community members and recent developments in Cambodia.

"WE KHMER ARE ALL BUDDHIST"

Despite the lure of American culture and the profound transformation in the organization of key religious institutions, Buddhist beliefs remain powerfully central to Khmer identity. When Khmer are asked about their religious affiliation, they consistently respond either, "To be Khmer is to be Buddhist" (*"Khmae preah pŭtĕsasna"*) or "We Khmer are all Buddhist" (*"Khmae yoeng tĕang ăh knea preah pŭtĕsasna"*).

Community religious leaders estimate that at least 85 percent to 90 percent of Boston's Khmer identify themselves as Buddhist. My own surveys and interviews confirm that 90 percent is likely to be more accurate. Of course, to identify oneself as a Buddhist says less about participation in temple rituals or belief in specific dogmas than about a sense of community and solidarity. Adult refugees commonly emphasize the need to maintain Khmer solidarity in the face of pressure to assimilate. This moral identification appears to reinforce or even strengthen their association between being Khmer and being Buddhist.

Thus far, Christianity has not had the effect on Boston area Khmer refugees that it reportedly has had on other Southeast Asian refugee groups. Christianity has widely affected Hmong, a hill tribe minority from Laos. Several accounts indicate that more than 50 percent of Hmong refugees have become Christian (Dunnigan 1986:47; Scott 1987:44; Tapp 1989:90–91). By contrast, few Khmer have converted, despite the large number who reportedly attended churches in the Thai border camps and the even larger number who have been involved with U.S. churches since resettlement (Smith-Hefner 1994:24).

Unlike Hmong, Khmer subscribed to a world religion long before coming to North America. Whereas Hmong are an ethnic minority in Laos and have struggled to distinguish themselves from the surrounding Buddhist majority (Keyes 1977; Tapp 1989), Khmer are the majority ethnic group in Cambodia and have a strong sense of national identity, an important element of which has always been Buddhism (Ebihara 1968; Keyes 1977).

Christian missionaries based in mainland Southeast Asia have long been aware of these differences of religious commitment and have therefore typically tried to convert ethnic minorities, particularly marginalized hill tribes. For those groups, Christianity has often served to reinforce ethnic boundaries (Tapp 1989; Kammerer 1990). May Ebihara, who conducted ethnographic fieldwork in Cambodia in the late 1950s, commented that efforts at Christian conversion in prewar Cambodia largely failed (Ebihara 1968:69). The cultural and historical factors that determined how different Southeast Asian groups responded to conversion pressures in their homelands continue to affect their religious affiliations in the United States.

Leaders of the Christian Khmer minority readily acknowledge that the link between Buddhism and Khmer identity is a major obstacle to their conversion efforts. Many Buddhist Khmer view conversion as evidence of a person's desire to adopt a new, non-Khmer identity (Barth 1969; DeVos 1975). As a result, converts to Christianity are often bitterly accused of having "forgotten their culture" *(něak phléch brâpey'ni/tŭmlŏap khmae)*. One Khmer Catholic lay leader, a man in his mid-thirties who had been raised Catholic in Cambodia, expressed his frustration over the small numbers of Cambodians in his parish in just those terms:

> It is very difficult to convert Cambodians because maybe 95 percent or 97 percent of them are Buddhists; they believe their religion is their culture. Those who convert to Christianity, they are criticized by their friends, who say, "Why did you convert? You forgot your culture! If you believe in Jesus, that's the religion for Americans or for the French!" So it's very difficult to convert them.

Just as Khmer identify Theravada Buddhism with Khmer nationality, they also identify Catholicism with the French—or, even worse, with their longtime historical rivals, the Vietnamese. The fact that the lay leader of the Khmer Catholics in one Boston area parish is a Vietnamese who happens to speak Khmer does not escape the attention of most Khmer.

The identification of Buddhism with ethnic identity remains strong among Khmer adults. The uncertainty about the Khmer homeland and the intense grief that many older Khmer feel for loved ones who died in Cambodia suggest that this identification will persist for some time.

The situation for younger Khmer, however, is less defined. Those who left Southeast Asia when they were small children or who were born in this country have no memories of Cambodia. Many young Khmer have only the vaguest understanding of Buddhism's social and historical precedents. The temple's displacement in everyday life also means that the naturalizing, daily exposure of young people to the temple and to Buddhist practice is quite limited. Conversely, young Khmer are exposed to competing cultural ideas and values through school, television, and friends. The commitment of these Khmer American youth to doctrinal Buddhism will depend heavily on their elders' ability to develop new institutions that can give new relevance to Buddhist traditions.

KHMER BUDDHISM: CORE BELIEFS

The Khmer variant of Buddhism is quite different from that which has recently become familiar to some Americans through popular literature and even through films about Buddhism, Zen, and high Buddhist doctrine. Khmer Buddhism is heavily interwoven with elements of an earlier, if now thoroughly indigenized Hinduism, or Brahmanism, as well as with native Khmer spirit beliefs (Ebihara 1968:364). Most lay Khmer do not consciously distinguish between the Buddhist, Brahmanist, and ancestral strains in their religion. Similarly, most grasp their tradition's deeper and more philosophical meanings to varying degrees, depending, most basically, on their previous education and involvement in temple affairs. In general, Khmer monks, particularly those of long-standing service, have the most discursively elaborate, esoteric understanding of Buddhist liturgical texts and ritual, whereas many laypeople express uncertainty about the meaning of some of their beliefs and practices.

Despite such variations in knowledge and depth of understanding, most Khmer Buddhists share certain basic beliefs. The most central of these is the concept of karma *(kam)*, the notion that one's actions in previous lives and the resulting store of merit *(bŏn)* that one has accumulated determine one's current life situation. All adult Khmer Buddhists are also familiar with, and generally accept, the related doctrine of reincarnation *(kaoet mauk vĕnh* or *kaoet m'dong tiet)*, the idea that every individual is caught up in a cycle of rebirths. Together, these two beliefs underlie many of the most basic Khmer notions of personhood and practical morality.

According to the law of karma, everyone accumulates merit and demerit as a result of good acts *(bŏn)* and bad acts *(băp)*. "*Tvoe l'ăh, ban l'ăh; tvoe akrŭak, ban akrŭak,*" people frequently say; "Good acts result in merit, bad acts in demerit." One can accumulate merit in a number of ways. The most common include observing Buddhist holy days, listening to monks' sermons, reciting the liturgy, and adhering to Buddhist precepts.[8] Time and time again, Khmer hear that they must always avoid the three cardinal vices—greed, anger, and delusion—and exhibit the qualities of compassion, charity, and mercy.

By far the most meritorious act is to become a monk *(buoh)*. This option is available only to Khmer men, but some of its spiritual benefits extend to women, especially the initiate's mother. Typically both parents sponsor the son's initiation into the monkhood, and this act of sponsoring brings them merit.[9]

Barred from the monkhood, women tend to achieve merit by dedicating themselves to smaller, ongoing acts of virtue (Ebihara 1974; Keyes 1977). The most beneficial acts tend to support the *sângha*. Women might donate labor or money to the temple or offer food, household objects, or clothing to the monks. Both genders can accrue significant merit by sponsoring a *sâng khătean*, in which they ritually feed the monks at their homes, or by organizing a *kăthĕn* ceremony to give the monks new robes and household items after their yearly retreat *(Chaul Vausa)*. All of these activities involve considerable investment of time and money.

Many Khmer invoke the concept of karma to make sense of social inequalities. The wealthy and powerful are said to be those who accumulated significant merit in their previous lives. Those who are poor or in difficult circumstances explain their condition by referring to putative misdeeds in a prior existence. Karma, however, is not absolute. One can never be certain, for example, when one's store of merit will be exhausted or when one's debt of suffering will be paid. Most important, the individual is always free to choose whether to engage in meritorious or demeritorious acts, thereby directing his or her future in a negative or positive way.

[Male, age 46] I want to make clear to you that all human beings do good and bad things in their life. When you die, your spirit will suffer for the bad things you did, and after that suffering, you will be reborn according to your karma, your good and bad acts. Buddhist doctrine doesn't say that you suffer and after that suffering, you will have a better life. The suffering doesn't save you, no. You pay off your evil by suffering, but then you have to choose to do good.

For example, I have problems with my family, and my wife has divorced me. I suffer about my wife and my problems, and my children are living with other people, not with me. That's suffering. So I have to look to myself to do something about that suffering. I don't want to repeat my mistakes. I have to look for a way, so I decide to go to the monks to learn from them the way of not suffering. I ask them to teach me so I can do well in this world.

But some people suffer and they do not want to learn about their desire and about suffering, and if they fall on the same path, they will suffer again. That is the world of suffering.

Khmer emphasize that karma says little or nothing about one's behavior in the present, only one's behavior in the past. Thus the concept accommodates even the rise to power of a despicable individual such as Pol Pot. It may be reasoned that Pol Pot came to power because of his previous meritorious behavior. He will, however, spend the next five hundred years suffering in hell, informants say, to pay for his behavior toward the Khmer people. More difficult for ordinary people to understand is why so many apparently innocent individuals suffered and died at the hands of the Khmer Rouge—particularly close family members and loved ones. By way of explanation, some Khmer make vague references to the Cambodian people's "collective karma"—a result of their involvement in the prior administration's abuses (see also Mortland 1994:80). Conversely, it is quite common for individuals to explain their personal survival by referring to their own past, meritorious lives.

Karma, then, offers the individual an explanation for a current situation and a means to improve it; simply put, the message is "Accumulate merit, avoid demerit." Part of the psychic economy of merit making, however, is that one can never be certain when its benefits will be realized. It can have important immediate benefits, such as the feeling of peace and well-being that comes from having given freely and with a pure heart (Tambiah 1970:53–54). Most Khmer believe, however, that the more substantial benefits of merit making will be felt only in some future incarnation. For those who are suffering in the present, this belief may prove unsatisfactory; it would be far preferable for them to experience the benefits of their meritorious actions in the present (Keyes 1977:87).

Karma, however, is not the only spiritual idiom through which Khmer interpret and enact the pattern of their lives. Like many other Southeast Asians, they look to other spiritual beliefs to explain (and relieve) many of their more pressing personal and social problems. These beliefs include ghosts, spirits, and the idea of fate. Some scholars of Buddhism, such as the distinguished American anthropologist Melford Spiro (1967), have viewed the existence of such alternate beliefs as antithetical to Buddhist doctrine, contradicting its emphasis on karma as the single and ultimate cause of events in the world. In his study of Burmese supernaturalism, Spiro concluded that Burmese spirit beliefs constituted a religious system so contrary to Buddhist principles as to make the two completely separate.

In a manner that accords more directly with the Khmer experience, however, the anthropologist Stanley J. Tambiah has argued that both religious traditions are elements in a "total field" of action and belief (1970:41). Indeed, inasmuch as Khmer believe that karma explains one's susceptibility to imminent good or evil (such as that associated with spirits), the two systems of ritual and belief need not contradict each other. On the contrary, both are subsumed within a religious system in which karma remains ultimately determinative (Ebihara 1966:189–90, 1968:364; Keyes 1977:88).

Consistent with Tambiah's analysis, I disagree with those who have questioned the importance of Buddhism for Khmer and who have suggested that spirit beliefs are somehow more central than Buddhism to the Khmer psyche. Such arguments are based on an idealized and excessively doctrinal definition of Buddhism, rather than, as I attempt to portray here, the "practical" Buddhism of ordinary Khmer. Khmer define themselves as Buddhists; most do not feel any contradiction between the more doctrinal elements of their religion and their less orthodox spirit beliefs. Even the monks do little to discourage spirit beliefs. Through their presence and silence (or even their active participation), many lend spiritual support to unorthodox practices.

One of my earliest field experiences, an exorcism or purification ceremony *(p'dâh kruoh)*, impressed upon me the interrelated nature of these varied elements of Khmer religious practice and belief. With a busload of Boston area monks, I traveled to the Bronx home of a prominent middle-class Khmer family. The husband in this household was having an affair with another woman. Unbeknownst to the husband, the wife had arranged an exorcism, "in order to chase away evil and restore harmony to their relationship." She invited an *achaa* (a Khmer ritual specialist) and several monks from Boston because she did not want the local Khmer community to learn of her marital problems. She told her husband only that the ceremony would be a *sâng khătean*, or a ritual feeding of the monks.

The monks performed their prayers and were fed. The head monk offered some commentary, which included an admonition to the husband to "listen to his wife if she tells him something is wrong." After the monks finished, the *achaa* began the exorcism, fashioning two "corpses" to represent the couple. The effigies were made of flour paste and were shaped into small human figures on flat sheets of cardboard. To ensure their proper identity, each was dressed with articles of clothing from their living models. Offerings of food, alcohol, and cigarettes were set out, and incense was burned to entice the evil spirits to enjoy the food and drink. The spirits would then be "tricked" into inhabiting the effigies, rather than staying with the host couple.[10]

From the perspective of official Buddhism, this exorcism was clearly unorthodox. Yet the ritual's sponsors made little effort to distinguish between its orthodox and heterodox, animist elements. Although the monks were not directly involved in the exorcism, they remained in the room while it was performed and were fully aware of what was occurring. At one point, a senior monk even joked with me about the two turtles that were released at the end of the exorcism to carry away sin and evil. He said, "You see? The one is carefree and happy like the wife, and the other is sullen and angry like the husband." Thus, the monks do little to discourage ancestral and spirit beliefs. Indeed, in subtle and unsubtle ways, many actually support such actions and beliefs.[11]

Khmer, like Spiro's Burmese, are familiar with a whole array of spirits (see Ang 1986). There are, for example, territorial spirits *(něak ta)*, who protect those living in the area they inhabit. Although they are usually harmless if deferred to properly, these spirits can cause misfortune if ignored. There are also ancestral spirits *(méba)*, who watch over living family members. *Méba* must be informed of all important life events and given offerings on important holidays. Normally quite benign, *méba* will attack an innocent person if his or her family member commits a sinful act, such as striking a child or having sexual relations outside marriage. Particularly worrisome is a category of ghosts *(khmaoch)* called *prĕay*, who are the unhappy spirits of those who died violently or in childbirth and who roam the middle world seeking victims.

> [Male, age 44] A *khmaoch prĕay* is a ghost, the spirit of a woman who dies in childbirth or from suicide—for example, following a rape. My neighbor, Mr. Bong, told me about a man in his village in Battambang who went with his wife to build a shelter to do their rice harvest. The man was a gambler, and his wife was pregnant. On the day the wife went into labor, the husband was away gambling in another village. His wife suffered alone, and finally she died trying to give birth to their child.
>
> The husband came home a few days later with some meat for his wife. He saw the woman still in the shelter, and he said, "Here is some meat for you to give you strength." But he noticed a strange smell around the shelter, a death smell, and he thought, Oh, maybe my wife is dead, and this is really her spirit. So he told his wife, "Stay here, and I'll get you some water," and he hurried away from that place. But as he left, his wife called out to him, "Please, husband, don't leave me!" And when he turned around, he saw that she was so ugly, with long matted hair and big popped-out eyes, and she began to chase him.
>
> He ran and ran all the way to the temple. The monks took him in quickly and locked the door. They recited Buddhist prayers. The ghost sat up in a big tree outside the temple walls. From this perch, she shrieked at her husband so everyone could hear, "If you ever come out and walk under this tree, I'll kill you, because you left me alone to die!"
>
> After many years, that man forgot about the ghost, and he walked under the tree. And his wife's spirit jumped on his back and broke his neck. When they found his body, everyone remembered that his wife's spirit had said she would break his neck if he walked under that tree. That spirit did not want to go away, because she wanted revenge.

Khmer in this country have given considerable thought to the possibility that spirits might relocate to the United States from Cambodia. The question is particularly vexing in terms of territorial spirits; they protect people in a certain place, but in the United States, they might easily be seen as "out of place." At present, there seems to be little consensus among Khmer on this issue, but, whatever the status of this belief, ritual practices directed toward this category of spirit seem to be declining. This pattern was reportedly already apparent among urban Cambodians prior to the war (Martin 1994).

There are fewer doubts, however, about the continued presence of other types of spirits, particularly ancestral spirits *(méba)* and unhappy ghosts *(khmaoch prĕay)*.[12] Spirit mediums *(mnŭh chaul rup)* and fortune-tellers enjoy considerable popularity among Khmer, and many individuals continue to offer spiritual explanations for misfortunes that occur within the Khmer American community.

> [Male, age 48] It seems that there are spirits now in the Boston area. In Lowell, for example, there are two places—a street and a house—where there is a spirit. The police in Lowell know that street because at night if you drive there, you will see that ghost. It will stop your car to talk to you. I never saw it, but I am afraid, because everybody told me about that, and there have been a lot of accidents at that spot. It is a bad ghost, a woman who was killed in a robbery in her car at that spot. The Lowell police know about that, too, and they stay on that corner at night to see if anyone stops. And if the car stops, they will call two squad cars to make sure you avoid that place quickly. If you stop and talk with her, the ghost will kill you.

Khmer also invoke the less anthropomorphic notion of "fate" *(veasna)* to explain events. Although it is an impersonal force at large in the world, fate obeys certain principles. Its logic can therefore be deciphered by a trained astrological specialist (a *krou teay*).[13]

Once people know their fates, however, they can take steps to adjust or manipulate events. For example, people typically consult with a *krou teay* to determine the auspicious day for a special event, such as moving into a new home or opening a new store. Even more important, before wedding negotiations can be finalized, a *krou teay* must determine the candidates' suitability for each other. If the appropriate date is not convenient or if the desired mate is deemed unsuitable, however, another ritual specialist may be called in to adjust the situation or to make the appropriate "fit" with special charms or magic potions. Love magic *(tvoe snae)* or its antidote may be used to induce or dissuade a suitor.[14]

Although the principles distinguishing fate from karma appear clear, ordinary Khmer do not consistently differentiate between the two. At times, their explanation of an event may invoke both principles. For example, in arranging a marriage, one may attribute the perfect match to fate *(veasna)*, while explaining that the family into which each individual was born is a matter of karma *(kam)*. The principles may be linked in such a manner in Khmer commentary, but they are nonetheless different. Karma offers an ultimate explanation for one's existential condition. It exerts a powerful and inalterable influence on the present but also offers the prospect of improvement in an indeterminate future. By contrast, belief in spirits and fate allows one to manipulate a situation in the present for a more immediate and (if done properly) positive effect.

SOULS, SPIRIT ESSENCES, AND THE AFTERLIFE

Khmer believe that the individual has a soul *(prâlŏeng)*. A vital life force as well as a spirit, the soul must remain in the body. Otherwise, the individual will become ill, suffer misfortune, or even die. Some Khmer distinguish between the *prâlŏeng tŭm* (the big soul) and the *prâlŏeng tauch* (the small soul or souls). Losing one or more of the *prâlŏeng tauch* causes disorientation or even unconsciousness. Losing the *prâlŏeng tŭm* is far more serious, however. If the *prâlŏeng* departs and cannot be called back, the individual will certainly die.

> [Male, age 44] Ordinary people call the soul *prâlŏeng tŭm*, but there are maybe twelve or nineteen smaller branches called *prâlŏeng tauch*. We are afraid about the *prâlŏeng tŭm*. If that soul flies away from you or *Yŭmba'bal* (the Taker of Souls) takes that from you, he takes your life. If the *prâlŏeng tauch* goes, then just a little of your soul is gone. You still remember. You can lose your [little] soul temporarily from shock or panic, like from an accident. But if the *prâlŏeng tŭm* leaves you temporarily, then you go into a coma or lose consciousness. And if you wake up, you may not remember anything at all.

If the *prâlŏeng* wanders, a special ceremony called *hav prâlŏeng* may be done to "recall the soul."

> [Female, age 56] Sometimes, you pass out and your body is still warm and they call you back. That's called *hav prâlŏeng*, "call the soul." They have a special kind of teacher *(krou)* who does that. And in my meditation group, we talk about that, too, with our meditation teacher. When you do meditation, sometimes you don't want to return to your body, and you want to live over there. You are very happy there. But the teacher knows you and knows where your *prâlŏeng* travels and calls you to come back. "Come quickly, because you still have a lot of things to do here!"[15]

Some Khmer say that the *prâlŏeng* may appear as a fireball that flees from the body when the individual dies. Some also say that on dark nights in Cambodia, such fireballs could be seen falling from the sky onto roofs, indicating that a woman in the house had conceived.

> [Female, age 56] When I traveled with my parents to the seashore at night, I would see something like a shooting star that fell down onto a house. We believe that in that house, someone gets pregnant. It is called *tep sayŭt* (*tep* means "god," and *sayŭt* means "come to be reborn"), a reborn soul, a falling star.

When the individual dies, the *prâlŏeng* vanishes, but the *vĕ'nhean* (the individual's "vital essence," sometimes translated as "consciousness") survives (Keyes 1977:116; Tambiah 1970:57).[16] Khmer believe that the continuity allowed by the *vĕ'nhean* is the reason some people can remember their previous lives. Such memories are common only among people who have performed many good acts in their lifetimes and who have thus died with a clean soul. In this case, Khmer say, the fact that the soul had no sin allows it to be reborn quickly, without the usual wait in *asaurâkkay*, the world of spirits.

> [Male, age 46] If someone is reborn and remembers his previous life, that kind of soul did good in the previous life and was reborn very quickly. That's why that person can remember his previous life. He didn't have to wait long in *asaurâkkay*, the world of spirits.

Other Khmer insist that when someone dies, that individual's *prâlŏeng* survives and is evaluated on the basis of that person's past actions. The soul goes before a judge *(Yŭmreach)*, who considers the individual's good and bad acts *(kam)*. Most individuals have a surplus of negative acts and will have to spend time in hell to pay for their misdeeds.

> [Male, age 44] People believe that when someone dies, their spirit *(prâlŏeng)* goes to a place that looks like a court, and there is a judge. The judge opens up the paper and looks at how many sins you did, how much good you did, and then he decides how many years you will spend in hell or in heaven or how quickly you will be reborn.
> He is called *Yŭmbi'bal*, the guy who comes to take your soul. *Yŭmreach* is the judge. There is another one called *Mach'reach*. He decides when someone will die or be killed. When they die, *Yŭmbi'bal* picks up the spirit to take to *Yŭmreach*, who decides how many years the spirit will spend in heaven or hell. It's like on earth, like a jail with a

> judge. It depends on that person's sin, like did he steal or kill or rape someone? Then when he dies, he will be sent to jail, and in jail he will be hit or beaten or have to eat something horrible like in our jails today.
> They have levels of punishment, different kinds of hell, that depend on the crime. And after the punishment is over, they send the spirit to be reborn as a man or a woman or an animal. The judge decides that.

Various kinds of sin require different punishments. Those who commit adultery, for example, are stripped naked and required to climb a thorny pole. Women who display their physical attractiveness before monks in the temple are suckled by worms. Individuals who commit acts such as torture or murder may be sentenced to five hundred years of suffering—being boiled in a vat of hot oil or being poked with sharp knives or hot irons. Only after these tortures have been endured can the individual be reborn as a human being or animal.

In contrast, those who are particularly meritorious in life spend time in a level of Buddhist heaven *(thansuo)* after death. Again, the level of heaven attained depends on the amount of merit and degree of insight gained in this life. No matter how pleasant or painful, however, all time spent in the invisible realm is finite, as is all time spent in the world of the living. Every individual is caught in an endless cycle of birth and rebirth *(vâdt'sângsa)*. After living out a sentence in heaven or hell, one is reborn according to one's karma. Only those such as the Buddha who gain true insight can reach the final "blowing out," the extinguishing of all desire that is nirvana *(ně'pean)*. With this achievement, they escape the suffering of birth, old age, sickness, and death *(kaoet, chah, chhoeu, slap)*.

THE BUDDHA'S LIFE AND TEACHING

Consistent with Theravada doctrine elsewhere, religious specialists in the Khmer community emphasize that Khmer Buddhism does not see the Buddha *(Preah Putth)* as a god but as an example to be followed, a teacher. There were Buddhas long before the Buddha of our era. Another, *Preah Se'amétrey*, will arrive sometime in the future. Contrary to some Western portrayals of high Buddhism, however, Khmer Buddhism (like many other Southeast Asian forms of Buddhism) asserts that there is a heaven and that godlike spirits inhabit this heaven.

Among the spirits figuring in Khmer descriptions of heaven, for example, are gods of Hindu origin, who are alternately referred to as "angels" *(tévoda)*, such as *Preah An* (Indra in Hinduism) and *Preah Prŭm* (Brahma in Hinduism). These gods are familiar figures in many Theravada Buddhist cosmologies. These Hindu deities are "Buddha-sized" through their identification as inhabitants of realms below that of Buddha.[17] In addition, these Hindu gods are depicted as being so absorbed in sensual enjoyment that they cannot practice the detachment necessary for the achievement of nirvana. There are also various spiritual entities inhabiting the different levels of hell; their suffering is so intense that they cannot concentrate enough to be saved. Thus, their only hope for relief from suffering is that they might share in the merit accrued by their descendants who remember them in their prayers and offerings (Lester 1973:40). The Buddha is always far beyond these deities, which indicates his unparalleled insight and his freedom from sensual entailments.

The story of the Buddha's life is recounted in the temple at least once a year on the day celebrating his birth, enlightenment, and death. This occurs during the month of *Meak Tŭm*, which normally falls between January and February. The story is a favorite of Khmer children, who may hear it at the temple or from their parents, teachers, or older relatives. In the United States, some Khmer children also learn the story by seeing movies about the Buddha. Some of these, such as Bernardo Bertolucci's *Little Buddha,* have become quite popular among Khmer. Here is an abbreviated version of the Buddha story as recounted by a temple *achaa* (a Buddhist lay minister) to a group of Khmer students on a field trip.

> Buddha was a prince, the son of an Indian king. When the Buddha was born, he came out of his mother's womb and walked. He took seven steps. He pointed his finger and said, "In this world, nobody knows better than I." He was a prince, and when he grew up, he would become king after his father. It was foretold, however, that if he saw the world outside of the palace, he would renounce everything and become a Buddha. So his parents did not allow him to go outside the palace walls.
> But Buddha was bored and went outside one day with his servant,

Chhan'mat. He saw an old man walking with a cane. "What kind of person is that?" he asked his servant.

"It is an old person. Later on, you will look like that, too."

Buddha began to worry about becoming old, and he returned quickly to the palace.

Again, he became bored and went out of the palace. This time, he saw a sick person. "What is wrong with that man?" he asked *Chhan 'mat*.

"He is sick, and later on when you become old, you, too, will experience sickness."

They returned again to the palace, where Buddha worried that later he would become sick.

Several months passed, and he went out of the palace again. This time, he saw a dead person. "What kind of person is that?" he asked his servant.

"That is a dead person, and later you, too, will die."

Buddha returned to the palace and worried about death, about suffering, about sickness.

A fourth time, he ventured out of the palace. This time he saw a monk *(lŏk sâng)*. "What kind of person is that who has a shaved head and saffron robes?" he asked *Chhan'mat*.

"It is a monk. He begs for food, and he goes to the temple to pray. That man who is a monk doesn't want to be born again, to get old, to get sick, to die *(kaoet, chah, chhoeu, slap)*. That's why he became a monk, to escape the cycle of rebirth."

"Where is the place where you don't suffer and die?" the young prince asked.

And his servant answered, "That place is nirvana *(nĕ'pean)*. It has no suffering, no sickness, and you don't have to be born again."

And then the young prince smiled. He said, "I want to become a monk, because the happy existence I have now is not happy at all. It is hell. All my fortune, all my possessions, all of that is sin, a dirty thing, a worrying thing. It is the cause of all suffering. That's why I must give it up and become a monk."

The king of the angels, the Evil One, Mara, then came to Buddha to try to dissuade him from his decision by saying, "Think about your wife and your child. Think of the good you can do with your fortune."

But the prince was not swayed. He became the Buddha and spent his life preaching the *dhamma*, "the right path," which is the middle way between extreme indulgence and extreme asceticism.

The Buddha shared his insight with the world through his teachings (the *dhamma*, Pali; *thŏa*, Khmer), which were recorded by his followers and are part of the Buddhist scriptures, the *Tripitaka*.[18] Central to the *dhamma* and the best-known of Buddha's teachings is his first sermon, "Setting in Motion the Wheel of the *Dhamma*," in which he enumerates the Four Noble Truths (Lester 1973:22). They are as follows:

1. Human existence is suffering.
2. The cause of human suffering is desire.
3. Where there is no desire, there is no suffering.
4. The way to avoid suffering is the Middle Path.

Although virtually all Khmer Buddhists know of the Four Noble Truths, the degree to which they worry about suffering and release varies greatly by age, gender, experience, and religious education. Khmer believe that a young or unreflecting individual may come to the temple to request love, popularity, or beauty in this life. This is to be expected, more sophisticated people say. In their commentary, Khmer religious leaders repeatedly emphasize that devotion has various motives and meanings, depending on one's life situation and capacity for understanding. According to these leaders, the Buddha himself taught that people must each realize the *dhamma*'s truth in their own time. An elderly temple *achaa* explained it in this way:

> Many young people come to the temple and make offerings to the Buddha and ask to be beautiful or popular. For example, there is a story about a young girl who didn't have any flowers to make an offering, and she saw some yellow squash flowers by the temple. She picked those flowers and offered them to the Buddha and said, "I want to be a lovely yellow color like this flower in my next life," and she became yellow like that—her skin was a beautiful yellow like that in her next life! But the older people don't ask for things like that. They ask for peace, and they ask that their offering will go to their ancestors, because they need that kind of thing. Young people have desire on their mind—they want to be this and that. They wish for everything. But not the older people. That's all right. It is acceptable. Buddha understands about that.

Many older or more devout members of the laity attempt to abide more closely by the *dhamma*'s teaching and to follow the middle path. Some even go on to study meditation, cleansing their thoughts and more carefully controlling their desires. In so doing, they prepare for death and future lives.

> [Meditation grandmother, age 67] I do meditation because I want light on my soul. That means when I die, I will have light on my body, on my mind, and I will have a good rebirth. I am old and sick and I will die soon. I am not afraid about that, because I am going home. I will look for the light to bring me to that place. I would like to go to nirvana, but at least I have light, and my life will be better. You have to learn to control yourself, your desire, and do good things *(tvoe bŏn)*. That way, when you die, your mind is fresh, and you remember those good things. And you will go to a good place, a peaceful place.

Most Khmer think it is not possible to achieve nirvana in this lifetime; it requires many lifetimes of meritorious behavior. By espousing this belief, people acknowledge their limited standing in the sociomoral order. At the same time, this self-perception relieves them of the more onerous disciplines required of a spiritual virtuoso. These people are, after all, merely ordinary, still far from the elevated status required to prepare for full enlightenment. They therefore focus their spiritual attention on merit making in all its concrete (and manageable) immediacy. By making and accumulating merit *(tvoe bŏn)* in this life, however, average laypeople hope to improve their chances for a better rebirth or perhaps secure a place in one of the sensual heavens after death. They leave it to the monks to achieve more lofty religious goals by donning the saffron robes of the order and dedicating themselves to following the Buddha's path.

MONKHOOD AND THE MONASTIC LIFE

Monks are integral to Khmer Buddhism's social functioning and cultural transmission. In their efforts to emulate the Buddha's life and uphold the *dhamma*, they serve as important moral models, as well as teachers and counselors to the lay community. Monks also act as conduits for merit making. Because the offering's power depends on the purity of both the receiver and giver, gifts given to monks are considered the most meritorious (Tambiah 1970:53; Lester 1973:46).

Before a man can become a monk, he must fulfill several conditions. He must be able to declare that he is debt-free, disease-free, sane, and indeed a human (not of the animal or spirit worlds). He must also have the permission of his parents (if he is a youth) or his wife (if he is married). Under such circumstances, there are strong pressures for the parents or wife to assent to the man's request. Most Khmer feel it would be sinful to refuse a man's request to join the monkhood.[19] The moral reciprocity at work in such requests extends in both directions, however, bringing merit not just to the aspiring monk but also to those around him. More often than not, in fact, it is the parents who ask the young men to *buoh* (become a monk) for a period of time; most sons feel obliged to consent.

> [Male, age 52] Even now, if my father asked me to become a monk, I would say, "OK." Because in Buddhism, we believe that ordaining is a duty, a repayment, the highest repayment for the debt to the parents. You understand how much your mother loves you and takes care of you, how much she suffered when you were born. So the child says, "OK, mother and father, to please you I will go." And if I did that, I would feel so good, so I would go.

There are two orders of monks in Khmer temples: the *lŏk néan* (Pali, *sammné*), "novices," and the *lŏk phŏek* (Pali, *pĭkhŏk*), "senior monks." *Lŏk néan* are young men under the age of twenty; *lŏk phŏek* must be twenty or older. *Lŏk néan* are required to follow only 10 major precepts, whereas *lŏk phŏek* must follow 227. Correspondingly, becoming a *lŏk phŏek* requires deeper study and self-discipline and is thus considered more meritorious than becoming a *lŏk néan*.

Khmer typically comment that novices and senior monks are held in equally high regard. After all, both are in the category of *âng*, "religious persons," and both are addressed with special terms of deference. Nonetheless, there are clear and far-reaching differences in status between the two. *Lŏk néan*, for example, may not eat with the *lŏk phŏek* and may sit with the senior monks only if invited to do so. The novices also sleep in a separate area of the *wat* and spend much of their day apart from the *lŏk phŏek*.

In Cambodia until the 1970s, young men and their parents still regarded initiation into the monkhood as an exemplary social act and as an ideal way to accrue merit for the initiate and his parents. Initiation rates were relatively high, particularly in rural areas (Ebihara 1966:177). Former monks were highly regarded because of their presumed moral stature and education. For the same reasons, former monks tended to hold positions of authority within village political and social life.

> [Male, age 52] Most people liked men who were ordained for a son-in-law. When you become a monk and then leave to become an ordinary person, you are considered a very good person, an educated person. In the village, when you are a monk and then become a regular person, they call you differently, like *bândĭt* (pundit). You have a high rank like a scholar.

Parents sent unruly or disobedient sons to the monastery to acquire discipline and to prepare themselves for adult responsibilities.

> [Male, age 52] Somebody who is like twenty years old and is no good and drinks all day, his parents would send him to the temple. And the monks would educate him, and he would become a monk. That young man would change completely.

Before public schools were widely established in the late 1960s and early 1970s, many men also joined the monastery to obtain an education. Their exposure to reading and writing was particularly important (Ebihara 1966:183).

> [Male, age 52] My father, he sent all of his sons to the *wat* to study and to become monks, beginning at the age of seven. My three brothers all stayed at the temple from ages seven to twelve. They stayed the whole time. Then, when my oldest brother was fifteen, my father had him ordained. He became a monk and then took care of all my other brothers in the temple, like he cared for them at the *wat*.
> I remember in 1962, there were still a lot of monk teachers, until about 1970. Then they switched over to the other [public school] system. I was the only one who didn't become a monk, because I went to public school. By the 1970s, things had already changed, and more of my friends went to school in town. Only two or three came back [to the village] to go to the *wat*.

Today in the United States, very few Khmer men, young or old, become monks, even for short periods. In eastern Massachusetts, only one or two ordinations take place in each temple per year, and almost all of the men ordained remain monks for extremely brief periods.[20]

School schedules make it difficult for young men to *buoh* (undergo ordination), except in the summer or during vacations. Those who do *buoh* often enter the temple as novices *(lŏk néan)* and stay for no more than a week or two. In the Boston area, small groups of young men, often high-school friends, sometimes come together from different temples to be ordained as *lŏk néan* during the summer. They are housed in a single temple and receive their religious lessons together—with a different temple taking responsibility for new *lŏk néan* so that no temple is overburdened. Many of the novices, however, must spend their time in the temple learning to read basic Khmer script. As a result, most fail to master any but the most rudimentary Buddhist prayers and doctrine.

> [Male, age 52] Here, maybe fewer than 1 percent of boys become monks now. As a parent, too, I don't want to pay for my son to become a monk for only a short time, like a few weeks, even a few months. We call that *buoh kŏm aoy chay kham*, "become a monk just to get rid of the lice" (because you shave your head when you become a monk). You can't learn anything in such a short period of time. So for me, I think it's better that my son stay in school and study hard for his future.

Given the chronic undersupply of ordination candidates, it is perhaps not surprising that most experienced senior monks *(lŏk phŏek)* in Khmer American temples were ordained not in the United States but in Cambodia or Thailand. In the early years of the Khmer diaspora, monks were recruited from Thailand or the border camps. Today, however, monks may also be brought from Cambodia itself, with a local temple committee acting as sponsor. Recent reports indicate a healthy revival of the temple and monkhood in Cambodia, with large numbers of ordinations and widespread temple construction (Keyes 1990a). A significant portion of the financial support for these events has come from Khmer who have resettled abroad. It appears that as public school opportunities have again become less certain in Cambodia, religious education is once more an attractive option. Indeed, reports indicate that there is considerable competition among young monks for positions in the Buddhist University in Phnom Penh.

Probably the majority of monks in Khmer American temples today, however, arrived as refugees. As noted earlier, doubts remain about the background and training of these individuals. Further complicating the situation, the majority of monks who survived the Pol Pot years came from the ranks of the less-educated, rural clergy. Many of them are thought to lack the training and spiritual standing to merit their congregation's confidence.

Concerns have also been raised about the monks' daily activities. Conditions in the United States have necessitated adjustments in the monks' ascetic regimens. Many of these adjustments represent a serious departure from the monastic discipline observed in Cambodia. In the United States, for example, it is impossible for monks to go begging from house to house for their daily meals. Instead, on Buddhist holy days, offerings of dry rice and canned goods are stockpiled in the temple. Food must be cooked either by the *yeichi*, the temple grandmothers, who live in a separate area of the monks' quarters, or by families in the community, who take turns cooking.

There are rumors that some monks have used their own money to "order in" from Chinese restaurants, whereas others have refused to eat food from certain families because it does not suit their tastes. (Monastic rules specify that monks must accept all that is offered to them without comment or evaluation.) Community members also complain that monks smoke, watch inappropriate television programs, and eat ice cream during the afternoon fast, all of which are explicitly against monastic rules (the *Vinaya*).

In the monks' defense, it should be pointed out that it is quite hard for them, and especially for aging monks, to adjust to the harsh northeastern climate and to a new social environment. They must don long underwear and hockey socks under their saffron robes and learn to deal with the cold and isolation of long winter months. Older monks grieve the loss of dignity and respect that their role once commanded. Young Khmer Americans are unlikely to know the terms of honorific speech and polite demeanor required in their interactions with monks. Moreover, many of the monks, like the general refugee population, suffer from health problems and require special diets and medication. Monks who are depressed and unhealthy have a difficult time supporting and counseling their community.

LAY RELIGIOUS SPECIALISTS AND THEIR KNOWLEDGE

Although monks are recognized as the most important religious specialists in the Khmer community, they are not the only religious practitioners. Former monks, those who spent a number of years of their lives in the monastery and then left again to become "regular people," also play an important role as intermediaries and interpreters of religious doctrine for the laity. Most important among these are the *achaa*, who are lay ministers or "ritual specialists."

Achaa are typically middle-aged men who spent many years as monks in Cambodia and who therefore know a lot about the monkhood and the temple. In Cambodia, some candidates reportedly undergo a written test administered by the *sângha* before they can assume the *achaa* role in the temple. The exam is designed to assess their knowledge of Buddhist doctrine and ritual. Because the *sângha*'s administrative structure does not exist here in the United States, the monks and laity within a particular temple usually invite men directly to become *achaa*. They continue to serve as *achaa* only as long as the monks and the laity are satisfied with their conduct. If an *achaa* oversteps the bounds of his role or fails to perform his duties, the religious community shuns him.

> [*Achaa*, age 62] If the *achaa* does something wrong, then he has to receive some kind of suffering from the regular people [the laity]. Like, the people will avoid you and not talk to you—that is a suffering. Nobody chases you out of the *wat* or out of the community, but nobody will ask you to worship at the temple or officiate at their home ceremony. They just don't do anything—they don't pay attention to you, they don't talk to you, they ignore you *(baek knea)*.

The *achaa*'s official duties include overseeing the daily upkeep of the temple and temple grounds, seeing to the monks' comfort, assisting the monks on religious holidays, and setting up and orchestrating rituals in the temple and private homes. *Achaa* may also play an active role in educating novice monks.

In Cambodia, *achaa* typically specialize in certain types of religious ceremony. There are, for example, temple *achaa*, house-blessing *achaa*, wedding *achaa*, funeral *achaa*, and many others. In the United States, a single *achaa* is usually called on to perform several or all of these ritual roles.[21] The role of *achaa* in Khmer American temples and communities cannot be overestimated, as they manage the temple's day-to-day operations and ensure that the life-cycle ceremonies so critical to Khmer Buddhism (and in which monks are only minimally involved) are carried out properly.

Temple *achaa*, particularly those involved in conducting official temple business, tend to be relatively orthodox in their religious knowledge and behavior. Other *achaa*, however, are often involved in doctrinally questionable activities, such as exorcisms of evil spirits or demons. In these rites the *achaa* acts somewhat as a lay minister and somewhat as a *krou*, another Khmer ritual specialist.

More peripheral to the temple's life and doctrine, *krou* are traditional healers. They practice several magical, medicinal, and spiritualist folk arts. Like *achaa*, *krou* may be former monks. They may have even learned their prayer formulas and healing techniques from a fellow monk during their time in the temple (yet another indication of the interrelated nature of doctrinal and less doctrinal elements of Khmer belief).

The knowledge of other *krou* has only a marginal relationship to Buddhist institutions, though. For example, some *krou* are said to have inherited their abilities from their fathers or grandfathers. Others have mystical powers because of some unusual circumstance of their birth. In still other cases, especially with black magic, they may secure their powers through illicit activities or even violence. There are reports of *krou* who possess a powerful demon spirit called the *kaun krák*, which the *krou* obtained by wrenching a fetus from the womb (usually killing the mother in the process). *Kaun krák* give their *krou* owners great magical powers as long as the *krou* make daily offerings of food, incense, and candles to the *kaun krák* (Marcucci 1986:156).[22]

The most common *krou* are healers who may be called on to administer traditional cures and to offer protective charms and spiritual insights. *Krou* healers typically cure illness by blowing or spitting *(phlŭm baley)* on an affected body part. They also use special Buddhist prayers or charms that they recite over the patient or that they engrave on a strip of paper or small piece of metal for the patient to wear around the neck or waist.

> [Woman, age 37] My husband is a *krou*. He can do things like spitting on people to heal them. He is very good at helping small children if they are sick. If they have a high fever, he spits and the fever is gone. In Cambodia, he did that all the time. But here, the people don't know the proper way to invite him to the house. Like, you have to put out a bunch of bananas, some money, a candle, and incense, and then invite him to come and see the child. One person didn't know to

do like that. She just paid him money—no incense, no candle. And so he got sick because his spirit master made him sick. He [his *krou* master] said, "You did wrong to accept that money without those other things." So I told my husband, "Stop. Don't do that kind of thing anymore."

Within the metropolitan Boston Khmer community, many *krou* of various kinds continue to practice healing and magical arts. Most middle-aged men who spent some time in the temple seem to know at least a few simple healing techniques, which they use if a family member falls ill.

Another category of religious specialist is the *yeichi*, or *daunchi*, "temple grandmothers," sometimes incorrectly identified as Khmer "nuns." Typically, though not always, the *yeichi* are older women, especially widows or women who have no family responsibilities. The *yeichi* live at or near the temple. They are recognizable by their shaved or short-cropped hair and traditional black or white silk pants and tunic. In the United States, they help clean the temple, prepare food for the monks, make tea for visitors, and participate in the monks' daily prayers. *Yeichi* take no vows, although they may follow an expanded number of Buddhist precepts. One index of their relatively unelevated status in the hierarchy of ritual specialists is that the laity does not consider them to be a source of merit.

> [*Achaa*, age 62] The *yeichi* are women who live at the temple and practice Buddhism by reciting the precepts. In the daytime, they cook for the *lŏk sâng* (monks). In Cambodia, the *yeichi* have to live in a different house, separate from the monks. But here, we accept that we have different conditions, and the *yeichi* live in the same house as the monks, but on a different floor. In fact, the *yeichi* should be in a separate building. In Cambodia, nobody will trust you if you live under the same roof, but here, we have to allow that.

As this comment illustrates, the *yeichi* tend not to be highly regarded within the community. This status is consistent with that of women in Khmer Buddhism generally (Van Esterik 1982). Older women may be respected community members and even outspoken leaders in many community affairs. (In the United States, Khmer women often exercise considerable public influence.) In the religious sphere, though, women are of a decidedly lower status than men. In the case of the *yeichi*, this marginalization is reinforced by the widespread perception that *yeichi* are poorly educated and lower class and by the constant suspicion of their involvement in sexual improprieties with the monks.[23] (To underscore this latter claim, community members are quick to recount stories of alleged liaisons involving specific individuals.)

Although *yeichi* have no particular religious training, they are typically well versed in Buddhist ritual and liturgy because of their constant presence at Khmer religious ceremonies. They attend most lifecycle ceremonies in the community as honored guests, offering their blessings and adding their voices to the monks' chants. The *yeichi* also make up the core of the worshipers present in the temple every *Thngay Sĕl*, or Precept Day.

A CORE RITUAL: *THNGAY SĔL*

Although there are no regular Sunday services at the Khmer temple, on Precept Day *(Thngay Sĕl)* elder and pious members of the laity come to the temple to present food offerings to the monks and to receive the precepts. All Buddhists are enjoined to follow five precepts in their daily lives. These doctrinal prescriptions are formulated as general exhortations to avoid excess, rather than as categorical imperatives (Tambiah 1970:89). They are as follows:

I undertake the precept to abstain from taking life.
I undertake the precept to abstain from taking that which is not given.
I undertake the precept to abstain from improper sexual acts.
I undertake the precept to abstain from telling lies.
I undertake the precept to abstain from imbibing or ingesting substances which cause heedlessness. (Keyes 1977:118)

On Precept Day, many older Khmer vow to follow an expanded number of precepts for twenty-four hours. Some spend the entire day (and night) at the temple, praying and meditating, listening to the monks' sermons, and fasting from noon until the following morning.[24]

Thngay Sĕl occurs approximately every eight days or, following the Khmer calendar, each quarter of the lunar month. Given the size of the Boston area congregation, though, and in an attempt to regulate the amount of food that the monks receive, Precept Day may, in fact, be celebrated over several days, with various neighborhood groups assigned different dates of observance.

The combination of prayers recited on *Thngay Sĕl* is recited at every Khmer Buddhist ritual. It is a version of the worship *(saut thŏa)* that monks perform each morning and afternoon in the temple. These prayers, referred to in Khmer as *thvay bâng'kŭm preah,* "paying obeisance to the Buddha," include the prayer of homage to the Buddha, followed by the three "refuges," the precepts, and, finally, the prayer to spread merit to all sentient beings. These prayers are of central importance because they express in abbreviated form basic Khmer Buddhist tenets.

Early in the morning of *Thngay Sĕl,* the monks, older women, and a smaller number of men assemble in the sanctuary. The men and women arrange themselves on mats in front of the monks, with the men seated closest to the monks, followed by older women, and younger women and children farthest back. The *achaa* opens the ceremony by leading the assembled laity in paying homage to Buddha. They chant the Pali formula three times:

> *Namo tassa bhagavato arahato samma sambuddhassa.*
>
> "Homage to Him, the Holy One, the Pure One, the Fully Enlightened One."

The *achaa* then invites the monks to give the three refuges to the group. The laity call the refuges *praputh, prathŏa, prasâng. Praputh* is a combination of *preah* and *Putth,* meaning "the holy Buddha." *Prathŏa* combines *preah* and *thŏa* to mean "the holy rules." *Prasâng* is *preah* plus *sâng,* translated as "the holy monkhood." In Pali, the refuges are the *tisarana,* the "three gems." Most older Khmer know the chant by heart, although they may not be able to assign meaning to the individual Pali words. Pressing their palms together at face level in a gesture of respect, the worshipers intone

Buddham saranam gacchami.	"To the Buddha I go for refuge."
Dhammam saranam gacchami.	"To the Dhamma I go for refuge."
Sangham saranam gacchami.	"To the Sangha I go for refuge."

One recites the refuges both to thank the Buddha and to affirm one's dedication to following his path (Narada 1990).

After acknowledging the three refuges, the *achaa* requests the precepts from the monks on behalf of the laity. Instead of the usual five, three additional precepts are offered on this day. The additional precepts are to fast from noon until sunrise, to avoid all forms of entertainment and sensual pleasure (including wearing jewelry and perfume), and to sleep on a mattress no higher than one's forearm. The precept regarding improper sexual relations is also expanded; one should abstain from all sexual relations for twenty-four hours.

The monks give the eight precepts, saying them first in Pali and then providing a Khmer translation—a liturgical innovation that apparently dates from 1926 (Kalab 1976:166). The laity repeat only the Pali.

> [Temple *achaa*, age 56] After the monk has finished giving the eight precepts in Pali, he explains each precept to the people in Khmer. For example, the monks explain that *panatipata* in Pali means "Don't kill." That means even if you kill some animal or you ask someone else to kill the animal, the sin is the same; don't do that. Don't ask someone to steal for you, it's the same as stealing yourself. You have to abstain from sex for twenty-four hours. Don't lie. Don't drink alcohol. Don't eat after 12:00 [noon]. Avoid entertainment. Don't wear perfume or any decoration. Don't sit in the high places; don't sleep on the high mattress. They ask, "Why do you come to receive the precepts? Because if you receive the eight precepts, in your next life you will be beautiful, you will go to heaven *(thansuo)*, you will be calm in your heart and have peace. If you follow the precepts, you will reach nirvana *(nĕ'pean)*."

After receiving the precepts from the monks, the laity intones "*Sathŏk, sathŏk, sathŏk*" ("I agree, I accept, it is good, it is right"). The *achaa* and his assistants begin to clear the area in front of the monks so that they may receive the food offerings. The laity kneel in front of the monks with bowls of rice and plates of food, always careful to keep their heads lower than those of the monks. As each food offering is given, the monks carefully place the dishes in front of themselves on the mat. When all of the food offerings have been delivered, the monks intone the prayer to spread the blessing or merit *(bŏn)* to all sentient beings *(phsay metaa kákrŏnathŏa)*. While they do so, individual laity may slowly pour water from one container into another, concentrating on spreading the benefits of their good actions to their parents and ancestors and to all sentient beings.

> [Temple *achaa*, age 56] The monks recite the *phsay metaa kákrŏnathŏa* (the prayer to spread the blessing) so that all sentient beings receive that blessing. At that time, you have to think about your parents, your seven generations of relatives, about whatever you did to the animals (like hitting the dog) so that *dhamma* is spread to them. We have to think about the sins that we have committed *(bietbien)*. That means when we are young, we are ignorant, and we don't know anything. We make the animals suffer and we don't think about them at all. So now we say we spread the merit to them, we spread the result of our good action *(bŏn)* to all sentient beings.

Their services completed, the monks file out of the room, and the laity eat together in small groups. *Thngay Sĕl* ceremonies thus combine important merit-making activities—feeding the monks and reciting the refuges and precepts—with significant rituals of communal solidarity. This is expressed most clearly in the sharing of food and the blessings of merit.

OFFERINGS AND MERIT TRANSFER

As we have seen from the rites performed during the *Thngay Sĕl* ceremony, Khmer, like most other Southeast Asian Buddhists, believe making offerings to the monks accrues merit that can be passed on to spiritual as well as human beings. When spirits receive this merit, it is said to appease them and ease their suffering in hell (Ebihara 1968:393).

> [Female, age 44] Of course, we do not know which of our parents or ancestors have already been reborn and which are still in hell. But you have to do that [make and transfer merit] anyway, because we know that some of them are probably still in hell and suffering.

There are several Khmer religious rituals that focus on transferring merit. The largest of these, and perhaps the most emotionally charged, is *Phchŭm Bĕn* (Souls' Day), which always occurs in September. During *Phchŭm Bĕn*, people deliberately make merit by offering food to the monks. They then pass the merit on to their relatives. During the prayer to spread the merit, worshipers think of their deceased relatives, particularly their parents; in the course of the ceremony, many are visibly overcome with grief.

Offerings made directly to spirits in the form of food, cigarettes, and alcohol are not fully consistent with Buddhist orthodoxy, but they are also a common element of Khmer rituals. During *Phchŭm Bĕn*, for example, people set out special offerings of food (especially favorite dishes of the deceased), alcohol, cigarettes, and small amounts of money at their homes. The offerings are for the ancestral spirits, who come to visit over a fourteen-day period (they return on the fifteenth). A woman who was at the temple on *Phchŭm Bĕn* commented on the logic of these ritual acts:

> [Woman, age 65] There are some ancestors who have a lot of sin and walk around on the river of death. They cannot become human beings; they have too much sin. The god of hell allows those dead souls to come visit their relatives on earth for only fifteen days each year during *Phchŭm Bĕn*. They are given permission to come to eat the offerings set out by their descendants.
>
> Those ancestors with a lot of sin have a very small mouth, tiny like the eye of a needle. They cannot eat like humans, so they must be fed special kinds of food. But we don't know for sure if our ancestors have a lot of sin or not, so we always have to make fried glass noodles [thin vermicelli] to offer them, because we know that those people can eat that.
>
> Because we miss our parents and our relatives, we always make their favorite food dishes, too. If you don't remember [what they liked to eat], it's OK, too. You just make something delicious.
>
> But if we forget to do offerings at *Phchŭm Bĕn*, the ancestors will become very angry and jump down to earth and curse us and give us bad luck. Everyone is afraid that their ancestors will do that.

During the Khmer New Year, or *Chaul Chnăm*, monks bless offerings of rice and curry on small banana-leaf trays and set them outside the temple at the foot of a special spirit mound made of sand, known as the *poun phnom khsăch*. These, too, are intended to satisfy ancestors and guardian or territorial spirits, so that they do not trouble their descendants.

Such "unorthodox" offerings are actually a vital part of most Khmer ceremonies. For example, I recorded the following observations at a *sâng khătean* (ritual feeding of the monks) ceremony in an East Boston apartment complex.

> [Fieldnotes] At Bâng Kamroeun's *sâng khătean* ceremony, four large bowls of rice are placed on a low table in front of the *bhikkhu*, one for each of the four monks present. As the monks chant their prayers,

Bâng Kamroeun's granddaughter quietly adds an additional container of rice to the dishes on the table. After the monks have finished their prayers and left with their rice bowls and stacked containers of curry, the young woman uncermoniously takes the foil-wrapped package and sets it out by the back steps of the apartment building. When asked for whom it was left, she explains that she put it there for the *nĕak ta,* the guardian spirits of the housing project, who are responsible for the well-being of those living in the area they inhabit. At the very end of the ceremony, the *achaa*–ritual specialist informs the guardian spirits [here referred to as *tévoda,* "angels"] of the offering's origin and expresses the hope that the gift might have a beneficial effect on the hostess: "Through the power of the food offering to the monks and of fruit for myself [the *krou achaa*], I proclaim to the angels *(tévoda)* who guard this area that if Ms. Kamroeun goes anywhere, those angels must protect her and give her peace and good fortune."

In his comments on this ritual activity, the *achaa* was careful to provide a doctrinal gloss on the transaction that did not explicitly violate Buddhist precepts. He made no mention of the exact food (the rice) left for the spirits but instead referred to the "power of the food offering to the monks and of fruit for myself." There is doctrinal support in the Pali canon for the notion that when one does something virtuous, such as feeding monks, one may ask spiritual entities to "empathize in the merit" so that one can receive protection and assistance in return (Gombrich and Obeyesekere 1988:18). Offerings made directly to spirits in this manner, however, are not officially sanctioned within Buddhism.

Even less orthodox are popular beliefs associated with death and funerals. In the *bângskaul* ceremony for the dead, people make offerings to the monks in the form of food, dishes, pots and pans, bedding, and even electric stoves and refrigerators. The monks accept these offerings on behalf of the deceased. Khmer say their relatives are "pleased to have those things" and then look favorably on their descendants. In popular understanding, the physical objects or their essences are actually "transferred" to the dead through processes similar to those used to spread blessing or merit among the living.

[Female, age 52] Our relatives who have sin and are not yet reborn will be happy to have those things. And when they are happy, they will bless us.

After accepting the goods and appliances, the monks recite the *bângskaul* prayer for the dead. Rather than confirming these popular ideas about the transfer of merit and goods, however, the monks' prayer denies the apparent logic of the ritual act. Their words instead remind the living that they, too, will eventually die, that the physical body is subject to decay.

> [Female, age 44] The *bângskaul* text has a translation different from what most people believe. They believe that the *bângskaul* is for the dead, like a blessing for the dead, but in fact the text recited by the monks has a meaning like, "You should not become too attached to your physical body. You have to be aware of the fact that your body is decaying, too, and that you will die eventually, just as your relative has died. So think about that." Because according to Buddhist doctrine, when someone dies, there is nothing left—no soul, no spirit—so how can they [the deceased] accept something like that [objects such as stoves and refrigerators]? But we believe those dead souls are suffering and we need to help them.

Although they convey this message in their prayers, the monks make little effort to dispel popular notions about merit transfer. They accept the gifts as a simple act of merit making in remembrance of the dead. Some especially orthodox monks do take care to distance themselves from spirit beliefs and rites. At most ceremonies, however, the monks simply recite their prayers and sermons and then leave. Afterward, the *achaa* is free to provide a comment on the ritual proceedings in a way that accords more with popular belief.

For Khmer elders, transferring or sharing merit and making offerings is a deeply important dimension of the spiritual reciprocities linking parents and children. Such ceremonies to create and exchange merit and to give offerings to deceased relatives are among the first rituals elders perform if they return to Cambodia either temporarily or permanently; many cite the desire to perform such ceremonies as their main reason for returning.

INDIVIDUALISM AND SOCIAL RECIPROCITY

Specialists in Southeast Asian Buddhism have long disagreed about the degree to which Buddhism is an individualistic religion dedicated primarily to saving individual souls. Textual studies of Buddhism underscore Buddhist doctrine's overwhelming preoccupation with the illusory nature of individual experience and the individual's need to transcend it.

Perhaps the strongest claims to this effect are found in Herbert Phillips's study (1965) of Thai personality and socialization (see also Phillips 1969). Drawing on a more-or-less orthodox understanding of Buddhist doctrine (centered especially on the idea of karma), Phillips argues that Theravada Buddhism emphasizes the individual, individual action, and responsibility. "The principal tenet of Hinayana [Theravada] Buddhism is the complete psychological freedom, isolation, and responsibility of every person" (Phillips 1965, cited in Keyes 1977:164). Subsequent studies of Theravada Buddhism, however, particularly those conducted by other anthropologists, have consistently demonstrated that practical Buddhism—that is, Buddhism as understood and acted on by ordinary people in communities—is also concerned with relationships of an intergenerational and socioreciprocal nature (see, for example, Ebihara 1966).

Indeed, contrary to textual Buddhism, such social and intergenerational reciprocities are at the heart of Buddhism and family morality for many lay Khmer. Parents struggle to support and educate their children; the children repay the debt owed to their elders by entering the monkhood and sponsoring ceremonies to transfer merit to their parents (Tambiah 1970). This is but one of many social reciprocities within and between families through which practical Buddhism becomes a living and thoroughly social reality.

As we have seen for Khmer in the United States, many of the institutional supports that were vital to the practice of Buddhism in Cambodia no longer exist. The Khmer Buddhist temple's influence in everyday life has clearly diminished, and the monk's role has undergone significant adjustments in this country. This situation is likely to have serious consequences for the future religiosity of Khmer American youth.

Nonetheless, in many important ways, it is still true that "to be Khmer is to be Buddhist." Enacted in daily exchanges within the family and community, as well as in familial and communal ritual, Khmer Buddhist values and understandings remain central to Khmer identity.

In the following chapter, I explore these themes of individualism and intergenerational reciprocity by looking at Khmer socialization practices and beliefs. Patterns of child socialization reflect many of the conscious and unconscious concerns of Khmer parents. In these practices, we find that Khmer Buddhism has a profound influence on parents' attitudes toward children's early behavior. Concepts of karma and reincarnation inform parental notions about just how much it is possible to influence a child's development. The beliefs and practices that accompany Khmer socialization reflect the interplay between autonomy and relatedness at the heart of Khmer American morality.

3

Early Socialization
Observing the Child

Khmer practices of early socialization are deeply informed by Buddhist notions of reincarnation and karmic destiny. In Khmer Buddhist worldview, every birth is a rebirth. Birth is considered a "dangerous passage" for the newborn, partly because the infant remains connected for some time to its former life and parents (Ebihara 1968; Wood 1983; Hansen 1988).[1] Parents thus focus on the infant not as an utterly new and natural being but as a preexisting social individual who brings from past lives inherent traits and abilities (Smith-Hefner 1990a).

In line with this view of the child, Khmer parents intervene in the early stages of child socialization considerably less than today's Western, middle-class parents do. Rather than immediately imposing a predetermined model of socially appropriate behavior on the young child, a Khmer parent first observes the child closely in an attempt to discern the residues of past lives and the child's karmic trajectory. The parent will then try to support the child's development in a way that enhances any previously acquired interests and aptitudes.

Khmer Buddhist and spirit beliefs reinforce this focus on the individual. The possibility that ancestral and other "protector" spirits could remain too close to the infant and jeopardize the child's well-being requires that caretakers be vigilant, paying particular attention to the infant's character and demeanor. Moreover, at this early stage, the child is deemed incapable of rational behavior and "deep" understanding. As a result, attempts to reason with young children are considered futile. Khmer child socialization practices thus appear indulgent (Ebihara 1968:115; Wood 1983:10; Kelley 1991:53) and noninterventionist and seem to be in broad accord with Theravada Buddhist doctrine, with its overriding focus on the project of individual salvation.

There is, however, a countervailing emphasis in Khmer socialization practices. From this second perspective, parents focus not on the individual, as in Buddhist doctrine, but on the child's sociomoral relation to the family and on the family's sociomoral relation to the larger Khmer community. More relational and less individualistic than conventional Buddhist understandings, this view accords with an earlier, Brahmanic perspective on the world and on social relations (see also Steinberg 1959:271). In this view, the child is first and foremost a social being. Born into a family with an established status and reputation, the child is morally obligated to maintain the family's social standing. The parents must therefore teach the child the behavior and demeanor deemed appropriate for the family's reputation. More specifically, the parents need to insist that the child uphold the family's "face" *(mŭk môt)* by behaving in a socially acceptable manner. From this perspective, then, the "embedded" or organic reality of the family and community takes precedence over the reborn soul's individualized identity.

Without understanding this tension between Buddhist ideals and everyday practice, one could misinterpret Khmer conceptions of self and identity. Some studies of Khmer Buddhism in particular, and Theravada Buddhism in general, have so highlighted the individualistic nature of doctrine and belief as to overlook the social, communitarian, relational, and even paradoxical dimensions of practical morality. Nonanthropological studies of Buddhism have been particularly prone to this excessive individualization of Buddhist society (by contrast, see Tambiah 1970; Ortner 1989).

This chapter details how Khmer socialize young children. These socialization practices reveal the foundations of the tension in Khmer conceptions of self and identity; on the one hand, practical interpretations of Buddhist doctrines focus on the individual, and on the other hand, the more embedded or sociorelational morality of community life emphasizes status, face, and family. This tension first appears in early childhood, but it continues to exert an important influence on personality development throughout an individual's life.

OBSERVING THE CHILD

In discussions of child socialization, Khmer parents often comment that a good parent "knows his children before they know themselves." Parents describe their role as one of "watching closely or ob-

66   *Early Socialization*

serving" *(moel, sangkét moel)* their children. Parental scrutiny of a child's character begins even before the child is born.

Not uncommonly, for example, the pregnant woman dreams of the fetus's sex. A dream that includes a necklace or the moon is taken to indicate a girl; a dream of a ring or the sun indicates a boy.

> [Fieldnotes, female, age 32] Sokkha's mother dreamed that a treasure was buried under her house. When she dug up the treasure, she found a beautiful white necklace. "That was my daughter," she says. "At that time, I knew I would have a daughter."

In the expectant woman's dreams or dreamlike experiences, the child's soul is often described as coming to the mother as a gust of wind or clinging to her ankles begging to be reborn. The unborn soul is said to seek out a mother with a store of merit roughly equal to its own. Babies lacking merit are miscarried or die during delivery; mothers lacking in merit suffer or die in labor (Hanks 1963:2). Meritorious mothers, by contrast, have easy births; their babies are healthy and give them no trouble.

> [Fieldnotes, female, age 36] Prum Peou's niece tells me the following story. During Pol Pot time, she was ordered by her group leader to go far from the village to get water. When she was deep in the jungle, she heard two boys call to her, "Mother, Mother, we want to come live with you. Please let us live with you." She felt a strong gust of wind blowing around her. The voices said, "We are hungry, and we want to live with you, Mother."
> But she was frightened and said, "No! Go away!"
> "We are good people," the boys persisted. "We want to live with you."
> Finally, she agreed, saying, "OK, if you are good people, you can come live with me." Then, she thought someone grabbed her by both ankles. At that time, she became pregnant. She later delivered twin boys.

Although not all Khmer women say that they have had such specific dreams or dreamlike experiences before their children's births, most Khmer women report having had some kind of premonition with at least one pregnancy. In some cases, premonitory insights even present themselves to other family members.

> [Female, age 40] When Samphos's mother was pregnant and the family was preparing to leave the refugee camp for a third country, she

sent her husband to a Chinese trance medium to ask about their future. He told the medium that the family hoped to be resettled in the United States soon where they would be reunited with his mother. The medium replied that he would never see his mother; she would die, and her soul would come to live with his newborn daughter. His new daughter, the medium said, would look just like her grandmother and would have the same two birthmarks on her leg.

On the day the family arrived in the United States, just as the medium had predicted, Samphos's grandmother died at eight in the morning, only hours before the family reached her apartment in East Boston. Samphos, now three years old, was born several months later. As her mother told the story, she lifted the little girl's pant leg to reveal the two birthmarks on her calf.

In many prenatal premonitions, family members learn details of the child's previous life or individual identity. The soul may be that of a deceased relative who is reborn into the same family, but it may also be a friend, an acquaintance, or even a stranger.

Prum Peou's niece [who heard the voices of two boys while fetching water] said she also learned her twin sons' identities through her dream. Some days earlier, she had "seen with her own eyes" the local Khmer Rouge leader kill two wealthy teenagers from Phnom Penh for their motorbikes. The fact that the spirit voices in her dream identified themselves as "good people" convinced her that these were the same individuals.

Taouch Sok reported a similar experience. She knew her youngest son was the incarnation of a young man whose death she had witnessed during the Communist regime. She, too, had dreamed that the dead man's soul came to her, begging to be fed and cared for. She later bore a boy. The child, Taouch Sok said, had a scar on his lower back in the exact place where an ax had struck the dead man.

Whatever its shape or origin, premonitory information such as this is discussed with family members and friends before and after the child's birth. It plays an important part in all Khmer narratives of childbirth. These stories illustrate the heavy burden of past lives on the individual's development, from the moment of conception.

READING THE SIGNS

Once a child is born, parents keep studying his or her character, seeking traces of past lives in current physical and behavioral signs. Typically, for example, parents and elders examine the newborn's body closely for birthmarks or unusual characteristics. They discuss these signs with people they know to determine what the signs reveal about the child's nature, as well as the child's future or past.

As in the stories above, a scar or a birthmark may confirm a child's link to a deceased relative or even to some unknown individual. (In Cambodia, family members' dead bodies were sometimes marked with ashes to facilitate their identification in a future incarnation.) Attention is also paid to any unusual or difficult aspects of the birth, as these may indicate that a child has special powers or will require special care.

Children who are born with a caul (enclosed in the placenta) or who are born with the umbilical cord around their neck or shoulders are said to *kaoet mean krou*, meaning to "be born with a teacher." This is considered a very auspicious sign (see also Hanks 1963:46), and care is taken to note the placenta's position or the cord's configuration. The "teacher spirit," or *krou*, is described as "owning" the placenta or umbilical cord and is believed to endow the child with special spiritual powers. When the cord is around the child's body (like a Brahman priest's holy cord), it is called *sângva*. When the cord is wrapped around the neck, it is called *srânŏm*.

Khmer believe that such children are more susceptible than normal infants to spiritual disturbances. As a result, parents may erect a small spirit altar *(sakkarăk bauchea)* near the child's bed, burning incense there and making periodic offerings to keep the spirit-owner content. If the child is born enclosed in the placenta, the spirit altar is made of green coconut with a red "leaf hat." If the child is born with the umbilical cord wrapped around the body, a white cotton string is wrapped around the coconut figure an equal number of times. (In the past, the placenta itself was sometimes kept and dried and later used as medicine if the child became ill, a practice still common in much of Southeast Asia.)

> [Fieldnotes] Phy was born with a caul. His mother told how she had brought a coconut altar made for Phy from the Thai camps into the United States. She laughed as she recounted the custom officer's puzzlement at the object, her inability to explain its significance, and the way the official finally waved them through in exasperation. This altar now sits on a dresser in the parents' cramped bedroom, which they share with their three youngest children.

[Male, age 43] Niep recounted the story of his son Ry's birth in a Thai refugee camp. The birth was unusually difficult. After twenty-four hours of labor, the doctor said that if the baby was not born in the next half hour, he would have to perform a cesarean. Fortunately, Niep said, the baby emerged soon after. Because he came out feet first *(prâchrah choeng)*, "with his hands up over his head as if in prayer," Niep and his wife believe that their son is endowed with the spiritual powers of a *krou khmae.*

Among these powers is the ability to dislodge small fish bones caught in the throat. The boy has already demonstrated this remarkable ability on several occasions. Once when his mother was choking on a small bone, he stood with his feet together in a posture of reverence. He then dipped one heel into a cup of water and gave the cup to his mother. After she drank the water, his father said, the bone disappeared from her throat. "Nobody told him to do that," his mother added. "It seems he has a skill like a *krou khmae* to do that kind of thing."

Only some children are thought to be endowed with an especially powerful protector spirit, or *krou,* as a result of some unusual feature of their birth. All children, however, are believed to be watched over by an "invisible mother."

THE INVISIBLE MOTHER AND OTHER GUARDIAN SPIRITS

According to Khmer elders, the "invisible mother," or *mday daoem,* who is said to be the child's mother from a previous life, still loves her child and wants to see the baby, especially when it is first reborn. (Some explain that the mother cannot be reborn herself yet because, unlike her child, she died with "too much sin" and must remain in the "invisible realm.") One can discern her presence by observing the baby's behavior closely. Parents feel that the *mday daoem* is near when the baby smiles, laughs, or cries for no apparent reason. These signs indicate that the invisible mother is teasing or playing with the child.

As is generally true of Khmer spirit beliefs, Khmer express some ambivalence about the *mday daoem.* She usually visits at night, say Khmer, and keeps the baby from sleeping soundly. Parents believe it is important that young children sleep next to their human mothers to protect against such bothersome (and potentially dangerous) encounters.[2]

The *mday daoem* is said to cause serious trouble only if the child's human parents do something wrong, such as striking or cursing the child. In such cases, the child may cry incessantly or develop some unexplained illness, such as a fever, convulsions, chills, or diarrhea, that Western medicine cannot cure. Parents, however, may not know why or how the *mday daoem* or the child's protector spirit was insulted; they may have forgotten or disregarded important details of the child's birth or subsequent behavior. In such cases, a *krou khmae*, or ritual specialist, must be called on to determine the spirit's identity and the reasons for its anger, and to perform a ritual cure, if necessary. According to the *krou khmae*, if the child is not attended to quickly when this type of disturbance occurs, he or she may die.

Neak Khmau told this story about her younger brother:

> [Female, age 52] When she was just ten years old, Neak Khmau said, her four-year-old brother was "taken back" into the invisible world after their human father beat him rather severely. After the beating, the boy ran out of the house and "just disappeared" into the forest out back. Neak Khmau's mother was beside herself, and the family called all of their neighbors and relatives to look for the boy, but no one was able to find him. Finally, they called the *krou khmae* to come and do a ceremony, so that the boy's father could apologize to the *mday daoem* for having beaten his son.
>
> The *krou khmae* burned incense and made an offering, and then Neak Khmau's father addressed the spirit mother, saying, "I know my sin. I hit my child. Please overlook my sin. I will change my behavior from this day on, and I won't touch your child again. Will you please accept my acknowledgment of sin? I know that I did wrong."
>
> Not long after the ceremony, the boy reappeared behind the house. When asked where he had been, he said, "I was here all the time. I could hear you calling, but I could not speak."
>
> "He was right there in the backyard but no one had been able to see him!" Neak Khmau explained. "It was the *mday daoem* who made him become invisible like that."

In these and other stories of spirit disturbances involving young children, the issue of whether the child deserved to be punished is considered irrelevant. In such cases, the *mday daoem* is always "on the child's side." Indeed, some guardian spirits are so protective, parents say, that their charges simply "cannot be hit" *(kaun ât aoy vai)*. These children become so ill at the slightest scolding that their parents fear disciplining them in any way.[3]

Early Socialization   71

Even if no particular symptoms of spirit disturbance manifest themselves, cautious parents try to protect their young children from visits by the *mday daoem* or other potentially dangerous entities. Sharp objects, such as scissors, may be placed under a child's pillow or mattress; as spirits are afraid of being cut, this practice keeps them away from sleeping children (see also Laderman 1983:202).[4] A relative may also ask a *krou khmae* for an amulet *(katha)* that is engraved with special religious symbols or Pali words. The child then wears this around the neck or wrist as protection.

Of course, some parents insist that they do not believe in either malevolent or protector spirits. These same parents often use traditional precautions and seek traditional remedies anyway—particularly when an unexplained illness occurs. One well-educated, urban woman explained her thoughts on the matter.

> [Female, age 42] We want to forget about those customs, but if my child gets very sick, I have to take the child to the *krou khmae*. And he will ask me, "Was your child born with a *krou*?" So we still pay attention to that. Even people who say they don't believe in those things, when their child is sick, they still follow the advice of their mothers and older relatives [and take the child to the *krou khmae*].

For one middle-aged father of four a fear of retribution prompts him to honor spirits.

> [Fieldnotes, male, age 45] "If you have a habit of feeding bread to the birds, they know the time to come and eat everyday. They expect that, and if we stop, they will be upset. Like that, the ancestors *(méba)*, they also expect it. But if you don't remember to feed the birds, they cannot make you sick or poor. The ancestors can. If [you] don't feed them and they are hungry, they will get angry, and they will cause you or your children harm."
>
> He explains his failure to perform spirit ceremonies for his own children, saying that for years, he was too poor to pay for the necessary offerings. Now, he is afraid to burn incense or candles because "if they come, they may think, 'Hey, why didn't he do this for us for a long time?' and they will be angry and do something really bad to me or to my family." He is waiting, he says, until he can afford to have an elaborate ceremony for his ancestors with lavish food and offerings to make up for his past negligence.

In such comments, the ambivalence surrounding Khmer spirit beliefs emerges quite distinctly. Spirits are seen as capable of being good, but they can also be unpleasant. Moreover, when upset by a descendant's misdeeds, they may vent their anger on an innocent party, often a child.

Although Khmer resist the suggestion, people sometimes use spirit beliefs for their own purposes. Claiming a causal relationship between a person's sudden affliction and another's misbehavior, they might demand that the wrongdoer acknowledge and stop the unacceptable behavior (Ebihara 1966:190). This pattern of "lateral" moral pressure is most clearly evidenced in instances of *méba kăch*, or "wrath of the ancestors." In such a case, a family member's sexual impropriety often causes a child to be ill. For example, ancestors struck Kang Ara's twelve-year-old brother blind because of a cousin's out-of-wedlock pregnancy.

> [Female, age 44] Ara said that when her brother was twelve years old, he suddenly became totally blind for no apparent reason. Her mother thought, "There is nothing wrong with him. Why is he blind?" Everyone told her to look around, to ask the relatives, "Is someone misbehaving to make the ancestors angry *(méba kăch)?*"
>
> Ara's grandmother and cousins and the rest of the family gathered together. They put an egg on the floor in the middle of the group and called out the names of various family members. (If you call out the wrongdoer's name, the egg will stand on end, Ara explained.) When they called Ara's cousin's name, the egg stood up. So everyone knew that this unmarried girl must have been pregnant.
>
> Ara's mother went to the girl's mother and told her that the girl and her boyfriend had to come to her house to do a release ceremony, or *p'dâh kruoh*, to beg forgiveness from the ancestors for their immoral behavior. The girl's mother protested that she didn't believe it; her daughter could not be pregnant. But Ara's mother said, "You have to do that! I will kill your daughter if my son goes blind permanently!"
>
> Only a few days after they had done the release ceremony and made marriage arrangements, Ara said, her brother regained his sight.

Such incidents continue to be quite common in the Khmer American community. Parents regularly admonish young people not to behave in ways that might upset the ancestors.

SAFEKEEPING THE CHILD

Previously, in Cambodia, the life-cycle ceremony called *pĭ'thy prâkăk kaun*, or "safekeeping the child," was automatically conducted shortly after a birth to ensure the child's well-being (Ebihara 1968:447–48). Khmer believe that dangerous spirits called *prĕay* are attracted to childbirth blood and may stay around to bother the newborn unless they are offered food and respect. As was discussed in chapter 2, a *prĕay* is the spirit of an individual who was killed or who otherwise died suddenly or violently. *Prĕay* seek revenge and may endanger not only the newborn but also any others involved in the childbirth, especially those who must touch the mother's blood, such as the midwife.

During the *prâkǎk kaun* ceremony, malevolent, ancestral, and other spirits are fed and honored; the midwife is thanked and paid for her assistance; and the new parents are established as the child's rightful caretakers. The child is sometimes also named. A critical element in the *prâkǎk kaun* ceremony, which is also referred to as the *pĭ'thy prâkǎk chmâb*, or "ceremony of apology to the midwife,"[5] is begging the midwife's forgiveness for requiring her to touch the mother's "polluting" blood.

Prâkǎk kaun ceremonies have become rare in the Boston Khmer community. Most elders attribute the disappearance to the ritual's high cost and the fact that most births now take place in a hospital without a midwife's direct involvement (see Marcucci 1986:188). Traditional Khmer midwives *(chmăb)* are not licensed to practice in the United States, and many now hesitate even to give advice. None of the people I consulted in the Boston area could identify anyone who had given birth with a Khmer midwife's assistance since arriving in the United States. As for the *prâkǎk kaun* ceremony, one father said simply, "Here we pay the hospital a lot of money to do that [deliver the baby], and besides, there is no *chmăb* or *krou* to pay." Moreover, there are often no family members present during the birth, because the medical staff members are expected to take care of everything. Children now typically receive a name in the hospital before they are brought home. In this way, American birthing customs have contributed to Khmer "disenchantment" with at least some traditional birthing practices (Hansen 1988).

Nonetheless, some of the *prâkǎk kaun* ceremony's spiritual functions are preserved in what Khmer prefer to call simply the child's first "birthday party" *(m'kuob)*.[6] These parties combine aspects of both American custom and Khmer tradition, although they are decidedly more Khmer when held for newborns, as in one birthday party that took place in an East Boston neighborhood.

[Fieldnotes] Tey's parents-in-law hold a first birthday party for Tey's four-month-old daughter, Chantha, the older couple's first granddaughter to be born in the United States. In the front room of their dilapidated clapboard house, they set elaborate food offerings on the floor on woven mats, as for a Cambodian wedding. The items include two chickens; two roasted ducks; two bottles of Hennessy cognac; and twin plates of fruits, noodles, and curried meat dishes.[7] The newborn's grandmother lights incense sticks, and family members take turns performing a *sampĕah* (gesture of respect). With the burning sticks in hand, they press their palms together high over the head in obeisance to the ancestral spirits. The grandmother even jokingly pretends to be the *mday daoem*. She tells her daughter-in-law, who sits with the baby in her arms, "I gave my daughter to you. I don't want my daughter back. I eat a lot of things. I don't want my daughter back." The baby's grandfather has tied a large gold ring to the infant's arm, explaining that it is to "weigh her arm down and keep her from trembling"—that is, to keep bothersome spirits at bay.

Though less prevalent than among Thai or Lao, some Khmer believe that young children are susceptible to soul loss (see chapter 2). If a child is shocked or experiences some traumatic event, Khmer believe that the soul, or part of the soul, may leave the body. As chapter 2 noted, a ceremony to recall the soul *(hav prâlŏeng)* must then be performed to entice the soul back.[8] The type of shock that results in soul loss may result from any number of things; in the story recounted below, the shock of seeing a thief's face in the night frightens a young child's soul out of her body.

[Female, age 44] When I was young, maybe three or four years old, my father got a government job in the province of Takeo. He bought a village house for us to live in, the kind built up on piles with a floor of bamboo slats. In the summertime it was so hot, I slept only in my underwear on a mat on the floor. Sometimes when I slept, I put my arm between the slats of the floor.

One night, a thief came underneath my house and felt along my dangling arm to see if I was wearing any jewelry. I wasn't sleeping deeply and when I felt that, I opened my eyes. In the moonlight, I suddenly saw his face looking up at me! I could see he was a very big man, a strong man. When he saw me open my eyes, he actually smiled up at me!

I yelled to my parents, *"Tao, tao,"* because I couldn't yet pronounce *chao* (thief), but the thief ran away very quickly. The villagers all came out of their houses. They said there were no thieves in that area. My parents told me not to cry, there were no thieves. But I cried and cried and ran out of that house. I didn't want to go back inside. I kept crying uncontrollably; I couldn't stop.

Finally, my parents called a monk and an *achaa* to come. The monk came to touch me and to recite some prayers to call back my soul *(hav prâlŏeng)*, and the *achaa* repeated those words. Then they tied a string around my wrist to tie the soul in and sprinkled some kind of blessing water to bathe me. The monk said something to me, and I believed him. It seemed that my mind was calm and then I could go back into the house without fear.

Virtually all Khmer agree that, because of a baby's physical and spiritual fragility, parents should constantly attend to the child. They should never leave a young child alone, especially at night, and should always keep a lamp on in the child's room. Such measures, say Khmer parents, are particularly important in the first six months to two years of the child's life; during this time, most young children sleep next to their mothers, usually in the same bed.[9]

In fact, when possible, the mother attends to most of the child's needs until the child is two years old. If it is a first child, a mother may rely on an older relative (a grandmother, sister, or aunt) to help care for her infant. Contrary to the pattern seen in some other Southeast Asian cultures (Geertz 1961; Smith-Hefner 1988a), however, care of the infant is only rarely entrusted to a young sibling. Khmer mothers in the United States often comment that they, unlike their American counterparts, never put their babies down, never leave them alone, and do not allow them to cry. A caregiver may swing sick, restless, or colicky infants in a makeshift hammock and sing them lullabies to ease them into sleep but will always remain nearby to ensure the child's comfort.

Because of such constant and close contact, Khmer mothers seem remarkably attuned to their babies' emotions and needs. In their interactions with their young children, mothers typically take their cues from the baby; infants are fed and entertained on demand and allowed to sleep when they want to, rather than according to any particular schedule. Interestingly, however, in contrast to American parent-infant interactions, Khmer babies are not typically engaged in prolonged playful, climactic interaction. The lengthy face-to-face exchanges American caregivers often engage in with their infants are uncommon.[10] Although Khmer babies are indulged by their caretakers, even moderate stimulation is avoided (see also Kelley 1991:53).

Good babies are quiet and complacent. Mothers insist that too much stimulation will produce an overactive and demanding child.

Once mobile, Khmer children are allowed to explore their surroundings free of the protective physical barriers American parents tend to erect (gates, harnesses, or playpens). Khmer caregivers prefer to distract their young children from danger rather than impede their free movement, shouting *"Heq, heq, heq!"* or clapping loudly to distract a child who is flirting with trouble. When children begin to understand verbal directives, they are often stopped in their tracks by threats such as, "Stop that, or the police will get you!" or "Don't go in there! There's a cat behind that door!" In most cases, or at least until the child realizes the emptiness of these threats, such directives will make the child scurry back to the caregiver.

In general, however, physical movement and curiosity are considered natural in young children, and most parents feel that such exploratory behavior should not be frustrated. A certain degree of independence is viewed positively, as is the value of learning from experience. Parentally imposed obstacles are regarded as a sure way to upset the delicate balance of strong feeling and limited understanding with which the infant is endowed.

As the child approaches the age of two, parents begin toilet training. Again, most do so in a relaxed manner designed to instill not a harsh new bodily discipline but a sense of personal and emotional balance. Inevitably, the mother assumes primary responsibility for the training. She begins familiarizing the child with the bathroom by seating the child on the toilet at intervals throughout the day. Her close observation of the child's demeanor also plays an important role in this process. Around the house, the child may wear no pants or diapers. Mothers say they can sense from the child's behavior when the child wants to urinate or have a bowel movement. In the case of boys, mothers say they know when the child has to urinate because the penis retracts; he is then promptly carried into the bathroom. None of this is performed with any particular pressure, however, and no one seems to make a fuss if a young child takes time mastering the mysteries of the toilet.

In these and other ways, young Khmer children are allowed to develop in a nurturing and relatively unobstructed social environment, largely at their own pace. When asked about the expected timing of a child's developmental achievements, parents uniformly insist that everything depends on the individual child *(srach tae kaun aeng)*. As we have seen, this theme of autonomy and individual character plays a prominent role in other aspects of Khmer social life. It is a feature of parental commentary on later socialization practices, as well.

TO KNOW ONESELF

Often described as lax or indulgent, Cambodian treatment of young children is informed by the Khmer Buddhist emphasis on the individual and by related spirit beliefs that underscore the child's independence and autonomy. Children are not viewed as shapeless clay to be formed and molded but as individuals born with a character and personality. It is the parents' responsibility to discover and nurture that character. The indulgent treatment of young children is, moreover, reinforced by the less distinctly Buddhist view of young children as naturally undisciplined and, to some extent, irrepressible and uncontrollable.

Infants and young children are described as having "unlimited wants, unlimited needs." They have no sense of self yet and do not know their proper place in the world. A mother excuses a young child who misbehaves by saying, "She doesn't yet know herself" *("Vea měn toan dǒeng khluon neou laoey")*. Similarly, a father threatens an older child with the words, "Someday, you will know yourself *(dǒeng khluon)* [and realize the serious implications of your behavior]!"

Only as children gain this self-knowledge do they learn to limit their needs and desires, to recognize right from wrong, and to accept their debt and responsibility to their parents. Although it is the parents' duty to help the child to come to such self-understanding, parents do not feel that achievement can be forced or imposed on the young child.

> [Male, age 37] You just have to talk to the child and say, "OK, now don't do this, or don't do that." You just give them advice and say, "If you don't listen to me now, you will know when you get older. You will know yourself. That's when you will learn to control yourself!"

A central feature of "knowing oneself," of course, is becoming aware of the karmic consequences of one's acts. According to the Khmer Buddhist view of the self and existence, an individual is the sum of merit or demerit amassed in past lives. The karmic notion that "you reap what you sow" *(tvoe l'ăh; ban l'ăh; tvoe akrŭak, ban akrŭak)* leads many Khmer to believe that every child is born with a particular destiny *(veasna, samnang)* determined by behavior in previous incarnations.

As mentioned in chapter 2, Khmer Buddhists believe in reincarnation *(kaoet mauk věnh* or *m'dang tiet)*; many insist, moreover, that some individuals can actually remember their "previous lives." In fact, it seems that virtually everyone in the Khmer community can point to people—friends, neighbors, or relatives—who knew their previous life identities when they were children. Those who remember usually begin to speak of their previous lives when they reach the age of four or five. Such stories are quite popular and widely recounted; they tend to be detailed and often very convincing.

Because Khmer have been in the United States for a relatively short period, many, though by no means all, of these stories are set in Cambodia or in the camps. Sok Chea, for example, told the story of her twin son and daughter, now grown. When the boy was old enough to talk, he began speaking about his previous life and the circumstances surrounding his death.

> [Female, age 52] At the age of four or five years old, Sok Chea's son told her he and his twin sister had been close friends who fought the French together as members of the Issarak.[11] (His sister had been male in her previous life.) His mother heard him say to his sister, "You are my friend from a previous life. We were both commandos fighting against the French, and we were ambushed and killed near the big road outside the village." The boy insisted on calling his sister "friend" *(mĭt)*. He said, "You are not my sister. You are my friend, so I won't call you sister. I'll just call you my friend. We were Issarak together!"
>
> Sok Chea asked her son, "Why did you both decide to come to live here? Why didn't one of you go to some other place?"
>
> He replied, "I loved my friend. We were both killed together near the national road. They shot us together. I loved him so much, and that's why I followed him here—to be close to him like a brother." The people in Sok Chea's village knew very well the story of two young men, allegedly Issarak, killed together not far from the village near the national road.

Nget Kan's older daughter began talking about her previous-life family when she turned four.

[Fieldnotes, female, age 50] Nget Kan's daughter told her mother, "You are not my real mother. My real mother lives far away." She named her previous parents, her sisters and brothers. Those names actually matched those of a family from a neighboring village, but Nget Kan said she didn't pay any attention to that.

One day when the little girl was playing in front of the house with some friends, her mother heard her tell the other children, "I know my real parents. Every day, my real father comes riding past the house on his bicycle on his way to his rice field. You will see him in just five or ten minutes." And in five or ten minutes an old man came riding past the house.

Nget Kan said she heard her daughter call to him, "Father *(Ŏv)!*" The old man stopped and scolded her, "I'm not your father. I don't know you! Call me 'grandfather *(ta),*' not 'father'!" She then told the old man that she was his daughter. She said she had died at the age of four and that every day for three days, he had come to cry at her grave. "Do you remember me now?" she asked him.

The old man said, "Yes, I recognize you now!" and he began to cry. Then he listened to the little girl tell him all about his rice field and the rice pot and how much rice he always put into the rice pot. She knew all about that, and the old man told her that everything she said was true.

Through stories like these, the child's previous identity is revealed, often confirming earlier signs or premonitions. Some parents insist they would be happy if their child remembered his or her previous lives; it would mean the child "died without sin." Such information is not always welcome, however, as it could link the child to previous family members who are still living. Many parents fear that if their children remember previous lives, they will run away to look for earlier families or will be claimed by previous relatives.

Parental anxiety over a child's relations in a previous life runs through many of these accounts. In much of Southeast Asia, parents fear that the child might abandon them, leaving them without support in their old age (Hanks 1963:68–69). Given their more recent experiences under Pol Pot and the Khmer Rouge, Khmer say that their fear of losing children has, if anything, increased. In the United States, many parents feel that their children are "all they have left" and cling to them tenaciously.

[Female, age 26] My cousin, who now lives in Washington state, remembered her previous life when she was three years old. She knew her previous-life husband, her mother, and father—she knew everything. For a while, she stopped talking about her past, because her mother would beat her. But in 1979, when the Vietnamese took over, she told the soldiers, "This is not my mother. I have another mother." And her mother got really mad and hit her really hard and said, "I don't want you to say that! I don't want to hear it!" Her mother was really afraid that my cousin would leave, because she was her only child and she had already tried to run away many, many times in the past. Finally, in the refugee camp, my cousin's previous-life husband came to find her, because he had heard about that story. He was maybe forty at that time, and she was only ten. My cousin recognized him immediately and called him *bâng* (older brother / husband). She described to him how she had died in childbirth. She said to him, "*Bâng*, I miss my mother and father and my siblings."

In these stories, as in earlier stories of spirit disturbances, one can see how people can use such beliefs to manipulate others. During Pol Pot time and in the refugee camps, for example, stories of children who disclaimed their parents this way were reportedly quite common, undoubtedly because of the increased tension placed on family relations during this period. Such beliefs and practices have understandably confused social workers, doctors, and service providers who work with Khmer in the United States.

A recent incident involving the tragic death of a Khmer teenager in Boston reveals the degree to which Khmer American parents still fear that children will be claimed by a "previous" relative.

[Fieldnotes, female, age 40] Heng Rath tells a story of how a teenage boy who lived in her Boston apartment building died in a horrible accident. He drove his car into a tree and was killed immediately. His mother was inconsolable.

After the accident, Heng Rath began to "see the boy's face everywhere." One night, she dreamed that the boy came to talk to her. He said, "I am very angry with my mother because she burned [cremated] my body, and I wasn't dead yet." The boy then grabbed at Heng Rath, throwing himself at her feet. She was so frightened, she said, that her body shook. At that time she was pregnant with her son, Sonnim.

The dead boy's mother heard about Heng Rath's dream and came to talk with her about it. Heng Rath assured her that it was probably nothing. But after the baby was born, the woman came to visit Heng Rath again and asked to see the baby. When the dead boy's mother saw the infant, she cried and cried and said he was exactly like her dead son. She told Heng Rath that her son had had the same scar over his eye and two cowlicks in his hair, just like Sonnim.

She gave Heng Rath money and clothes for the child and begged her not to feed the baby any eggs so that he would remember his past life. But Heng Rath said she was worried that the dead boy's mother would claim the child as her own. She refused the woman's gifts and told her, "The doctor says that my son needs his vitamins and protein, so I have to let him eat eggs." And as soon as he could eat solid food, Heng Rath fed the boy eggs. When her son was old enough to talk, she often quizzed him to be sure that he had forgotten. "Are you Sonnath?" [the name of the dead boy], she would ask. He insisted, "I am not Sonnath. I am Sonnim!"

To prevent a young child from remembering a past life, one must give the child an egg to eat. Khmer say they have no idea of the egg's significance, but the egg's connotation as "new life" seems fairly obvious.[12] If the child's previous life stories persist and the parent becomes worried, the child may be placed in a shallow rice-winnowing basket, and a brief ceremony can be performed.[13] In severe cases, a *krou khmae* may be called. Even if nothing is done, however, parents say that by age twelve or thirteen most children stop talking about their previous lives. It may be that at that age they are embarrassed to tell such stories anymore. More significant at that point, parents insist, is that children become conscious of responsibilities to their present parents and aware of the role they must play in caring for them. This awareness indicates that children have begun to develop the "deep thinking" *(kŭmnĭt chrŏu)* indicative of early adulthood (see chapter 4).

Perhaps the most striking aspect of these stories is the degree of parental insecurity they express. Whereas some accounts of Thai children's early socialization indicate that it is children who are insecure, afraid that they may be abandoned by their parents or given away to relatives (Piker 1975:102), among Khmer, it is clearly the parents who fear this separation. They worry that their child may not stay with them, either because they have angered protective or ancestral spirits or because previous-life relatives may come to claim the child.

Khmer insist that, in some cases, children who remember their past lives have gone back and forth between their previous-life family and present family. Others have decided to stay with their previous-life families permanently. Several parents cite the story of a fifteen-year-old girl who happened upon her previous-life husband after her family relocated from the refugee camps to Texas. He was, at that time, a widower of fifty-five with three children by his second wife. Against her parents' wishes, the young woman eventually (re)married the man, and the couple went on to have several children of their own. ("Can you imagine," exclaimed an elderly woman after recounting the story. "Two lives with the same husband!")

Interestingly, in studies of Thai, beliefs about the remembrance of past lives do not seem to play a similar role in socialization. This may reflect differences in patterns of indulgence and insecurity in Thai and Khmer upbringing. As we shall see, among Khmer, children tell stories of previous lives and prior parents roughly at the same time as parents begin to indulge them less. Such stories may be children's response to the loss of overt parental affection and indulgence and an attempt to recapture or compel parental attention.

DESTINY AND DIRECTION

Even when children are born remembering the past, parents insist that one can never know what is to come in the future. Nor can parents ever be sure of their children's destinies. Parents, therefore, continue to watch their children, evaluating their earliest actions, as well as their reactions to instructions and discipline, in an effort to discern their intrinsic dispositions. An elderly midwife put the matter this way:

> [*Chmăb*, age 85] You cannot know your child's destiny for sure. But you have to keep observing. You need to observe the physical acts of the child closely. When they play, you have to observe, Do they kill small animals, even an insect? I have to observe that kind of behavior, and I can tell. If a small child likes to kill a lot of animals, that kind of child is not good, and he was born to have sin. And because they are born with sin, the sin will show, and they [will] want to behave like that. But some children, we can observe their acts and we see they have pity on animals. They don't want to kill. Even with other children, they don't want to fight. They don't want to handle the knife or point it at anyone. They don't touch dangerous instruments.

Because one can never be certain of the child's destiny, parents must persist not only in their observations of the child's behavior but also in their efforts to teach the child to behave properly.[14] An observant parent notes the direction in which the child is headed and attempts to guide the child to the correct path gently but repeatedly if the child should go astray.

> [Chmăb, age 85] If you observe that no matter what you do, no matter what you say, he still is walking in the wrong path, you keep advising him over and over. You have to tell him, "In this life, they will put you in jail and hit you badly." You must tell him the consequences of his acts. "In your next life, you will still have that sin, be reborn with that sin." I have to tell him that.

Conversely, a child who is born with a particularly destructive personality or a birth defect may be viewed as carrying karmic retribution for something the mother or father did in a previous life. In other words, parents are believed to get the children they deserve (Hanks 1963; Leclère [1899] 1975). The young mother of a deaf child expressed this belief when she explained that her daughter's inability to hear likely resulted from some bad action that she, the mother, had committed in a previous life, such as killing an animal.[15] Similarly, a willful or disobedient child is often described as a kind of "hell"; the parent is thought to "owe" something to that child as reparation for some bad act committed in a past life.

> [Chmăb, age 52] They say that if you have a child who "comes to live with you" and they don't want to listen to you as a parent, then it means that in your previous life, you did something wrong and you owe something to that child. That's why they come to live with you. They don't want to listen to you, and they do negative things and even want to harm you. This is because of your previous life. You owe that child something, and you have to give it. That child will squeeze you and do very bad things to you. They won't reply when you talk to them. We say the child is like *moha chao* (a high thief, a high killer) for you, someone who will steal from you without end until the end of your life. We say that child is your hell.

Of course, one can never know which qualities result from the child's karma and which are related to one's own. The central challenge of the parental role, then, is to determine what must be endured because it is destiny (either one's own or one's child's) and what can be altered because it is only learned. Applying too much pressure or pushing children in a direction other than that for which they are destined is considered not only futile but also dangerous.

Parents must therefore apply pressure when it can do the most good and allow children to go in their own direction when it is inevitable.

TO KNOW ONE'S PLACE

At first sight, Khmer may appear passive, even fatalistic, in their parental roles. Parents focus on discerning the child's inherent capabilities. In principle as well as in practice, this emphasis accords the child considerable personal autonomy. Interestingly, however, as the child matures, this socialization pattern slowly undergoes significant changes. These changes eventually introduce a fundamentally different tension into the child's socialization and self-perception.

Specifically, as children show signs of beginning to "know" themselves, parents stress that they must also learn their place within the Khmer social hierarchy. They need to learn the etiquette and demeanor that this place entails. This information about status and role begins to be impressed upon children gently but insistently, even when they are still quite young. At first, it is conveyed almost entirely through intrafamilial relationships, especially those related to language socialization.

For example, caregivers stress that in speaking with very young children, one should use only "sweet words" or "good words" *(piek phâ'aim, piek l'ăh)* so that children learn to use appropriate, polite language in return. In the presence of their children, mothers should refer to themselves as *mae, måk,* or *ma* (mother), rather than using *aing* (a colloquial form of the first person). Children should be addressed with a term of endearment (*keo*, meaning "sweet dear"; *peou*, meaning "youngest"; or *mŏm,* meaning "sweet girl") or with *kaun* (child), or *aun* (young one), rather than with *haeng* (an impolite form of "you" for boys) or *ngaeng* (an impolite form of "you" for girls).

Like so many others in Southeast Asia, the Khmer language contains special status-marked vocabularies that are used to address those who are older or of higher status (Steinberg 1959:56; cf. Smith-Hefner 1990a). As soon as they begin to talk, children are instructed in the proper use of such forms by both modeling and direct tutoring.[16] For example, caregivers instruct children to use *saum* (beg) when requesting something of their elders, instead of *aoy* (give). Similarly, a mother encourages her child to imitate her usage when she says in the child's presence *"Pa, nhchoenh pĭsa bay"* ("Father, please come eat"). With this sentence, she models the respectful forms for "request" and "eat" and the kin term *pa* instead of *bâng* (both elder brother and the usual term of address for one's husband).[17]

By drawing the child's attention to status in her family and community, the caregiver impresses on the child the social hierarchy of which she is a part. Caregivers insist that this exercise is quite different from Americans' politeness to young children. In contrast to the common American pattern, Khmer rarely say "please" to a young child, and they certainly do not say "thank you" to their own children. The idea here is not to be polite to the young child, who has neither face nor status, but to teach the child that she must learn to recognize the status of those above her and be deferential to her elders. What is being learned is not the leveling politeness of autonomous individuals but a politeness keenly attuned to the contours of a decidedly uneven social field.

In perhaps the most common sociolinguistic exercise of this sort, the caregiver teaches the proper use of kin terms and the terms of address used in greetings. Khmer adults are horrified by the way in which American young people address their elders by their first names, as if they were equals. Khmer children are encouraged to address even their own siblings and cousins as either *bâng* (older brother or sister) or *aun* (younger brother or sister), depending upon their relatives' ages or, in the case of cousins, on the relative ages of their respective parents.[18] Children very quickly become sensitive to such usages and their meanings, and elder siblings may even demand that their younger siblings address them with the proper term.

Caregivers also tirelessly urge their charges to greet older relatives and guests in an appropriately formal manner. They typically do so by modeling the proper linguistic formula themselves, saying to the child, for example, *"Chŭmriep suo, ŏm!"* ("Respectful greetings, older aunt!"), while pushing or pulling a reluctant child forward. In greeting an elder, children must place their palms together at face level, bowing slightly. Although the words for leave-taking differ, children must learn to leave in a similar manner. It is also common to see caregivers physically molding a young child into the appropriate posture of deference, legs folded to the side, head bowed, and hands pressed together, in a monk's presence. Children who behave appropriately in these and similar situations are rewarded with praise from all present: *"L'ăh nah! Kaun kuosăm nah!"* ("Very good! That's a very polite child!") A child who does not behave appropriately may be gently shamed.

Caregivers take such etiquette exercises extremely seriously. What begins as gentle or even playful prodding and shaming when the child is young changes to more insistent, exacting demands as the child matures. At first sight, certainly from a North American perspective, the emphasis Khmer parents place on such sociolinguistic exercises may appear disproportionate to the actual dynamics of interaction. As will become clear in the chapters that follow, however, these small acts of deference are repeated in virtually all Khmer ritual celebrations over the course of an individual's lifetime. For Khmer, the expression of respect between individuals of differing status is, in effect, an elementary form in social life. Khmer elders view the ability to greet and address others as a critical index of the child's social status and moral upbringing and therefore also of the parents' social "face."

FACE AND FAMILY REPUTATION

Face *(mŭk môt)* and reputation or honor *(kétyuoh)* are major preoccupations for Khmer (see also Ponchaud 1977b; Martin 1994). A person with a good reputation is commonly said to *mean mŭk (mean) môt*, which is literally "to have face, to have voice," or to *mean mŭk khpŭah*, which is "to have a 'high' face, to be highly respected." The individual who has lost face is described as *ât mean mŭk môt*, being "without face or voice," or *bak mŭk, bak môt* "having a shattered face" ("so that even flies won't alight; even dogs don't bark when he passes"). As elsewhere in Southeast Asia, face is not a uniquely individual matter but a complex social evaluation that depends on the judgments of people in the community and the expression of those judgments in public ritual and etiquette.

Khmer parents emphasize that a child who acts or speaks disrespectfully reflects badly on the entire family. Parents explained this perspective:

[Male, age 42] If a child speaks well [and] says *"Chŭmriep suo"* ("Respectful greetings") well, the parents of that child are considered well.

That is, they are considered good parents. And throughout the community, people will speak highly of that family. The child reflects on his family. And status is gained by the appropriate use of language like *"Chŭmriep suo."* We have a rule in Cambodia to be peaceful and friendly with each other. Language use reinforces that order. Like in Cambodia, children say *"Chŭmriep suo"* and bow to their teacher every morning. They have to say that to be polite. If a child is impolite, people say, *"Kméng nuoh ât pouh"* ("That child has no roots, education, or upbringing") or *"Kaun nuoh batpsa"* ("That kid comes from the streets") [literally from "the bottom of the market"]. They will say *"Mae ŏv ât brâdav"* ("Their parents didn't teach them"). In this way, the parents will lose face. Everyone will say that family is no good.

[Male, age 59] If my son speaks to the old people and uses *a* [an informal epithet] instead of *lŏk ŏm* (honorable older uncle or aunt), *lŏk pou* (honorable uncle), *lŏk ming* (honorable younger aunt), those people will look at him and say, "Who is your father?" They will blame me as a parent and say, "Oh, what a terrible parent! He didn't teach his child how to address people in the right way." And I would be very ashamed.

[Female, age 42] I must teach my children to use the proper words to address the other people, because if my children know those words, then the other people will say, *"Nih kaun chav neak na?"* ("Whose family does that child belong to?") and they will say, "Oh, that family is very good, they know very good words, they know about hierarchy and the proper status of people. They have taught their children well."

Khmer parents consistently refer to others' evaluations of their own children's behavior. Conversely, parents are reluctant to praise their own children's behavior publicly. Parents note that they "don't dare say anything" *(mĭn hean tha)* about their children, because they "cannot take responsibility for such pronouncements." Even if one's children behave well today, they may misbehave tomorrow; even if one's children behave well at home, they may not do so away from home. And if children fail to live up to public praise, their parents will be called liars *(neak krâhâk)*. Social sins par excellence, lying and boastfulness are considered deeply offensive in the eyes of the community. Parents thus prefer to rely on others' comments in assessing their children's behavior.

[Widow, age 46] I don't want to say anything about my three sons, how well they are doing. *Khnhŏm mĭn hean tha* (I don't dare to speak about that). When I hear good things about my children from others, from people outside of my family, then I can know what I already feel in my heart. But I cannot say for myself. We cannot say because we don't know. We don't dare to take full responsibility for that. Like if I say that and then something bad happened to my son later on and I said he was so smart and so good, everyone would look at me and say that I lied. Then I would be ashamed to have boasted like that. That is considered very bad in the eyes of the community. I only want to say true words, so it is up to the other people to say. [It's up] to my neighbors to judge my sons. I cannot say.

The evaluation of others' speech and behavior is, in fact, a topic of endless conversation and gossip (*ni'yeay daoem*) whenever community members meet. The importance of gossip in Khmer society is captured in the popular Khmer saying "Vietnamese have their tricks, Thai have their schemes, Khmer have their gossip." When asked why young children do what they are told, one young person laughed and said, "It's simple. People always talk about anybody with bad behavior, and then that person feels embarrassed and they don't want to do that behavior again." A woman's comments illustrate how this works.

[Fieldnotes, female, late 50s] While waiting to interview Kaoet Roeung, my Khmer companion and I sit chatting with his wife. She takes the opportunity to complain to us about her neighbor's children, "who don't know how to speak proper Khmer." She tells us indignantly, "They only speak English with my son, and I tell them, 'I don't allow you to speak English with Samnang! *Ni'yeay khmae!* (Speak Khmer!)' I tell them, 'Do you know why I say that? Because when you go back to Cambodia, the Cambodian people will hit you and kill you if you speak like that [if you don't know how to speak correctly].'" She turns to me and explains, "Their parents don't teach them, and the son calls me *bâng* (older sister)! I told the mother and father, 'Your children address me incorrectly. You'd better teach your children!' And then the next time they talked to me, the children called me *ŏm*. That's correct, because I'm older than those children's parents."

This sensitivity to community evaluations makes Khmer parents strive to produce well-behaved children and constrains Khmer children to conform to community standards. Equally important, these pressures may result in parental behaviors that contradict the indulgent patterns of early infant socialization. Although caretakers are relaxed about a child's inability to speak or behave appropriately when the child is "not yet aware," as the child approaches the "age of awareness"—somewhere between seven and ten—parents expect, indeed demand, better behavior. They prefer to talk gently and repeatedly with the child, but if the child does not eventually adjust the behavior, more forceful methods of instruction are used (see Martin 1994).

DISCIPLINE AND THE WITHDRAWAL OF INDULGENCE

Parents' decreased tolerance for inappropriate behavior does not develop suddenly but is preceded by several key developments. One may be the arrival of a new sibling. As one might imagine, the withdrawal of indulgence that accompanies a younger sibling's birth often causes great distress in the elder child (Ebihara 1968; Piker 1975), who may respond by withdrawing or misbehaving. Rather than receiving indulgence, the child often then becomes the target of parents' teasing and playful threats.

> [Fieldnotes] Four-year-old Rethy is being cared for by his mother, who has a two-week-old daughter. When we come into the room, Rethy is clinging to his mother's sarong, looking sad and abandoned. Baby in arms, the mother keeps nudging him away. When the baby's bottle falls, Rethy's mother raises her hand as if to hit him, playfully threatening, "*Vai! vai!*" ("I'll hit you! I'll hit you!") Rethy scrambles to retrieve the bottle.

Other family members usually reinforce this practice, reorienting attention away from the older child and toward the newborn. Often, too, they use a similar mixture of admonition and teasing, not infrequently including playful threats to strike the unhappy older child.

> [Fieldnotes] During the first birthday party for Tey's baby, Tey's three-year-old niece inserts herself between the adults sitting on the couch, coming a little too close to the baby. Raising her hand as if to strike her, Tey immediately threatens her, "*Sngiem, vai!*" ("Be good or I'll hit you!") Seconds later, when the little girl tries clumsily to pat the baby's head, the mother yells, *"Aun chenh! Sngiem vai aun!"* ("Get out of here! If you don't behave, I'll hit you!")

Some families ease a baby's arrival by handing the toddler over to a new caregiver, typically a grandmother, aunt, or older sister, who may continue to indulge the child much as before. As a child reaches the age of five or six, however, with or without a new sibling, both parents become markedly less tolerant. The father's change in demeanor is especially pronounced, as he abruptly becomes emotionally distant (Ebihara 1968:117). Indulgent with his infants, the father begins to demand respectful behavior.

> [Female, age 54] In our culture, we believe the father should stop kissing the child after age five, but under five, that's OK. Fathers should be more severe with their children than mothers. The father plays the more severe role. It is necessary so that the children will listen to him. When the father says, "Stop hanging around, stay home," they stay home, they listen.

> [Male, age 35] When children are under the age of five, it's OK to show them my love. I handle them carefully and touch them very softly. It is all right to show them my affection. But I believe that the child later on will forget quickly the way I showed that affection. And [when the child is] five, I begin to change my behavior. I don't go quickly—just gradually until they know I am serious. I want to show that kind of thing until the child knows *khlach*. [You mean fear?] Not really fear, but respect. Like gradually I want them to know that when I say "Stop!" I mean "Stop! Don't play!"

As these comments indicate, the open expression of parental (especially paternal) affection is not regarded as appropriate for an older child; the parents must balance demonstrations of love with measures to instill fear and respect. When the child is between the ages of five and seven, both mothers and fathers say, you must be very careful not to let your children know you love them too much. You should no longer kiss and hug them or offer them too much praise, or they will not respect or obey you. A child who receives too much praise and affection, parents say, will become spoiled *(tŭmroeh)*.

> [*Krou khmae,* age 42] It is bad to tell your child you love him. We have to keep it to ourselves *(tŭk knŏng chĕt)*. We have to make the distinction between loving children and telling them we love them. The way we love them is not to show them. [If we show them], we will spoil them. If they know I love them so much, they won't listen to me.

> [Female, age 36] It is very rare [for Cambodians] to praise the child if they do something good. Very rare. Usually, we just correct them if they do something bad. We have to observe them *(samlŏeng moel*

kaun léng), the way they do something wrong, and then we correct them by telling them they did something wrong.

[Fieldnotes, female, age 19] One young mother is particularly insistent on this point, saying that she "never" shows affection to her eighteen-month-old son but instead hits him "every day so as to limit his need." She reasons, "If you show your love to your children, they will not be scared of you, and they won't listen."

The views of this young mother aside, such an unindulgent and undemonstrative posture is thought to be more difficult for mothers to achieve than for fathers. It is widely believed that mothers are more attached to their children, partly because they interact with them more than fathers do. As a result, children come to "know their mother's heart" *(dŏeng chĕt mae);* that is, they realize that their mother loves them too much to punish them harshly.

[Female, age 45] The father is very strict in the family. He says, "I'll hit you," and he means business. He will hit hard. For the mother, it isn't like that. She hits, but never very hard, or she just threatens and doesn't hit.

Nonetheless, if a child in middle childhood or older misbehaves, fathers and mothers alike will resort to physical punishment when verbal admonitions fail to produce the desired results. Typically, this takes the form of a sharp pinch or slap on the hands or legs with incense sticks or chopsticks. At the same time, verbal admonitions begin to take on a new severity.

Indulgence of a child during infancy is related to parental anxieties that the child may be taken by spirits or real people if mistreated. Later—once it is clear that the child is "staying"—parental demands increase and indulgence correspondingly decreases. As children become capable of more thoughtful behavior, parents believe they will "forget" the early indulgence; indeed, parents themselves are enjoined to deny that they ever indulged the child. To do otherwise, it is feared, is to risk creating children who will not listen to their parents and who refuse to do what they are told. Parents will, in turn, be judged by the community to be incapable of controlling their offspring. The point at which parental indulgence is withdrawn is also the point at which community members begin to evaluate the child's actions, seeing them as a direct reflection of the parents' standing or face.

FACE AND MORALITY

This belief that continued indulgence spoils the child contrasts with that of some other Southeast Asian cultures, in which people consider it both natural and good to indulge children.[19] In those other cultures, one finds a similar concern with status and reputation, but Khmer culture differs in the degree to which children's behavior is considered to reflect the family's social standing. As we have seen—and contrary to other, more individualistic themes in Khmer Buddhism—the Khmer Buddhist view of karma affirms that parents get the children they deserve, reflecting the parents' store of merit. Thus, poorly behaved children indicate not merely social negligence but also a moral, indeed karmic, failing on the part of parents, in line with a family's collective lack of merit (bŏn). A child's misbehavior is an embarrassment to the parents, as well as to older brothers and sisters, grandparents, and aunts and uncles.

Khmer parents thus feel a complex, mutually reinforcing array of moral constraints enjoining them to produce well-behaved children. Even extended family members will aid in the effort. For all these reasons, the child's moral training is an important and enduring focus of parental socialization.

The following chapter continues this discussion of identity, face, and morality by examining the roles and responsibilities of the older child and adolescent. Here, as well, there are two views of the child and two cultural moralities, one emphasizing the child's individuality and the other emphasizing the child's embeddedness in an intricate social grid. As children become more capable of understanding and reasoning, parents focus more of their moral tuition on explicit, discursive training, emphasizing above all the child's debt to parents and elders. Equally significant, the parents also begin to distinguish more forcefully between what is proper and expected for girls as opposed to boys.

It is this capacity for reasoned and moral behavior, Khmer emphasize, that distinguishes human beings from animals (sat). A key feature of reasoned understanding is the recognition that humans, again unlike animals, have different statuses that must be acknowledged in social interactions. As children develop self-knowledge and social understanding, therefore, they must also form a respectful attitude toward parents and other senior family members. By extension, building respect for their parents helps children develop a sense of respect and fear *(khlach)* for people beyond the family, from neighbors to government officials and monks, and even to ancestral spirits and the Buddha. This relational understanding is a central theme of Khmer moral education—one that has encountered serious challenges in the more individualistic milieu of the contemporary United States.

4

Moral Education
The Child within the Family

For Khmer, young children are not yet completely "human" *(mnŭh)*. Parents often say that their children "don't yet know themselves" *(mĭn toan dŏeng kluon)*; "don't yet have deep thoughts" *(mĭn toan dŏeng rǎk chrŏv)*; and "don't yet know how to think" *(mĭn toan chéh kĭt)*. Only with the onset of puberty—marked loosely by menarche in young women and, at least traditionally, by investiture in the monkhood for young men—do children seem to gain self-knowledge and understanding, the qualities of "deep thinking" that differentiate humans from animals. This maturation ideally culminates with marriage, childbirth, and participation as an adult in rituals of merit making and intergenerational reciprocity.

Until adolescence, youths are also considered to have very little face *(mŭk môt)*. Consequently, adults in most situations speak directly, even bluntly, with young people, telling them what to do without using the gestures of politeness and the respectful speech that are obligatory when addressing equals or superiors (Steinberg 1959:56–57). Typically, for example, children and youths are addressed with the terms *kaun* (child) or *aun* (youngster). Alternatively, adults might address them by name without using any kin term; addressing adults this way would be considered insulting. In the larger scheme, then, children and youths count for rather little.

Recognizing face and trying to maintain it are critical elements in becoming a Khmer adult. Knowing oneself means knowing how to behave properly according to one's status within the family and community; with self-knowledge, one would be aware of social obligations and would accept responsibility for one's actions.

This concern with social status and reputation is expected to develop only gradually; it cannot be forced. Ideally, a young person should be allowed to develop at an individual pace. As is the case with other aspects of Khmer socialization, however, there is a tension between this focus on the child, who has individual developmental rhythms, and the family's more relationally oriented status concerns.

As youths become able to understand and reason—a development particularly noticeable between the age of seven or eight and the onset of puberty—they are expected to start behaving properly, thereby upholding the family's good name (Martin 1994). At the same time, parents intensify their efforts to *brâdav*, or teach (literally, "to discipline") children the responsibilities that they will assume in early adulthood.

FIRST GODS

A key feature of Khmer parents' moral training involves inculcating in children the proper attitudes toward superiors. This begins with the way children regard their parents. Khmer say that children must learn that their parents are their "first gods" (*ŏvpŭk mday chea preah knong ptĕah*), literally, their "gods within the house." When making food offerings to the monks, for example, the child is routinely asked, "Have you remembered your first gods [your parents]?" If children learn this first lesson well, elders say, they can later extend that understanding to their teacher, the child's "second mother" or "second father." Ultimately, this same sense of respect will apply to ancestral spirits and the Buddha, as well.

> [Male, age 40] As parents, we have to teach our children well so that when they grow up they remember, "I owe my parents. And when they are sick, I have to care for them, to remember them." Children must respect their parents and know that they owe them many things. *Respect* means you have to take care of your parents. That is respect.

Children are said to owe "unlimited things" to their parents, because their elders sacrifice everything for their offspring in bringing them into the world and nurturing them. This filial debt is described as "so great that it can never be fully repaid." Nevertheless, in actual practice, there is an expectation that preadolescent sons and daughters will begin to recognize their obligation to their parents by helping out at home. Daughters, in particular, are expected to assist with housework and child care, and sons should help do household tasks requiring greater strength. When old enough to seek employment, children of both sexes are expected to get jobs and to give all or part of their wages to their mother. All the while, they should reassure their parents of their respect and devotion through proper speech and bearing. Khmer elders stress, however, that children's most important obligation to their parents is to care for them in their old age. Freed from subsistence and household concerns, elders can then devote their final days to making merit and observing precepts in anticipation of rebirth (Piker 1975:92).

Yet, here, as in so many areas of Khmer American moral life, this seemingly secure moral edifice is laced with anxiety. Even the most exemplary children, it is said, may fail to reassure their parents of their love and devotion. Like the northern Thai that Piker (1975) described, Khmer acknowledge that human nature can be volatile. Radical changes in character and life direction can occur at any time. "The child who is good today," Khmer say, "may very well behave badly tomorrow." One can never know for certain when the store of merit amassed in previous lives may be exhausted, causing a person's character to change suddenly.

Many parents fear that such changes in a child's character will occur when the parents are elderly; they worry that the child will ignore their filial debt and abandon the parents to a lonely fate. This fear of abandonment by one's children pervades the conversations of Khmer parents in the Boston area. No doubt the trauma of the Khmer holocaust has added to this parental insecurity; the anxiety has been further exacerbated by the newly Americanized behaviors of Khmer youth and the perception that "in America, at age eighteen, children leave home and forget all about their parents."

It is thus not surprising that Khmer moral education focuses on filial obligation and, more specifically, on children's responsibility to reciprocate the care and affection their parents have showered on them. Reiterated over the life of a son or a daughter, this theme of unlimited debt serves as the linchpin of intergenerational morality within the family.

GENDERED SOCIALIZATION

Khmer insist that sons and daughters are equally desired as offspring and equally cherished as they grow. The birth of a son is not regarded as a more blessed event than the birth of a girl (Ebihara 1974:323). In fact, Khmer cite examples of couples with many boys who continue to conceive in hopes of producing a girl, as well as those with girls who continue to bear children in hopes of having a boy. Despite this lack of preference, Khmer do have markedly different expectations of daughters and sons. These are apparent even in early socialization and underscore broader differences in attitudes toward sons and daughters.

Many parents say that girls are more difficult to raise than boys, insisting that "you have to be more careful *(prâyat nah)* with a daughter than with a son." For girls, they explain, there are certain gender-specific behaviors that must be taught when the child is young so that she will "follow" *(tam)*, that is, do what she's asked when older. A daughter, in particular, must learn early on to mute her sexual desires so that she does not ruin the family's reputation through sexual misconduct.

Parental efforts to constrain undesirable behaviors in young girls ideally begin in infancy. For example, Khmer mothers from rural backgrounds insist that it is best to stop breast-feeding daughters before sons. The reasons for this have to do with a basic characteristic of gender in Khmer worldview: Khmer maintain that girls are naturally more "passionate" *(kaun srey mean tânaha chraoen)* than boys and less able to control their emotions. If girls are breast-fed too long, it is said, their passion will increase so much that they will be impossible to control. "They'll always talk back and never do what they're told," Khmer say. They see a lack of control in girls as extremely dangerous. Even when speaking about infant girls, they link its deleterious effects to the threat of uncontrollable sexual appetite in later life. Boys, in contrast, need to be breast-fed longer to become strong enough to support a future family. The problem of boys' sexual appetites looms much less prominently in parents' commentaries.

> [Female, age 39] If girls drink milk too long, *vea rŏeng* ("they will be naughty"). Boys, if they drink milk, *vea kamlăng* ("they will be strong"). Boys have to drink milk, to breast-feed longer, because they need that so when they grow up they are very strong and they can help their families. For the girls, it isn't good for them to drink so much, because when they grow up, they will want to have sex too early and they will go looking for a man. When you ask her to do something, she will always answer back and reply that she doesn't want to do it. She won't follow you. She won't do what you ask.

A related practice requires the mother to rub breast milk on the female newborn's vulva. One Khmer mother (cited in Kelley 1991:60) insisted that the practice reduces any puffiness or swelling of the genitalia and even "keeps the [vaginal] opening small." More important, the milk's cooling power is said to quell the girl's passionate nature, thereby ensuring her circumspection and obedience "so she won't do anything embarrassing later on."

Today, most young Khmer mothers in the United States prefer bottle-feeding to breast-feeding. Although a few report that they weaned their daughters from the bottle sooner than their sons, the deciding issue for the majority of mothers appears to be convenience rather than social control. Health services have made parents aware of the benefits of breast-feeding. Young women consider bottle-feeding more "modern," however, and say that breast-feeding "feels funny" and is bad for one's figure (Kelley 1991). Despite this shift away from traditional childrearing practices, they are of special interest because they express a fundamental point of contrast in Khmer conceptions of male and female; Khmer see the male as strong and rational and the female as passionate and emotional.[1]

Women are often described by others and by themselves as "soft and weak" (tŭan khsaoy), whereas men are "strong and powerful" (khlăng poukae). Men are thought to be stronger not only physically but also mentally. The father, for example, is often said to be "bigger than the mother" (tŭm chieng mday) within the family because he is stronger and better educated. The father is also said to deserve more respect because "he gives more as the family provider" and "has more strength and knowledge." In contrast, women are conceived of as passionate and emotional.[2]

Thus, it is women who are more prone to emotional outbursts. It is women, too, who are said to suffer to a greater degree the pain and loneliness of having lost family members during Pol Pot time. As in many other Southeast Asian societies (see Geertz 1960; Laderman 1983; Peletz 1996), women are also reported to be more susceptible to spiritual disturbances, particularly spirit possession.

The belief that males are strong and rational and that females are weak and emotional has a concrete and profound impact on gender socialization. Among other things, it reinforces the tendency to encourage boys to develop autonomy and independence while encouraging girls to be dependent and emotionally restrained.

RULES FOR GIRLS

In discussing the behavior and upbringing of girls, parents often mention *chbab srey,* or "rules for girls." This refers generally to "appropriate" behavior for girls and more specifically to a manual written in traditional Khmer verse form. Titled *Chbab Srey,* it describes ideal female behavior (see Chandler 1984:271; Ledgerwood 1990a:70; Martin 1994:10). These written rules were initially codified in the mid–nineteenth century. In a revised form, this manual later became part of the core curriculum in Cambodian schools in the twentieth century. Today, although few Khmer American households have access to the actual text, many mothers are familiar with it from their parents' instructions and from their own school years. They frequently invoke *chbab srey* when teaching their daughters. Beyond its details, the text owes much of its popularity to the widespread conviction that social behavior in general, and girls' behavior in particular, is not a matter of individual preference or choice. Rather, girls must know and abide by socially prescribed canons.

> [Female, age 54] We still follow that *[chbab srey].* The girls have to follow those rules. We don't want to forget our culture, to throw away our rules. We believe the law for girls is very good, so we teach our daughters to respect those rules. For example, girls should talk softly and walk softly without making any noise. No screaming or yelling. If you have a ceremony at the temple, the good girls, the perfect girls *(srey krŭp leak),* they know how to greet people appropriately. They talk softly and politely, and they bow and sit correctly in the way girls should sit, with legs to the side.

The theme of expressive constraint is prominent in all descriptions of proper female behavior. Young women are expected to control their physical movements, to walk softly and unobtrusively, and to sit modestly with knees covered and legs to the side. They must especially control their speech, speaking softly or otherwise remaining silent. Equally important, they must learn to keep their eyes downcast and avoid direct eye contact, particularly in the presence of males. It is considered especially important that a girl be shy and demure *(ean khmăh).*

> [Female, age 50] It is important for girls to be *ean khmăh* (shy, ashamed). That is *leak robâh srey,* the behavior of women. Cambodian girls, in our

culture have to be shy. Their physical behavior *(leak)* also has to be very careful. These are secret things for the girl that she cannot show off. She has to be careful how she walks and talks, not to open her mouth, to keep herself covered.

Through their gestures, comportment, and self-presentation, Khmer elders say, young women must learn not to draw attention to themselves, not to "show off their femaleness"—their "seductive power."

Given the weight of these expectations, daughters are more closely supervised than sons. From an early age, boys are allowed the freedom to roam about and do as they please. By contrast, beginning at age seven or eight, girls are expected to stay close to home whenever they are not at school, returning home directly after their classes. When they do go away from home, they are expected to have a companion—a sibling, cousin, or girlfriend—at all times.

> [Male, age 40] I don't want my daughters to go out after school. They have to come home on time. If they need to go out to do something, they must tell me in advance so I know about that and I know where they are and what they are doing.

> [Male, age 59] My daughters have to do the housework, to dress neatly, to cook. I don't want them going out after school. No hanging around with boys, so there is no gossip. Just stay at home. Don't do anything wrong.

Not surprisingly, efforts to shelter girls and limit their freedom intensify as girls approach puberty. For Khmer, menarche signals that a girl has become marriageable. Her new status leads people to expect that a young woman will now behave in an even more circumscribed manner (Ebihara 1974; Ledgerwood 1990a). Household sleeping arrangements may even have to be adjusted to allow a daughter to sleep in a room with a door (her brother may be exiled to the couch), so as to maintain proper appearances and to shield her from the eyes of male visitors.

THE MORAL SIGNIFICANCE OF MENARCHE

One Cambodian tradition required sheltering young women at menarche with an elaborate seclusion ritual known as *chaul mlŭb*, or "entering the shade." *Chaul mlŭb* involved keeping the young woman in a darkened room and out of male view (Ebihara 1974:311). This period of social isolation lasted from three weeks to three months; in some instances, it was even longer.

Just a few of the older women I spoke with had undergone *chaul mlŭb*. The practice seems to have been widespread only among higher-status, wealthy families. It appears that only wealthier families could afford to forgo a daughter's help during the seclusion period. In addition, only wealthy families had the resources and status interests to sponsor the expensive ceremony that accompanies the young woman's emergence from seclusion. For those who did "enter the shade," however, the experience was powerful, and the memories are still vivid.

> [Female, age 54] I stayed in my room for three months. And every day, I had to eat only sesame seed with rice and coconut. I was so bored. I wanted to go out to take a bath! My mother put mats up over the door and the windows. It was dark in there, and I prayed the days would be short and the nights would be short. I didn't want to stay in my room. It was so terrible. I was not allowed to do anything. Only at midnight, my mother would come to take me out to have a bath.

During her seclusion, the young woman was instructed in the behaviors and demeanor appropriate to her womanly status. When she emerged, her transformation was supposed to be apparent to all who saw her.

> [Female, age 54] When I came out, I was very weak, and my skin was yellow! All yellow! And my skin was very soft. Everybody said, when we came out, because of our skin, "Oh, that's a beautiful girl!"

Parents who did not make a girl undergo this ritualized seclusion at first menstruation instead kept her home for several days. Often, they would tie a white cotton string around her wrist to ensure that her "soul would not leave her body."[3] One has to do that, a young mother explained, "to protect the girl so that evil spirits cannot touch her."

> [Female, age 42] In my time, we didn't *chaul mlŭb*, but my parents wanted me to stay at home [at first menstruation]. They didn't want me to go out. And they tied a string around my wrist to make my soul and my memory strong and to [keep my soul] inside my body.

Khmer believe that the loss of blood during menstruation or childbirth makes women physically and spiritually vulnerable. This is why they seek to "tie the soul in the body" to protect a girl's soul from evil spirits.

Although parents may prepare for menarche by mobilizing spiritual resources, they typically do not anticipate its onset by explaining its physiological meaning to their daughters. Even in Massachusetts today, older women refer to menstruation as a "secret thing" and lower their voices when discussing the subject in front of young men or prepubescent girls. Most women report that they were ignorant of menstruation before their first period. Now in her late forties, Mok Sophal can recall the private terror of her first menstrual period:

> [Fieldnotes, female, age 48] Sophal remembers one day when she was nineteen and her father sent her out to the fields to watch for birds who were eating the rice. She walked in the rice fields, shooing away the birds, and she caught crabs in the shallow water. When she came back to her hut and sat down, it felt very sticky between her legs. She touched the area with her hand and found blood on her fingers. She was so frightened that she rolled up in her mat and stayed there the rest of the day. Her brother came looking for her, but she refused to respond to his calls. "I was thinking that maybe that crab bit my vagina!" she said. "I was so scared that my whole body was shaking!"

For many Khmer girls in the United States, the situation has not changed dramatically; most receive little or no counsel from their mothers before menarche. Mao Vanna, who came to this country at age seven, said that when she first menstruated at age twelve, she was certain that something was seriously wrong with her, "like cancer." She waited several days before telling her mother that she thought she was going to die. Some young women learn privately about menstruation from an older female relative, sister, or friend, but even then the matter is treated with considerable circumspection and, in general, much misinformation.

In American schools, Khmer parents have consistently opposed their children's involvement in sex education courses. They believe that it is particularly dangerous for girls to know about sex before marriage. Parents say they fear that if their daughters know about sex, they will become sexually active. So strong is this parental conviction that an irate father threatened one bilingual teacher who spoke out in favor of sex education in the schools. He told her, "If you had a daughter, I would send my son to rape her!"[4]

Although young women are told little about the physiological aspects of menstruation, they learn through stories and admonitions that female fluids have a certain power that requires their restraint and control. Even prepubescent girls are taught that they should never step over a man or allow any of their lower garments to touch his head; to do so would diminish the man's potency.[5] At the temple women make a wide path for any passing monk, trying to avoid proximity or contact. Mothers even rush to gather up infant girls as the monks pass.

When they reach adolescence, young women are more directly admonished to handle and dispose of feminine products carefully. Anne Hansen (1988:26) reports that in the past, the blood from a girl's first period was sometimes dried on a white cloth and saved. It could later be boiled in water and thereby made into a medicine. Today, young women are warned that it is highly improper to leave dirty undergarments lying about where male family members might see them; even hanging laundered underthings in the shower where they might be positioned "over a male member of the family's head" is unacceptable.

Through stories of seduction and black magic, young women *(krâmŏm)* also learn of the possible disequilibrating effects of female fluids on men.[6] For example, menstrual blood is said to be a powerful ingredient in love potions *(tvoe snae)*. It overwhelms the man who inadvertently imbibes it; he loses all his strength and willpower and falls under the woman's spell. This happened to the husband of Krang Sophy, an airline pilot from Phnom Penh. One day, he was seduced away from her by a "prostitute," who put menstrual blood in his coffee and gave it to him to drink.

> [Female, age 50] She used that kind of love magic, and after that, my husband started fighting with me all the time. One time in the camps, in the middle of a terrible fight, a friend of my husband's came by and said, "Hey, why are you fighting with your good wife? You should treat her better. Why do you fight over that prostitute? She was with me before you. Before you, I slept with her!" But my husband didn't even care. The love magic made him forget me, his real wife, and his kids. So he just left, left everything, and married that other woman.

Female sexuality is thus potent but dangerous. It must be constrained or controlled, and its bearer must be imbued with virtue (Hansen 1988; Ledgerwood 1990a).

Although many traditional rituals associated with the onset of menarche are no longer observed in the United States, some Khmer have attempted to improvise, adapting American customs to Khmer values in an effort to create functional equivalents to rituals performed in Cambodia. In the Boston Khmer community, for example, one young mother equated a sixteenth birthday party held for her daughter—who had recently reached menses—with *chaul mlŭb*. For her, the celebration marked her daughter Srey's new, marriageable status and her withdrawal from a youthful social life.

> [Fieldnotes, 16th birthday party] At Srey's sixteenth birthday party, there are, as usual, more adults in attendance than young people. In fact, Srey is not even present. Her mother explains that Srey will remain secluded in her room until given a signal to come out. "It is like *chaul mlŭb*," she says, "because my daughter is now sixteen and just recently began menstruating."
>
> When Srey finally emerges, she walks very slowly, her eyes downcast. She is led to her mother by several of her girlfriends, who act as attendants. Her mother hands her a bouquet of flowers, and her girlfriends lead her slowly around the room to a seat behind a table laden with gifts and a birthday cake. During the rest of her party, Srey sits there quietly and demurely, speaking only when a friend comes up to chat. Her mother says that now that her daughter has had her first period, she will no longer have any more birthday parties. "It would not be right for her to have a party, to go out like that. So I wanted to do this for her now, to make her happy, because she has not had a very happy life."[7]
>
> For her daughter's party, Srey's mother has decorated the walls with cardboard placards. They bear Khmer proverbs written in Khmer script: "To behave well is the flower of civilization"; "Mothers love their children who are like tiny fish; children love their parents like a Buddha who turns his back"; and "Truthfulness, patience, and mindfulness of one's elders." She explains that she put these signs on the walls because they convey important moral lessons for young people. "These sayings are things Cambodian children should know," she observes. "They are important lessons for their lives."

As in the menarche rituals conducted in Cambodia, the focus of Srey's ceremony highlighted her progression toward moral maturity and familial responsibility. No effort was made to hide the fact of her first menstruation—at least not from the adult women present. Nevertheless, little symbolic or ritual attention was directed toward the physiological aspects of the experience. In a later conversation, Srey's mother confided that her daughter still knew little if anything about sex. If she were to know, her mother added, "she would go out and get pregnant!"

THE VIRTUOUS DAUGHTER

Even when menarche is no longer marked in a ritual manner, it impels mothers into action; they intensify their campaigns to make daughters behave in a proper, virtuous manner. Again and again, they remind their daughters that if they do not conduct themselves well, they may not secure a husband. In these admonitions, mothers refer to *chbab srey*, the "rules for girls."

> [Female, age 42] If the girl is cooking and she drops the knife, her mother says, "If you are clumsy like that, you will never get a husband." If the girl does not dress neatly and modestly, her mother will say, "Oh, if the boys see you like that, they will never want to marry you." If the girl speaks too loudly in the house, her mother says, "According to *chbab srey*, you mustn't talk so loudly, or they will hear your voice ten houses away *(phtĕah dâb leu samleng neang aeng ni'yeay haoey)*."

According to *chbab srey*, a young woman must know how to take care of the household, cook and clean, and serve elders and guests. She must be industrious, shy, and modest *(ean khmăh)* if she is to please her in-laws.

> [Female, age 24] My mother taught me about *chbab srey*. You have to know how to do all of the housework. Otherwise, when you get married, your in-laws will not like you. Maybe you won't get married at all. And you have to respect older people and guests, say *"Chŭmriep suo,"* find them something to drink, and talk respectfully, then go away and sit in another room. Because if the daughter stays around too much, it means that you show off your daughter.

Many of the behaviors prescribed by *chbab srey*, including those cited by this young woman, are still widely practiced in the Khmer American community. During visits to Khmer homes, it is common to see a teenage daughter wearing a traditional long, gathered skirt (*sarong*), her long hair pulled back neatly. She will quietly and unobtrusively prepare meals, wash dishes, serve refreshments, or entertain younger siblings. Adolescent boys rarely, if ever, engage in such tasks and are generally much less visible in Khmer American homes.

In fact, it should be pointed out that although Khmer parents insist that boys and girls are equally desired, mothers frequently comment that having a girl first is a blessing *("Khmae yoeng, srey mŭn, l'ăh,"* or "For Khmer, a girl first is good"). On the most obvious level, Khmer link this preference for girls to the fact that, as described above, daughters typically help with the housework and relieve mothers of tedious chores. The potential value of a daughter's contribution to the household is captured in the well-known Khmer saying *"Kaun srey chŭmnuoh dai choeng mday"* (literally, "The daughter replaces the mother's hands and legs"). A related aphorism points out the economic benefits of having a daughter even more explicitly: *"Ban kaun srey dambaung raok si thou"* ("Have a girl first, and you can do business" or "earn a living"). In Cambodia previously, young women often assumed major household responsibilities, freeing their mothers to work in the fields or to open a small store "so that the family could survive."

Equally important, a daughter is thought to be more likely than a son to support and care for her parents in their old age. "Even if she is a prostitute, a daughter will always remember her parents and care for them when they are old," it is commonly said.

> [Mother of two sons, age 42] Khmer say *"Kaun srey kĭt mday nah"* ("The daughter always thinks of her mother"). Even after they marry, *"Kaun srey nŏek mday"* ("A daughter misses her mother"). But boys, when they are young, they just play. They never help the mother to cook or to clean. And when they are older, after they marry, boys just walk away.

Thus, although their socialization is seen as requiring more parental diligence, daughters are regarded as a more likely source of long-term affection and support in old age.

RAISING SONS

Just as there are *chbab srey,* "rules for girls," there are corresponding *chbab proh,* "rules for boys," which focus on proper behavior for boys. *Chbab proh* were also a part of the curriculum in both Cambodian public schools and temples. These rules place particular emphasis on physical strength, knowledge, and discipline. Interestingly, however, these rules are given considerably less emphasis in boys' socialization than *chbab srey* are for girls. Indeed, for Khmer in general, masculinity is less rule-encumbered than femininity. In comparing the roles of sons and daughters, then, parents more readily recite "rules for girls" *(chbab srey)* than they do "rules for boys" *(chbab proh)*.

> [Male, age 22] I don't really know too much about *chbab proh*, but my sister, she follows *chbab srey*. You know, like stay home, do the dishes, prepare the food.
>
> [Female, age 54] In Cambodia, when boys go to the temple or to school, they also study *chbab proh*. There is a book about that. The boys usually learn their duties then, but even in Cambodia, they don't really follow that. Like they study the *chbab proh*, but they keep forgetting. Not like the girls—they cannot forget that kind of thing.

Although parents discipline daughters more comprehensively than sons, boys tend to be subjected to more—and more severe—physical punishment. By one researcher's count, in fact, boys are physically reprimanded two and a half times as often as girls (Wood 1983:14). This may be true because girls internalize rules for proper behavior more thoroughly than boys. Clearly, however, it is also related to differences in the two gender roles themselves. In particular, girls are encouraged to be quiet and unobtrusive; by its very nature, this behavior is less likely to offend. Conversely, boys are expected to be more outgoing and assertive, especially as they move into adolescence. Encouraged to be independent, boys have more opportunities to get into trouble.

In contrast to their sisters, young men have duties that are said to lie "outside the house." Men generally avoid interfering in the domestic sphere, leaving household responsibilities to women. This identification of males with the public sphere and females with the domestic sphere is familiar in cross-cultural studies of gender.[8] In Cambodia, village boys were responsible for all heavy work and outside chores, such as chopping wood, carrying water, and tending large livestock (which, in other parts of Southeast Asia, is often gender-neutral labor).

Parents value strength and industriousness in sons (Wood 1983:11).

> [Female, age 44] Cambodian men are very concerned with their strength. It is the most important characteristic of a man—not necessarily physical strength but the strength to work either physically or mentally to support a family. A man should have "a five-span chest" *(proh mean daoem troung bram hat).* That is, a boy should grow up to be strong, to have a job, to support his wife. That's the most important thing for a man—the ability to support his family.[9]

This emphasis on male industry and physical strength existed even among the urban middle class. There, too, physically taxing outdoor chores were regarded as the responsibility of the young men of the household. Among the urban middle class, however, this theme of male prowess underwent additional elaboration, with comparatively more emphasis on a man's steadiness, industry, and intelligence. These three qualities were in turn linked to a boy's education for future employment, preferably in a white-collar, government position (Smith-Hefner 1995). Perhaps the clearest example of this middle-class masculine ideal is the frequent claim that "in Cambodia, one man could work and support his whole [extended] family." People say this to emphasize how things have changed; in the United States, both husband and wife must work to generate adequate household income. This is seen as undermining the earlier masculinist ideal.

Today, in most Khmer American households, there are few physically taxing chores specifically identified as male. Nonetheless, there is still a strong sense of gender-specific tasks. These are primarily defined as those that men perform only reluctantly. For example, many fathers will clean, cook, and wash clothes only in dire circumstances.

Without a clear division of labor, even parents from rural backgrounds focus on the middle-class masculine ideal and insist that sons concentrate on studying and preparing themselves to support a family.

> [Mother of five, age 48] A girl has to do the housework, watch her brothers and sisters, wash the clothes, do the cooking, clean the house, everything. [As for boys], in Cambodia they had to do all the work outside the house, like carrying the water and gathering the firewood. But here, where there is no farm, they have to study. And when they grow up, they have to go to work.

This focus on a son's education for future employment, however, poses serious problems for uneducated Khmer parents from rural backgrounds (which describes the great majority of Khmer in eastern Massachusetts). As most of them have only a vague understanding of the day-to-day requirements for school achievement, they find it difficult to reinforce the expectation that their sons apply themselves in school. Few parents have the educational background to help their children with homework, and few regard such assistance as a parental duty (see chapter 5). Moreover, since young males are allowed to spend much of the day outside of the house, parents can supervise their behavior only indirectly.

MASCULINE PUBERTY

When a young man reaches puberty, exhortations about proper behavior intensify. Teenage boys are expected to curtail any activities that undermine the goal of obtaining a good job; their priority should be preparing to support a family and to contribute financially to their aging parents' household.[10] Although there is no male puberty ritual equivalent to the girls' *chaul mlŭb*, in Cambodia temporary initiation into the monkhood was viewed as an ideal prelude to marriage and thus an esteemed rite of male passage (Ebihara 1966:177; Kalab 1976:161; Keyes 1977:160).

Because few young Khmer enter the monastery in the United States today, Cambodians have lost one of the most significant rites of male passage—and a critical opportunity for religious education. Many parents regard the decline of participation in the monkhood as a major cause of immorality in young people. From the perspective of traditional Khmer identity, they are probably right, although the decline is more the symptom than the cause of broader sociomoral changes.

Many Khmer parents complain that their teenage sons prefer to spend their time and money eating in restaurants and amusing themselves with friends instead of studying. Although they may be idealized as "more rational" than girls, young men are widely regarded as all too prone to squander their money on clothes, cars, stereos, and expensive entertainment. Dressing well and driving a nice car symbolize a young man's social status and financial acumen. Unlike young women, young men encounter no rules about dressing and acting modestly. Indeed, many proudly display their physical prowess and masculinity.

Similarly, adolescent sons are not prohibited from dating with the same vehemence as daughters are, although many parents do worry that involvement with young women will interfere with a young man's studies. The issue here is not merely technical; it touches on perceived moral differences at the heart of gender roles. Sons are warned that "girls are the enemies of education" (*"satrey chea satrauv nei kasĕksa"*), and those who hope to go far in school are told to avoid any involvement with the opposite sex. To ensure that this is the case, mothers are not above intercepting their sons' mail in search of "love letters." A mother will even intervene directly and scold a young woman who is "pursuing" her son. Mothers' comments make plain just who they blame for such attempted liaisons.

> [Mother of 18-year-old son] There were girls in my son's class who were chasing him, and they would send him love letters in the mail. I just took those letters and tore them up! I don't want him to be involved with that kind of girl. He should keep his mind on his studies. [Did your son mind that you took his letters?] My son saw me do that, but he just shrugged and laughed. He knows I am right, and there is nothing he can do.

> [Mother of 16-year-old son] There was a girl who kept calling my son, like she was a prostitute or something. And when I answered the phone, I screamed at her. I told her to leave him alone and never to call again or I would find someone to go and hit her!

As these comments suggest, Khmer culture maintains a double standard in evaluations of male and female sexual behavior. Everyone knows that young women from "good" families are not allowed to have boyfriends. Thus, if a couple is premaritally involved, the young woman must be at fault. This is the case despite the fact that, in general, male sexuality is thought of as more forceful and assertive. Both fathers and mothers are quite explicit about holding the girl responsible for such behavior.[11]

Khmer elders, then, want young men to avoid material enticements and romantic involvements and to concentrate their efforts on studying and preparing themselves for work or a career. Most young men adhere quite conscientiously to these role expectations. Although some are distracted by fast cars, romantic involvements, or gangs (see chapter 7), most appear anxious to do what is required to get a job and begin to help out their families financially. To do so, of course, is to take a critical step toward achieving the social autonomy that marks one as a man.

GENDER ROLES AND RITUAL RESPONSIBILITIES

The respect and care that sons and daughters owe their parents is not limited to household tasks and economic support. Children are also expected to attend to their parents' present and future spiritual well-being. Even young people who are otherwise exemplary—sons who are diligent in their studies and daughters who are polite and restrained and helpful around the house—are considered seriously deficient if they fail to honor their parents in this manner. By paying ritual obeisance to their parents while they are still alive, children reassure their elders that they will continue to do so after their death.

Ritual responsibilities differ for sons and daughters. Girls typically become involved in temple-related activities, such as preparing and delivering offerings, at a much younger age than their brothers. Girls' participation in such activities is a natural and easy extension of their gender role, because it is defined within the context of the household. Not insignificantly, however, their involvement is also an expression of their lower religious status.

In popular Buddhist understanding, being reborn as a female is viewed as a lesser incarnation than that of a male (Hanks 1963:28; Ebihara 1974:320). Because women are physically weaker and more emotionally attached to their families, it is argued, they are less capable of the detachment required for religious devotion. For religious and "natural" reasons, then, women are barred from monastic life.

As a result of her lesser religious status, a young girl is obliged to seek merit not through grand acts of renunciation but through an ongoing assortment of small meritorious behaviors performed over her lifetime. Again, girls learn to engage in such merit-making activities at an earlier age than boys (Ebihara 1974:336).

> [Female, age 28] I began to *tvoe bŏn* (make merit) when I was ten. I used to go to the temple with my grandfather all the time.

> [Female, age 26] I began to *tvoe bŏn*, to offer food to the monks and to give money and some clothes and some food for my parents, at age fourteen. I listened to the *yeichi* (temple grandmothers) and I learned from my parents, because they do that for their parents and so I do it

for them. Boys don't think about that kind of celebration. Maybe sometimes at age twenty they might think about that.

Although boys may be less active in temple activities than girls, boys can amass a great deal of merit for their parents in a single gesture: becoming monks (Steinberg 1959:80). During their stay in the monastery, young men learn to recite Buddhist prayers, to follow the numerous precepts associated with the monkhood, and to study Buddhist scripture. This monastic education also reinforces the depth and extent of a man's responsibilities to his parents. For this reason in particular, young men who became monks even temporarily in Cambodia had no trouble finding a wife when they left the monkhood. They were considered desirable spouses because they were deemed more likely to respect and care for their families.[12]

The significance of a young man's entering the monastery is the theme of a well-known Buddhist story, "Blessings of Ordination" (see Keyes 1984:227). Still widely recited in Khmer American homes and in the temple on holy days, it is the story of a poor widow whose son begs for her permission to become a monk. She hesitates because she has no other source of support. The story is recounted below by a woman whose sixteen-year-old son was recently ordained. (He stayed in the monastery for two weeks, which is longer than most Khmer American youths today but considerably shorter than it used to be in Cambodia.)

> [Female, age 42] There was once a poor widow who had only one son. The young man asked his mother repeatedly if he could become a monk. The mother said, "We are too poor, and you are my only son. If you don't help me plow, we cannot survive." But the boy begged her to let him become a monk. Finally, his mother felt that she could not oppose her son any longer, and she let him *buoh* (undergo ordination). He entered the monastery, leaving her to live alone. Eventually, she ran out of things to eat, and so she had to go searching for food in the forest, killing and eating small animals, even frogs. One night as she slept, the god of hell asked his subordinate to come take the woman's soul. Thus, she died.
>
> In hell, the god said to her, "What good things did you do in your life?"
>
> And she replied, "I am afraid that I killed a lot of animals."
>
> The god said, "So, you have a lot of sin!" He told his subordinate to throw the woman into hell—that is, into a big cauldron filled with hot oil.

The cauldron was very, very hot, but the woman was not burned, because suddenly a lotus flower arose out of the cauldron and lifted the woman up, away from the boiling oil.

Everyone wondered why, why did this happen? Why was such a woman spared? And she thought, Oh, I think maybe it was my son who became a monk who saved me. And the god said, "Yes, you have been spared from death because of your son."

Then she came back to life and lived on sesame seeds and white rice and became a *yeichi,* dedicating her life to the temple.

The woman recounting the story explained that it shows the "power of a boy becoming a monk." She observed, "If the son becomes a monk, it is possible for him to save his mother, his parents, from sin." The gender-differentiated moral is clear.

RITUALS OF DEFERENCE

Although few young people are actively involved in the temple these days, large numbers attend celebrations of the most popular Khmer holidays, *Chaul Chnăm* (the Khmer New Year) and *Phchŭm Bĕn* (Souls' Day). During these times, people invite ancestral spirits to their houses to enjoy special foods. Khmer offer obeisance to these spirits, first taking offering foods to the temple for the monks to bless. At the temple, the congregation listens to sermons about the suffering of their ancestors and the obligations of descendants.

People then repeat the ritual gesture of presenting food to deceased ancestors by presenting small offerings of food or money to their living parents. This is a central element of many Khmer religious celebrations. At these times, young people apologize for any sin they may have committed against their parents in the past year and ask for their forgiveness.

> [Female, age 60] At the time of *Chaul Chnăm* and *Phchŭm Bĕn*, children have to give something to their parents and to ask their forgiveness. When the parent receives those things, they say, "Yes, you have no sin toward me, and I wish you prosperity and good luck" (*"Khnhŏm aoy pau"*). And the child says yes (*sathŏk*) three times with the hands together at head level.

In the absence of other rituals that were common in Cambodia, these small ritual activities have taken on a special importance in the

United States. Parents regard these rites as times for youth to receive vital moral instruction about their filial responsibilities.

Moral instruction is also offered whenever parents sponsor a religious or life-cycle ceremony in their home. On such occasions, monks are invited to the home to eat, lead prayers, receive various offerings, and give sermons. Ceremonies that take place in the home include engagements and wedding ceremonies, the ritual feeding of the monks, and rituals to raise money for a new temple or school (often back in Cambodia).

I observed one such offering ceremony—a ritual feeding of the monks *(bŏn tean)*. This event took place in Bâng An's daughter's apartment. The ceremony revealed how moral and religious training in Khmer ritual occurs on several levels simultaneously. In this ritual, the monk's prayers and sermon contain official religious messages that draw words and images from high Buddhist doctrine. On another level, ritual offerings of food and gifts to monks, as well as offerings of money and blessings to family members, all give visible form to valued social relationships. Finally, at a less formal but deeply important level, caregivers make insistent efforts throughout the ceremony to impress upon young people the proper words, gestures, and meanings of Khmer ritual.

> [Fieldnotes, *sâng khătean*] In Bâng An's daughter's cramped living room, two saffron-robed monks are seated on a makeshift dais. All the male guests sit close to them. [Only four or five men are present, compared with twenty or twenty-five women.] The monks respond briefly when the male guests speak.
>
> When the monks begin to pray, the guests respond in unison. A group of children between the ages of eight and twelve are playing in a back bedroom, but they occasionally emerge to see what's happening. The adults repeatedly tell them, "Be quiet!" (*"Sngiem!"*)
>
> Younger children sit quietly in the living room with their parents. One mother has her one-year-old son in her lap. As the monks pray, she takes the child's hands and holds them between her own, palms pressed together. The child pulls his hands away, and she presses them together again.
>
> Another woman sits with a three-year-old girl, adjusting the child's dress repeatedly to cover her legs. She gently pushes the child's knees to the side in the appropriate position and presses the child's hands together in the conventional gesture for prayer. When a guest enters the room, the woman instructs the little girl to bow and say, *"Chŭmriep suo, ming. Chŭmriep suo, ming."* ("Respectful greetings, younger

aunt. Respectful greetings, younger aunt.") When the guest offers the child a stick of gum, holding it in a familiar gesture of respect, her palms pressed together, the child's mother instructs her daughter to receive the treat in the same fashion. The mother says for her, "Sathŏk, sathŏk, sathŏk."

When it is time for the main meal to be served to the monks, various family members bring in plates of food and deferentially kneel to offer them. Plates are given to younger children, who are pushed forward and urged to recite the appropriate words of offering. Although the language differs somewhat, these are the same gestures of deference that are impressed upon children whenever they offer greetings or food to their parents and elders.

After the main meal has been served, household goods have been offered, and the monks have given their sermon and been escorted back to the temple, the family comes forward to offer money and apologies to the mother, Bâng An. First, Bâng An's married daughter offers her mother an envelope of money held between her hands, palms pressed together. Tears stream down the young woman's face as she begs her mother's forgiveness. The older woman, who is also tearful, receives the money in the same gesture and offers her daughter a blessing in return. Her daughter's seven-year-old son then comes forward to make an offering to his grandmother, followed by his five-year-old brother. Their grandmother receives the money and blesses each boy in turn.

Rituals such as these are powerful reminders of individuals' filial responsibilities to their parents—reminders that are now often intermingled with painful memories of lost loved ones. Many who witnessed this ceremony were visibly tearful. They later explained that the occasion reminded them of parents and older relatives left behind or killed in Cambodia. In the United States, Khmer have few occasions in which the recollection of shared memories, and the expression of emotions they provoke, is publicly sanctioned. As one of the older women present explained, "When the people see that ritual, they think about their own parents and how they owe their own parents something like that. Then they remember." For Khmer Americans, more is remembered on such occasions than merely the formal bond of child to parent.

MORAL DISCIPLINE AND THE PURE HEART

Khmer repeatedly stress that offerings must be given freely and with a pure heart; offerings made without such intent lack merit. Parents point out that they cannot coerce their children into making such offerings. Nor can they force children to embrace moral responsibilities. The awareness of moral responsibility that marks a mature youth comes only gradually. One mother explained, "When they are ten or twelve and they go visiting their friends and relatives on *Chaul Chnăm* or *Phchŭm Bĕn*, children see their friends offering their parents food and money, and they think of their own parents and feel ashamed if they have not given anything." Other parents insist, however, that they do not expect to receive anything from their children until after the children marry. Before then, they say, children have nothing to give, as they promptly hand any earnings over to their mother.

> [Male, age 50] In the Buddhist way, the children will learn how to stand in his or her place. What I mean is that they learn how to make some offerings to their parents and do some religious ceremonies. They have to do that, because they owe their parents some kind of ritual thing, and the monks, too. But I don't want to force them to do that for me. They must do that from their real heart. Like, if my daughter has to fight with her husband to do a ceremony for me, I don't want that. I want only her good heart, her pure heart, to give that to me.

Khmer see it as futile to pressure young people on such issues. Indeed, it is said, such coercion often has negative repercussions. One cannot, for example, force one's daughter to make offerings at the temple in one's name. Nor can one force one's son to become a monk.

> [Male, age 39] I would like my son to become a monk, but I cannot push him. It's up to my son. If I push him to do that and he doesn't want to, it will make my son crazy. I believe that.

Despite this ideal emphasis on voluntarism in filial obligations, however, verbal and physical coercion of children does take place. Not surprisingly, matters involving morality and family face most commonly provoke severe disciplinary measures. Behaviors that contravene the five Buddhist precepts about lying, stealing, drinking, being sexually immoral, and killing are considered especially serious.[13] More generally, when adolescents behave in a manner that threatens the family's status and reputation—and when other measures fail—parents may resort to corporal punishment.

[Father of 12-year-old son] If I heard my son had stolen something, I would talk to him quietly at first. I would try to reason with him like that. But if he would not listen and if he stole again, I would beat him. Even if they put me into jail for that, when I came out, I would beat him again!

[Mother of 18-year-old son] He came home from school, and I asked him, "Did you steal my check?" And he lied to me. He said, "No, Mom, I didn't do that." So I hit him in the face, slapped him really hard, and he just put his head down, and I kept hitting him. That's all he can do, bow his head like that and let me hit him and listen to what I say!

[Father of 19-year-old daughter] All this time, I thought she was a good girl. No boys. Just always studying. I even bought her a car so that she could go to [a community] college. And I told everyone that I worried she studied too hard. When I heard that she had a boyfriend at school, I just couldn't stand it. I hit her until she was unconscious.

The strength of parental anger in incidents such as these is perhaps surprising, especially in comparison with the loving indulgence exhibited in early childhood socialization. Such forceful physical discipline also appears unusual, of course, in light of Buddhist injunctions against violence. Incidents of child abuse within the Khmer American community have been widely reported in popular American media. Most observers assume that they reflect culturally sanctioned disciplinary behavior exacerbated by parents' feelings of powerlessness in their present situation.

It is useful, however, to compare such incidents with stories of severe physical punishments that occurred in families in Cambodia. Having done ethnographic research in Java, where the physical punishment of children is uncommon and unsanctioned, I was initially disinclined to believe these stories. As I compared them with ones about Khmer in the United States, though, an important theme appeared. In Cambodia, many stories revealed that the child's relatives or even unrelated community members were almost always close at hand when a child was punished and would often intervene if the discipline became too severe. Furthermore, children often ran away to stay with a nearby family member or neighbor until a parent's anger had passed (see also Ledgerwood 1990a:185). Relatives or neighbors might also admonish the parent for treating the child too severely.

[Fieldnotes, female, age 42] Noeu Sopha tells the story of her twelve-year-old brother, who stayed out past midnight after watching a movie in Phnom Penh. When he came home, his father, was waiting. At first, the father talked calmly to the boy, but after the boy apologized, the father hit him several times with a rattan stick, because he was still angry. [How did your brother respond?] "He just stood there with his head bowed and said nothing. That is the proper way for a child to respond to punishment," Sopha observes.

Then the boy was told that his father would no longer give him pocket money for the movies or for anything else. So Sopha's brother started going to his grandmother to ask for money. At that time, his grandmother happened to notice the welts on the boy's back. She immediately came and chastised her son for beating her grandson. "What, are you an animal to beat your son like that?" she said. "Don't you ever do that again or I will hit you badly!"

[Fieldnotes, female, age 52] Ong Ra tells a similar story. She broke the family's large water urn by carelessly throwing a ball when she was six or seven years old. Her mother was very angry and told Ra that she would beat her. First, she hit the child with her hand. Then she went into the house to get a stick. While her mother was in the house, Ra climbed up a banana tree and hid. She could hear her mother looking for her and yelling. Her mother said, "If I find you, I'll beat you to death!" (*"Vai tăl tae slap!"*) Ra was so scared, she stayed up in the tree until nightfall. After a while, Ra's mother began to worry and called to Ra's grandmother. The whole family came over. They all blamed Ra's mother. They said, "You know it was just an accident that she broke that urn! Why did you say that you would beat her to death?!" Ra heard that from up in the banana tree. After her relatives all went home, Ra climbed down from the tree and ran to her grandparents' house. They brought her back home and told her mother, "If you ever dare to do that again to our granddaughter, we will kill you!"

These stories from Cambodia can be compared with the comments of a Khmer American woman, Mok Saroeung. School officials reported her husband to state authorities for beating their son. The husband reportedly had a serious drinking problem, and his son was often the target of his drunken rages. When Mok Saroeung was asked if there were somewhere her son could go when his father became angry, she replied, "No, no, he cannot go. If his father hits him, he has to stay with us, even if his father hits him badly. We have no relatives here in Boston, and the neighbors do not want to get involved."

Parental accounts of physical punishment in Cambodia (though no doubt idealized) indicate that cultural and social constraints there may have guarded more effectively against the disciplinary excesses that now occur in the United States.

DISCIPLINE AND FACE

Khmer are careful to distinguish between using corporal discipline to teach a child to behave appropriately and losing all control when beating one's children. In the latter case, the parent is described as behaving "like an animal" *(dauch sat)* and "without reason" *(kmean kĭt pi'charo'na)*. (The three examples of physical discipline cited above would certainly fall into this category.) Such behavior is very shameful for Khmer.

> [Male, age 50] If, for example, a parent is drinking and he beats his child, that is not the child's real parent to act like that. If they drink and then beat the child unconscious, the law is good to protect the children. I agree with that. Or the parent who beats the child for some small thing, who just loses control and hurts his child, that is the parent and not the child who is wrong. But those parents who are good parents, they want their children to do good in the family, not to steal things like cars, not to steal in the stores, not to hang out with the gangs and get into serious trouble. Those parents want to correct by explaining. But if the child still does that kind of thing, at that time, the parent has to correct them by hitting them.

It is widely considered appropriate for parents to beat their children to correct them—above all for behaviors that jeopardize the parents' face or family reputation. These parents are viewed as acting honorably in their effort to uphold the family's face and reputation, even though such physically abusive practices violate doctrinal Buddhism's tenets about violence. Parents justify this contradiction between high principle and actual practice by invoking another, somewhat less idealized, Buddhist principle about human fallibility:

> [Male, age 42] If my son does something very bad like stealing, and he does that several times, and he will not listen to me, I will hit him badly so he knows. In this case, we don't think about Buddhist doctrine. Nobody is perfect. We are human, not God *(Khnhŏm mĭn maen dauch preah té)*. I cannot yet do like God! *(Khnhŏm mĭn ach tvoe preah ban té!)*

If a family fails to discipline a wayward child who then gets into serious trouble, the family is twice shamed and loses face: first when the child misbehaves, and then again when the police intervene. In the eyes of the community, that family is deemed incapable of controlling its children.

> [Male, age 38] My son, if he goes to steal in the store and my friends see him and they say, "That's Niep's son," then I am ashamed and I lose face. After that, if the police come to my house to warn me that my son is stealing or because someone calls them to say I hit my son, I lose face again, because they say that I cannot control my children.

As this and other situations indicate, Khmer do not see a family as a union of autonomous and equal individuals, as middle-class Americans often do (see Shweder, Mahapatra, and Miller 1987). In ideal cultural terms, Khmer parents exercise near-total authority over their children, especially when they use that authority to teach moral behavior and to prevent loss of face in the community's eyes.

Khmer parents have often been baffled by the way American teachers and social workers react to their disciplinary measures. State authorities' efforts strike Khmer parents as ill-conceived attempts to limit parents' authority and thereby to undermine their children's socialization. They have difficulty understanding why the police would take the side of the child who is misbehaving over that of the parent who is trying to make the child behave. One father beat his son unconscious for associating with a gang and for acting disrespectfully to his elders. The father later said, "Children here have the police on their side, but I know myself [I know what I am doing]!" *("Khnhŏm dŏeng kluon khnhŏm!")*

> [Male, age 50] Khmer parents have a duty to lead their children so they will walk in the good way. That's why they become so angry when their children do something wrong, and that's why they are right to hit them.

MORALITIES IN TENSION

Khmer American parents are persistent in teaching their children to behave in morally acceptable ways. The ethical education of daughters differs significantly from that of sons. Daughters are more consistently restrained; their brothers always enjoy greater freedom, even when they are young. In adolescence, boys experience intensified social pressures to succeed in school and to work hard. They also are physically punished more frequently. However serious their effect, though, these disciplinary measures are not as restrictive as parental controls on girls.

Above all, sons and daughters are expected to behave in a manner that upholds the family's reputation or face and to honor and care for their parents in their old age. Although parents feel that a young child cannot be forced to understand these responsibilities, parents hold adolescents to a stricter moral standard. In particular, behaviors that jeopardize the family's reputation invite punishment, sometimes of a severe physical nature.

Back in Cambodia, the two cultural moralities—the one focused on the individual and the other on family, face, and honor—do not appear to have been experienced as contradictory or antagonistic. Instead, they seem to have been accommodated easily in prewar Khmer society. In particular, shaming and community opprobrium seem to have deterred improper behavior effectively, and physical discipline was used—with some exceptions—sparingly.

Khmer life in America, however, has strained the relative balance between the morality of autonomy, on the one hand, and that of honor, on the other. Parents' fear of losing control over their children exacerbates their concern with maintaining the family's reputation. As a result, Khmer socialization practices have come to face serious and potentially disequilibrating challenges. At the same time, the extended family and integral community that both reinforced patterns of appropriate behavior and protected children from disciplinary excesses are largely lacking in the United States. The resultant physical discipline for behaviors deemed inappropriate by community standards can be severe.

This tension in Khmer socialization practices intensifies as Khmer children move out of the home. Whereas in Cambodia, moral training in the schools reinforced values taught at home, the mutual reinforcement of domestic and public moralities is largely lacking for Khmer in the United States. Indeed, the tension between domestically sustained morality and the morality of American society is a recurring source of conflict in the Khmer American community. Discrepancies between the expectations of home and the requirements of school, in particular, have created serious intergenerational conflicts. These problems have sometimes been exacerbated because school personnel and state agencies do not entirely understand Khmer culture. In the following chapter, we see how the tension in Khmer socialization practices is both expressed and exacerbated in the context of Khmer children's involvement with American schools.

Figure 1. Khmer Buddhist temple in Lynn

Figure 2. Altar with three seated Buddhas

Figure 3. Temple painting of the judgment of souls

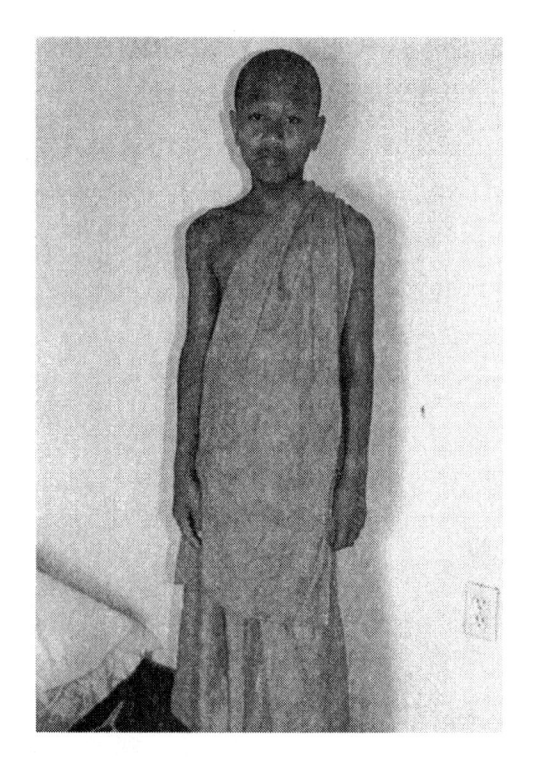

Figure 4. A young novice

Figure 5. Senior monks

Figure 6. Ritual specialist *(achaa)* and his wife in front of home altar

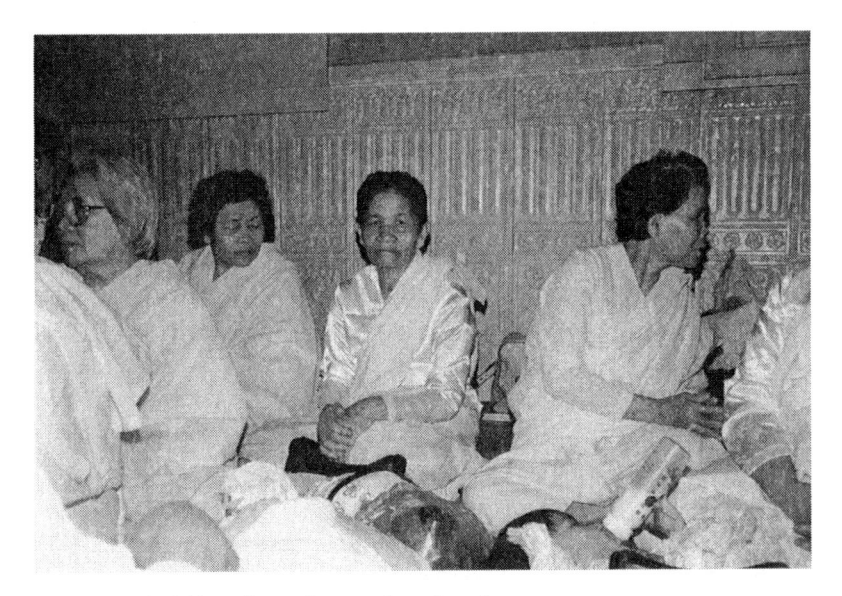

Figure 7. *Yeichi*, or "temple grandmothers"

Figure 8. Teaching the art of obeisance

Figure 9. Paying respect to the ancestors at a first birthday party

Figure 10. Grandson asking for his grandmother's blessing and forgiveness

Figure 11. Birthday child paying respect to her teacher

Figure 12. Paula Abdul and offerings for ancestors in the bride's bedroom

Figure 13. Bride (left) and her attendants

Figure 14. Engagement guests and offerings

Figure 15. "Tying of the wrists" at a home wedding ceremony

Figure 16. Ritualized teasing of the bride and groom at the wedding reception

Figure 17. *Châng dai* offerings at the wedding reception

5

Schooling in America

Khmer parents expect schooling not to be value-neutral or ethically relativistic but to reinforce the moral training children receive at home. Parents view teachers not primarily as inculcators of knowledge or skills but as honored partners in the project of moral education. Thus, parents often comment that they "give" *(aoy)* their children to the teacher, which makes the teacher a "second mother" *(mae chŏng)* or "second father"*(ŏv chŏng)*. Elders exhort children to view the teacher not as an equal but as a moral superior who deserves respect and obedience. In line with this view, parents expect that teachers will deal firmly with their children if they misbehave in school. Parents themselves may severely discipline children who skip school or behave badly in class.

Khmer elders derive their attitudes toward schooling from the strong links between Cambodian education and Buddhism and from their own educational experiences in Cambodia. Throughout most of Cambodian history, education was a matter for the Buddhist temple, and monks served as the teachers. Even after the development of Cambodia's national educational system, this remained the case in many rural areas, where renovated temple schools were the only available source of education (Ebihara 1966:183). Because of its long association with Buddhism and the temple, all education in Cambodia was seen first and foremost as moral education. Even in modern, urban schools in Cambodia, moral instruction remains central to the curriculum (Vickery 1990:51; Martin 1994).

In addition, there has long been a widespread belief among Khmer that education confers not just intellectual superiority but also moral superiority. Khmer teachers are revered both as knowledgeable people and as role models for proper behavior. As such, teachers are expected to be able to advise adults and guide children. And just as parents are responsible for their children's behavior, teachers are viewed as responsible for the behavior of their students.

Khmer American parents are keenly aware of the economic importance of education for their children. They often express the hope that their children will obtain good educations, so that they can find secure, long-term employment. Parents want their children to have more job opportunities than their own limited schooling has given them in this country.

Even as they enunciate such views in support of education, however, Khmer parents rarely attend school meetings, typically do not assist children with homework, and are usually not involved in school activities. Most parents feel that in turning their children over to the school, they have done their part; the rest is up to the teacher and the individual child.[1]

It is in the educational sphere that Khmer immigrants have experienced some of the greatest dissonance between their high expectations and the realities of American society. American schools do not reinforce the moral training Khmer children receive at home. Although some Khmer values are congruent with those expressed in American schools, others are quite different. When Khmer have worked as bilingual teachers in schools, they have helped provide some continuity between Khmer educational values and the practice of education in the United States, but not all Khmer children have the opportunity to enroll in bilingual programs. Even when children are in Khmer bilingual programs, their experiences in American schools differ profoundly from their parents' experiences and expectations. To understand Khmer interaction with American schools, it is important to examine Khmer elders' educational background and the way it affects their aspirations for their children.

SCHOOLING IN CAMBODIA

Historically in Cambodia, many young boys, especially those from poorer families, lived at the monastery for varying periods, assisting the monks as temple boys *(kaun sĕh lŏk)* and performing menial tasks such as fixing the monks' tea or sweeping the compound. During this time, boys learned manual skills and sometimes the rudiments of reading and writing.

Sending a boy to live with the monks was also one way for parents to deal with delinquent youths. Steinberg (1959:68) and others (Piker

1975; Wood 1983) have argued that for young boys who lived at the temple, the monk supplanted the father as disciplinarian and moral mentor. This role expectation is dramatically expressed in the words parents would utter when turning over a child to the monks: "Do whatever you want with him. Just leave me the bones and the eyes." *("Tvoe ey tvoe chŭa tŏk tae chh'ŏeung nĕung phnaek aoy khnhŏm.")*

Until well into the modern era, most young men entered the monkhood for at least a month or two (see chapter 2). Those who stayed for several years learned to read and recite Pali (Kalab 1976:161). Girls, of course, were barred from monastic life. In Cambodia, as in neighboring Thailand, there was no system of Buddhist nunneries such as that seen in some Mahayana Buddhist countries (see Van Esterik 1982:58). As a result, the vast majority of women in premodern Cambodia received no formal education and remained illiterate.

In 1917, the French set up a uniform system of education throughout Indochina as part of their "civilizing mission" (Ouk, Huffman, and Lewis 1988:30). In Cambodia, however, the effects of this initiative were limited at best. Classes were taught in French, and the curriculum was modeled on that used in France. These "French schools" (as some older Khmer still call them) were confined for the most part to large towns and cities. Despite laws that made education compulsory for children between the ages of six and twelve, many youths did not attend because of economic hardships and widespread Khmer ambivalence toward their colonizers (Whitaker 1973:110; Ouk, Huffman, and Lewis 1988:30).

Following the Thai example, the French also developed a limited number of "modernized" temple schools in the Khmer countryside that the population reportedly received more warmly (Whitaker 1973:110; Kalab 1976:162). Nonetheless, even after the establishment of the French system, most Khmer boys continued to receive educations in monasteries and traditional temple schools. Girls continued to have no access to monastic education, and, in general, their opportunities for formal education remained extremely limited.

Education in Franco-Cambodian schools was rigorous; few students managed to pass the required exams, and many could not afford to continue to the *classe terminale* (the thirteenth grade). The new educational system created new status criteria in Khmer society, whereby a small, educated, and somewhat Europeanized portion of the population was distinguished from the uneducated majority (Steinberg 1959; Vickery 1984). The legacy of this system is evident from the small number of Khmer who managed to obtain a high school diploma before World War II. In 1939, only four Cambodians had graduated from high school. By 1941, there were only 537 secondary school graduates from a total population of nearly three million people (Strand and Jones 1985:22; see also Chandler 1983:165).[2]

After Cambodia achieved independence from France in 1953, the national education system developed rapidly, as the government built public schools in cities and in some rural areas. Under new government programs, monastery and temple schools were also reinvigorated. "Renovated" temple schools adopted the same curriculum as national public schools, although monks continued to provide instruction and the temple school program's Buddhist elements were otherwise retained (Ouk, Huffman, and Lewis 1988:31).

Meanwhile, public school instruction was still organized largely on a French model. French-language instruction began in the second grade. The schools' language policy was to restrict the use of Khmer progressively after the first grade; by the time students reached high school, most or all of their instruction was in French.

In principle, national independence offered genuine educational opportunities to Khmer girls and boys. Girls of all social backgrounds could attend not only public schools but also, for the first time, the renovated temple schools (Ouk, Huffman, and Lewis 1988:31). However, in rural areas where temple schools remained the only source of schooling, many families were reluctant to send their daughters to "study with the monks." Few girls in these areas received more than two or three years of education; many received none.

Educational change did eventually come to Khmer society. In the 1960s, the government began a campaign of "Khmerization" of the educational system. By 1967, Khmer replaced French as the language of instruction in public schools. All subjects were taught in Khmer, except for six to eight hours per week of French or, rarely, English. Much of the core curriculum remained the same as that in France, however, its content having simply been translated into Khmer (Ouk, Huffman, and Lewis 1988).

By the late 1960s, mass education was finally becoming a social reality in Cambodian society. Government statistics indicate that at that time, 70 percent of Khmer children between the ages of six and twelve were receiving public education (Whitaker 1973:112).

Despite these impressive gains, girls were still significantly underrepresented in schools. In 1964, only 32.8 percent of Cambodian schoolchildren were female. In secondary education, female participation declined to 21.7 percent of the school population. In higher education, women constituted only 10.8 percent of students enrolled (Ministry of Education 1965, cited in Ledgerwood 1990a:92). In 1970, the last prewar year for which there are accurate statistics, girls' enrollment in grade school was 70 percent of that of boys. But by the sixth year of primary school, girls' enrollment was still only one-fourth that of boys (Whitaker 1973:112).

EDUCATION AND GENDER IDEOLOGY

Khmer elders attribute Khmer women's comparatively low educational achievement to traditional gender roles. In rural Cambodia, women were generally considered to have little need for formal education (Ebihara 1974:310–11). They were expected to marry and stay home to care for the children, a pattern that many Khmer women report with considerable regret. Boys, in contrast, had to be strong and well educated in order to provide for their families.

> [Female, age 40] I didn't study at all in Cambodia. My mother didn't want me to go to school. She wanted my brothers to go to school, not me. The girls had to stay home. I had to take care of all of the work in the house, to help my mother.

Young girls who did attend school normally did not continue past the elementary level. As puberty approached, girls were required to stay close to home. In rural areas, where continuing one's education necessitated traveling long distances, such restrictions often meant the end of a girl's education.

Many women who were denied access to schooling in Cambodia stress that they were needed at home, especially in poorer families. From an early age, these women assumed major household responsibilities, freeing their mothers to work in the fields or to open a small housefront store "so that the family could survive." Often, when a parent fell ill or died, young girls terminated their educations and "replaced their mothers" (*chŭmnuoh mday*), in fact.

[Female, age 33] I didn't have much education in Cambodia, maybe just to the fourth grade. My mother died, and I had my little sister, just two years old, and nobody to take care of her. So I had to quit school.

Older women in their fifties and sixties also recount ruefully that their mothers did not want them to attend school, fearing that they would learn to write and send love letters to boys (see Ledgerwood 1990a). Because a boy's parents traditionally initiated talk of marriage with a girl's parents, it was considered inappropriate for a girl to be directly involved in courtship or engagement. A girl's proper role in the matter was simply to agree or disagree once arrangements had been made. Parents worried that young girls might meet boys at school and become romantically involved, circumventing their elders' role in marriage arrangements and causing a family to lose face (see chapter 6).

[Female, age 51] I wanted to go to school, but my parents said, "We don't want you to go because if you learn how to read and write, you will have a boyfriend and you can write to your boyfriend." They don't like that. But all of my brothers went to the *wat* to study.

Although boys had greater freedom and educational opportunities, some rural boys did not fare much better than their sisters. Schooling in prewar Cambodia was compulsory only to age twelve. Continued education depended not only on intellectual aptitude but also on the ability to pay for school supplies, uniforms, and books. In many rural areas, children had to move to larger villages or towns to continue their studies (Ouk, Huffman, and Lewis 1988:38). Parents who depended on sons' or daughters' labor could afford neither to lose their help nor to pay for boarding them closer to schools. For all these reasons, village children were at a real disadvantage in the educational system. Most young rural boys left school after only four or five years to work their parents' fields or to take jobs to augment the family's income.

Compulsory and long-term education for both genders is thus a relatively new idea for parents from rural Cambodia (Ebihara 1974). They grew up viewing school not as a right but as a privilege for those with connections, capital, and aptitude. Although education in prewar Cambodia was believed to be important for upward mobility and financial security, it was widely recognized that few could actually attain these goals through education.

THE EDUCATION OF KHMER ELDERS

Most Khmer adults in the Boston area come from the Cambodian countryside. As a result, most have had little formal education. I surveyed some one hundred Boston area Khmer parents and grandparents about their education. Men in this group reported an average of six years of schooling (Smith-Hefner 1990a:255). Much of it occurred in village temple schools or in the monastery during temporary monkhood. Out of the men in the sample, 81 percent said they had some ability to read and write Khmer.

In contrast, women from the same sample had had only three years of schooling, on average; less than half were literate in Khmer. Even among the literate women, some had never attended school as children. They had learned to read and write only as adults during Cambodia's national literacy campaign (1964–70) or in refugee camps. Many of these women are semiliterate; they can read simple material but cannot write. Others have stopped using the skills they once had and have become functionally illiterate.

> [Female, age 32] I never went to school in Cambodia. I don't know how to read or write. My brother-in-law taught me with the other people in the village at night, but I got sick and forgot everything.

Although they hope their children will take advantage of American educational opportunities, parents who never attended school acknowledge that they have little understanding of how American schools work. Citing their lack of school experience and their limited English, parents say they feel they can do little to help their children do well in school. When asked about efforts to assist their children academically, parents typically focus on the teacher's important role: "I trust the teacher to help my children" or "I have confidence in the teacher." When I asked, "Do you help your child with his or her homework?" by far the most common response was, "We depend on the teacher for everything."

CAMBODIAN EDUCATION AND THE TEACHER'S ROLE

In Cambodia, teachers were strict disciplinarians and moral mentors, as well as educators. When children entered school at age six or seven, the father had already begun distancing himself emotionally from them (see chapter 3). In effect, the teacher both assumed some of the father's role and also complemented it.

> [Male, age 38] In our custom, the teacher is on top. At home, I am the father, and at school, the teacher is the father, the mother. So the teacher will help my children [and teach them] everything that is good for them. I believe the teacher will help them with everything.

As the child's "second mother" or "second father," teachers received the same respect and obedience from their students as they expressed to parents at home. At the beginning of each school day, students in Khmer classrooms would put their palms together at face level and bow slightly as a greeting, reciting, *"Chŭmriep suo, něak krou"* ("Respectful greetings, Ms. Teacher"). This is the same gesture of relational etiquette that parents impress on children in ritual and daily interaction. At the end of the school day, students take leave in a similar manner. In these interactions, teachers often did not respond to these gestures of obeisance. They might just nod. If they decided to make an example for the class, they might repeat, *"Chŭmriep suo"* ("Greetings"), or simply say, *"Chéh kuosǎm nah"* ("Very polite").

Cambodian schools often lacked books, paper, and chalkboards. Classes were large. In the classroom, information flowed in one direction, from teacher to students; children were expected to pay attention, listen, and memorize (Ouk, Huffman, and Lewis 1988). Students rarely asked questions, because doing so would challenge the teacher's status and authority. Individual students were rarely singled out and asked to perform; more often, they were called on to respond as a group.

The techniques used in the Khmer classroom generally drew on socialization practices first developed in the home. Instructors almost never praised children, as compliments were thought to spoil the child. "Good" teachers focused on correcting errors and considered correcting to be more important than giving explanations. One former teacher put it this way:

[Female, age 43] If you praise children and let them know you love them too much, they won't respect you. Khmer children don't need to be told what they do correctly; they only need to be corrected when they do something wrong.

These practices obviously differ from those common in American classrooms, where teachers emphasize praise and public displays of mastery by individual students. In American classrooms, students are expected to ask questions. Those who do not are assumed to be unprepared or uninterested in class material. Even more important, American schools generally place more emphasis on critical thinking and intellectual creativity than on rote memorization of correct responses.

As surrogate parents, Cambodian teachers had the same authority over their students as the parents. Students who did not know their lessons or who failed to pay attention could have their ears boxed, their knuckles rapped with rulers, and their arms and legs whipped with bamboo switches. Parents recount being thrown out the classroom window, made to kneel on sharp stones while holding bricks, forced to balance on one foot for the duration of class, and left standing at attention for hours in the midday sun. Teacher-monks had a reputation for being particularly harsh.

[Male, age 55] I remember when my parents took me to the monk teacher and they said, "I need back only the eyes and the bones, and everything else you can have—take it," I was very scared. You see this? [He shows the scars on his knuckles and hands.] My teacher gave me this souvenir.

Another attributed his deafness in one ear to the repeated boxings he received from his monk-teacher.

Some adults say they resented this harsh treatment, but most indicate that they respected and cared deeply for their instructors anyway. After all, they explain, the teacher is "like the parent," and children "owe" the teacher "something," just as they owe a parent.

[Male, age 45] We Cambodians believe that children owe something to their teacher—that is, respect and obedience. They owe that to their teachers, to their parents, and to the older people. So, if the teacher hits the student, then the student deserved that punishment and they should not be surprised or angry about that. Like the parents, teachers hit to correct the students, to make them good people.

As with the parent-child relationship, bonds between teachers and students tended to be deep and long-lasting. Refugees recall that former teachers led them to the Thai border when they escaped or sponsored their resettlement abroad. Conversely, former students offered teachers food and lodging in the countryside and carefully hid their identities from the Khmer Rouge. In America today, teachers are honored guests at life-cycle rituals and other celebrations. Their former students continue to call on them for advice and support. Years after a student has left school, a teacher may help that student find a job, a place to live, or even a spouse. In other words, teachers may act, or be expected to act, as patrons to their student-clients.[3]

The respect and deference accorded teachers stem in large part from Khmer Buddhist beliefs about merit and social status. According to the karmic understanding of social hierarchy, educated persons are believed to have amassed significant merit in their past lives in order to have achieved such an esteemed status in this life (Steinberg 1959:88). As respected experts, they are expected to make all decisions about classroom discipline and teaching methodology. They are rarely if ever questioned about the form or content of their instruction.

> [Male, age 38] [Here], sometimes the school asks me something, like what do I want my children to study, what is good to teach my children? But I don't know what my son should study in school. I don't have any idea, because in my custom, we depend on the teacher. The students follow the teacher and obey the teacher more than the parents. So I don't worry about that [what the teacher teaches].

Not surprisingly, Khmer parents are reluctant to voice any complaints about American schools. Many parents remark that the schools must be good, or there would not be so much technical progress and such a high standard of living in the United States (Ouk, Huffman, and Lewis 1988:53; Smith-Hefner 1990a). Many Khmer insist that "everything is good" about American education.

Despite these positive comments, when pressed, Khmer parents indicate that they are much less approving of the schools' social and moral content. This ambivalence especially emerges when they discuss the controversial issue of bilingual education. Their attitudes toward bilingual education illustrate important debates within the community about Khmer culture and identity. They also reveal the degree to which Khmer notions of personhood and achievement affect parental decisions about their children's education (Smith-Hefner 1990a).

EDUCATION IN AMERICAN SCHOOLS

The educational situation of Khmer children in American schools is particularly complex, as it depends on a number of variables, especially language ability. In 1971, Massachusetts passed the nation's first mandatory Bilingual Educational Act (Crawford 1989:33; MDE 1976). By state law, schools must provide bilingual instruction if they have at least twenty limited-English-proficient (LEP) children from a group whose native language is not English (MDE 1976:3).

The program is intended to be transitional, with most children moving into mainstream classrooms within three years (Crawford 1989). Under this arrangement, children are supposed to receive some form of native-language instruction until they are capable of moving into an all-English-language classroom. Native-language maintenance is specifically not a goal of these transitional programs, and the actual percentage of native language used in the classroom varies considerably by school and teacher. Although some school systems in metropolitan Boston initially had trouble finding qualified Khmer bilingual teachers, by the late 1980s, the overwhelming majority of young, LEP Khmer children in the area were placed in bilingual classrooms and received at least some form of bilingual education (MDE 1987, 1988).

The actual style and quality of instruction in these programs vary considerably, depending on the number of Khmer children in a given school or district, the child's level of English proficiency, the child's age or grade level, the availability of ethnic Khmer teachers, the parents' and child's wishes, and the school's interpretation of bilingual education laws. If parents put their child into a neighborhood school rather than in a district school with a bilingual program, only minimal language assistance may be available to the child. Moreover, what schools call bilingual programs can vary considerably.

Under the rubric of bilingual education, some schools offer instruction in English as a Second Language (ESL) and provide ethnic Khmer classroom aides who act as "translators" when needed. Other schools offer LEP students only "pullout" ESL instruction in forty-five minute sessions each day; students miss other classes to receive this instruction. In still other schools, ethnic Khmer teachers instruct in Khmer (usually along with an ESL component) until the child is proficient enough in English to move into a mainstream classroom. This is typically done in stages or steps; depending on their level of English proficiency, bilingual students may be placed in a mainstream classroom for one or more subjects each day.

The situation of older Khmer children who initially came into the system during middle school or high school was particularly complex, partly because of their histories in Cambodia. In 1970, when the American-backed Lon Nol government overthrew Prince Norodom Sihanouk and the 1970–75 war began, many Cambodian schools closed (Whitaker 1973:128; Banister and Johnson 1993:100). Teachers fled the countryside to join their families in the city. In urban areas, teachers who were still available and willing taught double shifts and private classes in the evenings. During the subsequent period of Democratic Kampuchea (1975–79), Pol Pot abolished formal education. Many, perhaps most, teachers and educated Khmer were murdered. After 1979, for the children of those Khmer who managed to flee to refugee camps, education was mainly limited to basic literacy and math. Most Khmer now in the United States who were children in Cambodia during this period thus experienced considerable disruption in their education.

Many older youths in Boston area schools today are secondary migrants; they came from states that may have offered little bilingual support, further complicating their situation. Some of these students have run away or have been sent by parents to live with relatives or friends because of disciplinary problems.[4] Schools have a particularly difficult time providing for these children because of their varied educational backgrounds.

In Boston area middle schools and high schools, LEP students can take ESL courses. Khmer students are grouped with LEP students from other language backgrounds. In the mid-1980s, a few high schools offered elective classes in Khmer literature and culture. Today, there are no longer any classes or programs at the secondary level that are specifically for Khmer students.

When they arrived in the United States, Khmer parents often differentiated the academic situation of their oldest children (those who entered American schools as teenagers) from that of younger ones.

Parents compared their older children with themselves, saying that they shared the immediate and practical challenge of learning enough English to get jobs and make a living.

In contrast, most Khmer children now in American schools were born in either the camps or this country and have received all their education in American schools. The parents of these children confront different options. As parents watch their children achieve fluency in English, many have begun to wonder whether something important is not being lost in the process. However marginal to their initial interests on arrival in the United States, issues of language and identity have now become central concerns for many Khmer.

CAMBODIAN ATTITUDES TOWARD BILINGUAL EDUCATION

Most Khmer children now in Boston area schools have grown up in largely Khmer-speaking households. Adults in the Boston area community speak Khmer almost exclusively; at community and religious events, one hears very little English. Some elderly Khmer will probably never learn English, because of their living situation, health, and lack of involvement in American workplaces or social networks. Typically, then, preschoolers, adults, and elders use Khmer for intergenerational communication.[5] As young children enter the schools, they are exposed to English, though, and some young people, particularly teenagers, come to prefer speaking English with their siblings and friends.

Khmer children are tested for English proficiency when they enter the school system. If they are designated LEP, they are normally placed in some form of bilingual program. Although parents can oppose this decision, teachers and bilingual coordinators report that most Khmer parents agree to the school personnel's recommendation.

Despite their apparent compliance, however, teachers and administrators often regard Khmer parents as uninvolved in their children's education and unsupportive of program initiatives. For example, they note that parental attendance at school functions and even at parent-teacher conferences is poor. Indeed, school administrators and bilingual program coordinators report that Khmer parents appear uninterested in Khmer-language programs and only want their children to learn English.

Language barriers and parents' reluctance to question school policy have complicated communications between parents and non-Khmer educators. Even bilingual teachers, themselves ethnic Khmer, cannot explain Khmer parents' seemingly contradictory attitudes. In interviews and informal discussions, Khmer parents, teachers, and community leaders consistently stress that bilingual education is necessary *(mean brâyaoch; mean samkhan)* for their children. Furthermore, these parents say that knowing how to speak Khmer is not enough; they also want their children to learn to read and write in Khmer. This attitude is shared even by parents whose children are not enrolled in a Cambodian bilingual program and who are, therefore, receiving no instruction in Khmer (Smith-Hefner 1990a:258).

Parents offer a variety of reasons for their concerns. Many speak movingly of reading and writing Khmer as a critical part of maintaining one's membership in the Khmer community. This is not just an abstract matter or an idealized commitment to the idea of a Khmer community. On the contrary, it can have enormous practical implications; if parents are not literate in Khmer, they may want their children to correspond with relatives in Cambodia.

> [Male, age 35] [Speaking of his son] He has his relatives in Cambodia. When they want to contact him, how can he respond? Can they write English? No, they cannot. So he has to know Khmer.

Many Cambodians want their children to learn Khmer in hopes that the family can return to Cambodia one day. Of the roughly one hundred parents and grandparents of school-aged children surveyed, 90 percent indicated a strong desire "at least to visit" Cambodia. A number of older parents and many grandparents said they hope to return to Cambodia eventually to stay—to the dismay of their children.

> [Male, age 52] I compare my life before and now, and I think it's better for my kids' education if we stay. But I might go back if there's peace and it's good again. I would go back because the weather is good and I know how to find money easily. Everything that I want to do is easier back there. My mother wants to go back, too. She complains that she doesn't understand English. She hopes Cambodia has peace soon so she can go back.

> [Male, age 60] I want to go back to my country. I miss it, my neighbors, my neighborhood, everything. I have a lot of friends still in

Cambodia and a lot of relatives. Some are dead, some are still living. So, if my country makes good, I want to go back. My wife also wants to go back, but I'm not sure about my children.

Among younger adults, the desire to return is often linked to the possibility of starting a business in Cambodia, such as opening a computer store, an import-export business, a travel agency, or even a laundromat. Some parents hope their children will be able to assist Cambodia in the future, "when there is peace." This will be possible only if their children know how to read and write Khmer.

[Female, age 31] [The] Khmer language is very important for his future. Like if my country becomes free, then my son can work for an international agency.

[Male, age 64] When Cambodia is at peace and then the American government [wants] Cambodians living here to help Cambodia, if they cannot speak their language at that time, maybe at that time only the Americans will be able to speak two languages, Khmer and English. And they will serve in Cambodia, and the Cambodian children will stay [in the United States] and work in the factories. Right now, if you visit Cambodia and you speak English very well, you will not get a bowl of rice, nothing. They don't care about that. In the village, nobody can speak English. And they are not happy with you. Like your relatives, they are not happy. They have a feeling—Cambodian people in Cambodia—if you use English, you boast about yourself. "I don't care if he can speak English," they say. "Speak *khmae!*"

Such comments have become increasingly common since the UN-sponsored elections in Cambodia in August 1993. As the situation in Cambodia improved between 1993 and 1997, and Cambodian immigrants obtained green cards or became American citizens, more have felt secure about returning to Cambodia for extended visits. Some have begun to explore the possibility of setting up businesses; many others have plans to return soon.[6] Such visits have only reinforced parents' desires that their children become literate in Khmer.

In virtually all of their comments on bilingual education, parents at some point make a strong identification between Khmer language and ethnic identity.

[Male, age 39] I want my daughters to know our culture and our race, as Cambodian people, to be able to identify themselves as

Khmer. If my daughters grow up and someone asks them, "What nationality are you?" sometimes I am afraid they will say, "I don't know if I am American or Cambodian or *cham* (Khmer Muslim)!" So they need to know their language and identity.

[Male, age 31] My son must learn to read and write Khmer, because we are Cambodian. When he grows up and his American friends ask him, "Where are you from?" and he says, "I'm from Cambodia—my father's from Cambodia." And then if they ask, "Can you speak Cambodian? Can you write Cambodian?" if he can't, that's a terrible thing.

These parents feel, as Khmer do in general, that to be Khmer is to speak Khmer. Language and literacy remain critical elements in Khmer identity.

LANGUAGE AND HIERARCHY

The Khmer spoken in the community and in Khmer bilingual classrooms is a more or less standard variant of Khmer, similar to that spoken by more than 90 percent of the Cambodian population. Compared with other Southeast Asian languages, Khmer is relatively homogeneous; regional variation is limited to minor differences in pronunciation and vocabulary (Ouk, Huffman, and Lewis 1988:67–68; see also Gorgoniyev 1966; Huffman 1970a; Ehrman 1972).

Historically, the Khmer language is related to Vietnamese. Because of some two thousand years of Chinese influence, however, Vietnamese is today monosyllabic and tonal, with many words borrowed from Chinese. In contrast, Khmer is atonal, and most native Khmer roots are disyllabic. Influences on the Khmer language have come not from China but from India. Many Khmer terms that refer to politics, royalty, religion, and literature were borrowed from Indic Sanskrit or Pali. Even today, Pali has remained a source of Khmer neologisms (Huffman 1970a:3). Polite, refined Khmer forms often draw on Sanskrit precedents, as well.

Cambodians become familiar with Sanskrit or Pali forms almost exclusively by studying Khmer literature. Many bilingual teachers cite this as an important reason for teaching children to read and write Khmer. When adult Khmer say that young people today "don't know how to speak their own language," they typically mean that the youth do not control this Sanskritized vocabulary. "If you want to know the deep words, the deep meanings, you must study Khmer literature," they say.

Like many other Southeast Asians, Cambodians borrowed their writing system from India, adapting it to fit their own language. The Khmer writing system is syllabic; each basic symbol represents a consonant-vowel combination. Huffman (1970a:4) notes that the Khmer writing system exhibits more consistency and a better "fit" between sound and symbol than English does. Nonetheless, learning to read and write in Khmer is daunting, because one must memorize so many symbols and rules for combining them. It is not uncommon for young people (and adults) to learn the system, only to forget it with a lack of practice.

An Indian influence can also be found in Khmer social hierarchy. Although Khmer do not recognize separate castes, they have a strong sense of status groups and social classes. Cambodians consider hierarchy to be an integral and natural part of their social order (Steinberg 1959:7; Martin 1994:17). Although many say they appreciate the equality of social relations in the United States, Khmer feel that recognizing social distinctions through appropriate speech and behavior is essential to harmonious relations.

Khmer are quite straightforward about the associations between language and hierarchy. In the Buddhist view, all living beings are ranked according to their status. Animals are ranked below humans, gods are above. There are distinctions within the ranks of humans and gods, as well. Khmer use titles, terms of address, and other status-marked language to indicate these and other social distinctions (Gorgoniyev 1966:73; Ehrman 1972:39; Center for Applied Linguistics 1981:8).

> [Male, age 59] The Buddhist doctrine says you have to use respectful words to speak to your mother, to your father, to the older people. Buddhist doctrine doesn't want all people to be equal. You have to have a hierarchy so that everybody listens to each other. If they don't have the hierarchy and everybody is equal, then who listens to whom?

The pivotal role that terms of address and reference, honorifics, and special vocabularies play in articulating the Khmer social hierarchy made them a prime target of the Khmer Rouge's revolutionary cultural policies. To "equalize" social relations, Pol Pot outlawed elements of polite speech. In particular, the Khmer Rouge abolished the use of terms that were most critical in marking social distinctions among interactants.

When asked about Pol Pot's language policies, Khmer uniformly responded that it was not an attempt to equalize social relations at all but an effort to wipe out "everything good." Especially distasteful to adult Khmer were Pol Pot's attempts to equalize relationships between parents and children. Under such programs, parents were to be called *mĭt* (friend), and unmarked forms such as *haub bay* (eat) were to replace polite forms such as *pĭsa bay* that were normally used in speaking to elders.

> [Male, age 55] Cambodians don't want to give up their language distinctions. In the United States, they don't want to hear those bad words, those dangerous words; they don't want that education from Pol Pot to be used. They want to kill those [Pol Pot] people. Why? Because the children who were taught like that, when they grew up, they didn't care about their mother or father. Some of them even told the soldiers their parents did something wrong, and then the parents were killed!

Many adults reported that they continued to use respect-marked forms in their private interactions with parents and elder relatives, despite Khmer Rouge policy. One man was so enraged by the policy that he announced his refusal to comply at a weekly village political meeting, an act that seems suicidal.

A woman reiterated the important connection between social control and the hierarchy expressed in speech.

> [Female, age 36] In our culture, we have levels of people, like the royal family, the king, and then the ministers and nobles. After that, we have the monks, and then the regular-class people and the lower-class people. That's why we need to know the correct Khmer language, to know all the words to use to talk to different kinds of people in our country.
>
> Pol Pot tried to make it equal between parents and children. He told the little boys and girls to call their parents "friend-mother" (*mĭt-mae*) and "friend-father" (*mĭt-ŏv*) to wipe out the hierarchy, even in the house. But if we don't have hierarchy, if the parents are not on top, then who will rule the house? The children didn't want to listen to their parents and they didn't want to follow them, because they were the same rank. A world without someone to lead is very difficult and very impolite in our culture.

Because appropriate speech is felt both to express and to reinforce Khmer social hierarchy, failure to speak properly has serious social repercussions. One bilingual teacher explained his extreme distress at being addressed with the disrespectful epithet *a* by his students in this country:

> [Male, age 37] When my students here call me *a krou*, it's like being called "crazy teacher." To be called like that is so shameful. You lose face. When someone calls you inappropriately like that, you feel yourself come tumbling down from your level, your class. When that happens, everything, everyone, all order is upset. If someone from my culture addresses me incorrectly like that, we say it is like he "cuts my skin."

Adults commonly associate children's inability to speak Khmer with other unacceptable behaviors, such as the desire to live away from home and the refusal to care for parents in old age.

> [Female, age 32] I have a niece living in East Boston who knows only English. I cannot talk with her, because I don't speak English. Her mother doesn't allow her to study in the bilingual program, so those children act and talk like Americans. They eat American food like pizza and McDonald's. They don't want to eat rice! And they say to their parents, "I don't want to live with you! I want to move in with a roommate!"

Many elders link language to the more general problem of maintaining Khmer identity. Parents express sorrow and dismay that some children have lost or never learned Khmer. Not to know proper Khmer, according to parents, teachers, and community leaders, is to risk losing one's identity as a Cambodian.

EDUCATION AND AMBIVALENCE

Despite the enthusiasm parents voice for instilling Khmer literacy and culture in their children, many display paradoxical attitudes toward actual instruction in Khmer. Interestingly, in discussions with parents who put their children in bilingual classrooms, only two parents cited the issue of their child's inability to understand English as a reason for their decision. Instead, many parents stated that "English is easy" for the child, "whereas Khmer is difficult." Only one parent mentioned, rather indirectly, that the program might help the child transfer skills from Khmer to English.[7] Most Khmer parents see bilingual education as a way for children to maintain their native language and identity.

Khmer parents' positive assessment of the bilingual program is consistent with both the important role they assign to appropriate language use and the high value they place on children's learning to read and write Khmer. While praising the virtues of learning Khmer, however, many parents do not actually keep their children in the bilingual program. Even some Khmer bilingual teachers have not placed their own children in bilingual classrooms. In other cases, they have enrolled the children but keep them in the program for no more than one year.

This pattern seems typical of parents from middle-class backgrounds who want their children to succeed economically. The pattern is also reported among many Vietnamese refugee parents; they feel that enrolling their children in English-only classrooms, or "mainstreaming," will contribute to their children's academic success. Similarly, Khmer bilingual teachers feel that their children can better obtain English-language skills by enrolling in a mainstream classroom. Besides, they add, they can teach their children to read and write in Khmer at home when the children are older. Despite these parents' professed intentions, however, many of these children never learn to read and write in Khmer. One teacher described a typical pattern.

> [Female, age 38] I planned to teach my son Khmer when he got older. But now he is in high school, and he is too busy studying other subjects, like French! He has no time to study Khmer. I don't think he will ever learn to read and write in Khmer. I feel very badly about that.

Parents cite many other reasons for not placing or keeping their children in bilingual classrooms. Although one mother wanted her eight-year-old daughter to attend a school with a bilingual program, her daughter had taken it upon herself to answer a questionnaire asking parents to choose a school; she chose one without a bilingual program. The mother seemed resigned, declaring, "I don't know anything about that. I want her to learn Khmer and English, but she is now at a school without a bilingual program." Another father said that although he wanted his son to learn Khmer, he had enrolled him in a nearby all-English school, because the boy kept missing the bus that serves children in the bilingual program. Other parents said their children "were not smart" or "were easily confused" and could not handle learning in two languages at the same time.

Parents' ambivalence toward bilingual classrooms is surprising, given the status parents accord teachers, especially Khmer teachers, and the very significant role parents expect teachers to play in educating their children. Many parents insist that the teacher plays a greater role in forming the child than even the parent does.

> [Male, age 57] The parent's role is only to take care of the child, to feed them when they are hungry, and when they are sick, to give them medicine. As for education, it's the teacher who has responsibility for all kinds of knowledge.

But whereas parents repeatedly stress that teachers are responsible for all aspects of teaching, they emphasize that ultimate responsibility for learning lies with the child. Several parents note, for example, that their children are not doing well in Khmer and find it too difficult.

> [Female, age 36] When Sokha [age six] is given homework in Khmer, she cries and has headaches and says it is so boring and she doesn't want to do it. She says it is very hard for her to learn Khmer.
>
> [Female, age 35] It's up to my son [age ten] to like to study Khmer or not. But he doesn't like to study it. He wants to play instead of studying.
>
> [Female, age 50] I want my daughter [age eleven] to study Khmer, but it depends on whether Saren likes to study Khmer or not. At this moment, she says she doesn't want to study Khmer.

It is especially interesting that parents take their children's complaints seriously. Despite their own desires for their children to learn to read and write Khmer, parents resign themselves not to push (*chŭmrŏnh*) their children.

> [Female, age 34] Some children, like Sochiet [age seven], he doesn't like to study Khmer. But I like [for him to do that]. For example, if I push him, maybe he's not going to study well.
>
> [Male, age 31] To know how to speak two languages is good for him [age eight]. But it depends on him. If he doesn't want to study Khmer, it's up to him.
>
> [Male, age 62] I want them to study to read and write and speak, too, but I don't know yet about my children, if they can do it or not.

These and similar comments would seem to contradict parents' emphasis that teachers and parents are the enforcers of discipline and that adults are the ultimate decision makers for children. Khmer parents stress that children should respect and obey their elders and do what they are told. This, they insist time and time again, distinguishes Khmer children from Americans. Through discussions and observations, however, it becomes clear that whereas a young child's failure to speak or behave appropriately and respectfully—including misbehaving in class or skipping school—is considered just cause for discipline, in matters of academic performance, most Khmer parents hesitate to oppose the child's interests or desires.

These attitudes shed light on research on the academic performance of Khmer children in American schools. Although research has generally confirmed reports in the popular media of the academic success of Southeast Asian children (Caplan, Whitmore, and Choy 1989; Whitmore, Trautmann, and Caplan 1989), a California study that included large numbers of Khmer (Rumbaut 1989) found significant differences between Southeast Asian groups. By both local and national measures of school achievement, Vietnamese did best, followed by Sino-Vietnamese and Hmong, with Khmer and Lao ranking lowest (Rumbaut 1989:169; Portes and Rumbaut 1996:203–5).[8]

The results for the Vietnamese and the Sino-Vietnamese are not completely surprising, because a higher percentage of these immigrants come from more Westernized, urban, and educated backgrounds than other Southeast Asians. The educational data for Hmong, Khmer, and Lao, however, are more perplexing. For example, one would have expected Hmong to perform well below Khmer and Lao, because Hmong households report the lowest levels of literacy and education among all immigrant groups and come almost exclusively from rural backgrounds. Acknowledging this anomaly, Rumbaut (1989:181) suggests that although social class and economic differences explain much of the pattern of achievement observed among Indo-Chinese youth, additional factors must be taken into account to explain the lower levels of Khmer and Lao achievement.

One explanation may lie in the common lament of Khmer parents that they cannot discipline their children in this country. They complain about American laws that protect children against child abuse; such laws, parents say, prevent them from disciplining their children as they would in Cambodia (see chapter 4). Many parents report that their children no longer fear parental threats of discipline and instead respond with threats of their own.

> [Female, age 47] In Cambodia, I have to hit my children so they will listen to me. But in the United States, it's very hard for me to hit or spank them, because U.S. law prohibits hitting children. Now if I hit my son who is thirteen, he will hit me back. And my daughter [who is fifteen], if I hit her, she gets a knife! I am afraid she will kill me! They all [talk] back to me, and they don't want to listen. In Cambodia, I wouldn't allow them to do that to me. If they did that in Cambodia, I would tie them up and hit them. I would hit them until they had a scar on their body. But in the United States, it is very hard to do that.

> [Female, age 54] The parents here cry because they can't do anything. The children say, "I can go anywhere I want. You can't do anything. If you hit me, I will call the police!"

Because they cannot discipline their children properly, parents say they are unable to push their children to the degree that they would in Cambodia.

What Khmer often do not recognize is that the level of control parents feel they have over children in this country is also closely related to Khmer notions of personhood, motivation, and achievement. These notions seem to be singularly Khmer, moreover; other Southeast Asian groups do not share them.

Even while citing their inability to discipline their children, Khmer parents also state their belief that certain aptitudes ultimately depend on the child's character. Many parents believe that their attempts to direct children's lives are deeply constrained or limited by each child's character.

> [Female, age 34] It depends on the child what he wants to study. We cannot push them to study. It depends on the child. If the child likes to study, whichever subject, then they go in that direction. In Cambodia, my parents pushed me to learn all subjects, but here I cannot push them.

> [Mother of a 10-year-old girl, age 48] You can give her advice, but she makes her own decisions. She takes an action and then we say, "Oh, this is what she likes." Sometimes our advice is ignored. We give it to her, but we cannot force her to take a particular course. She chooses, herself. Somehow, she has interests in her already; pushing her in some other direction is no use.

Khmer parents believe that a child's intrinsic disposition strongly influences growth and achievement. Particularly in the area of academic performance, Khmer parents insist that personal predilection and destiny play important roles.

> [Female, age 51] With my son, he decided to drop [out of] high school and study mechanics [in a vocational training program]. I am not happy about that, but I cannot [change] his idea, what he wants to do.

A child's behavior, it is thought, provides the best guide to that child's potential and likely achievement. A child who gets good grades "can do it"; a child who does not do well in school "cannot do it." Parents intervene when they feel intervention can be effective and otherwise resign themselves to a child's inalterable native disposition.

This attitude is also evident in parents' reluctance to speculate about their children's futures. Here again, Khmer attitudes contrast strongly with those of other Southeast Asian immigrant groups. If asked what they would like their children to become or how far they would like their children to go in school, Khmer parents typically make comments such as the following:

> [Female, age 29] I would like Buen [age twelve] to study a lot, if he can do it. It depends on his goal. I don't know his future.
>
> [Male, age 37] I don't know Seyha's [age fourteen] future. I don't know what he likes. It depends on him. I don't know my son yet.
>
> [Male, age 32] I don't know if he [age ten] can do it. I have to watch and see the direction he takes.
>
> [Male, age 37] We cannot decide or choose for Sitha [age ten] what she wants to do. It's up to her to choose for herself.

These and similar statements reveal the widespread belief that a child's future fundamentally depends on the child's predetermined nature. The resonance of these ideas with Khmer Buddhist conceptions of personhood and achievement is striking.

PERSONHOOD AND ACHIEVEMENT

In commenting on their children's school performance, many parents explicitly mention their belief in destiny or fate *(veasna* or *samnang)*. Some also cite the influence of reincarnation or the transmigration of the soul, discussed in chapter 3. According to both beliefs, one's past behavior determines one's present state. Good acts done in a past life will bring good things in this life. One parent even said that he could not learn English and was illiterate in Khmer because he performed bad acts in a previous life.

> [Male, age 57] I believe in destiny. For example, as a teacher, you have a good destiny *(veasna)*. In your previous life, you did very well. That's why you know how to speak, how to read, how to write in English and in Khmer, too. But for me, maybe in my previous life, I did something not very well. That's why I cannot learn English very well, and I cannot write or even read my own language. For my children, it's up to their previous life, too. If they did well, they carry good things to this life. I believe in that. If in their previous life they did a lot of good things and they want to be a policeman or a doctor or a teacher, they can do it. It depends on the previous life.

Another woman said the following of her eight-year-old son:

> [Female, age 55] What he does with his life, it's up to his destiny. I cannot push the destiny far from my son. It is really difficult to do that. According to my son's desire to become a doctor or a teacher or a policeman, it's up to him to choose, not up to me.

Many parents expressed the futility of pushing children in a direction other than that for which they are destined. "We Khmer have a proverb about that," explained a middle-aged father of five. "Human strength cannot change destiny" (*"Kamlăng kŏm brâchhăng nĕung veasna"*).

A young mother expressed her resignation with regard to her children's educational futures by referring to destiny:

> [Female, age 34] I want to push my children to finish college, but it depends on my children if they want to go far with their education or not. For example, people want to be rich, but destiny says, "No, you are still poor." What can I do?

Another said the following:

> [Female, age 47] I believe God gave my child a particular destiny, like a character *(smathpeap)*, and if God says, "This child has to drop out of school," yes, they will drop out. They cannot go farther than that. The Khmer say, *"prum lĕkhĕt."* That means "according to Brahman doctrine or destiny." It means God gave you some kind of thing that you have to do. You cannot go far from what God gave you. *Prum lĕkhĕt* is like the paper that Brahma reads. It says, "This child has to be a doctor, according to the list from God." And that child will be a doctor.

Some Khmer parents, particularly those with some exposure to American views of achievement, insist that they do not believe in destiny, karma, or reincarnation. Nevertheless, their behaviors with regard to their children remain consistent with these beliefs. The most common Khmer views of intelligence and achievement have derived from these religious concepts and from other beliefs, such as the immutability of social categories and the importance of being moderate or taking the "middle road" *(phlauv kandal)*. As one parent explained, taking the middle road means not aiming too high or too low but maintaining the present balance, doing the average amount. Taking the middle road means not demanding too much of a child, not expecting more than the child can deliver—and, as always, protecting one's own face in the process.

> [Male, age 45] For me, I cannot push my children. I cannot say, "My children have to finish this much school." I cannot say they have to be on the top in education. Just so-so, in the middle. I know my children. That's why I suggest to them, "You have to study hard to be in the middle. I don't expect you to go over the middle. I don't want you to be lieutenant, to be captain, but to be in the middle."
>
> I think it's like in Buddhism. Everybody wants to reach nirvana, but I observe that nobody can really go there. Nobody. Even if you work very hard, even if you work like Buddha, you cannot go to nirvana, too. That's why I cannot tell you that I expect my son to be on the top like Buddha.
>
> I know my son, I know my children. They cannot do that. That's why I say, "In the middle, the middle path. If you cannot go to the top, if you fall down, OK. In the middle."

Parents vary, of course, in the degree to which they will push their children in a particular direction before giving in to the child's predestined path. "I have to push my child over and over again before I can say he falls on his destiny," declared one father. Parents agree, however, that to push one's child in a particular direction and to fail is to risk losing one's face and one's standing in the community.

Parents hope that if children receive the appropriate moral training when young, they will choose the right path and achieve great things. Parents encourage and support children who show promise. Ultimately, however, what the child becomes depends on mysterious, invisible forces. In education, as in other domains of social life, achievement is ultimately shaped as much by individual destiny and disposition as by the urgings of teachers or parents.

It is noteworthy that Vietnamese, Sino-Vietnamese, and Hmong refugees—most of whom are not Theravada Buddhist—indicate very different attitudes toward personhood and achievement. In various accounts, parents consistently emphasize clear career and educational goals for their children. They also stress that children must make sacrifices for the benefit and prestige of the group and put strong pressures on children to succeed against all odds (Rumbaut and Ima 1988:47–48, 74–77; Caplan, Whitmore, and Choy 1989; Rumbaut 1989; Whitmore, Trautmann, and Caplan 1989).

In contrast, Khmer parents tend to see their children as individuals with distinctly personal capacities, goals, and frailties. Parents believe that their role is as much to discover these native dispositions as to direct the child. Khmer parents regard their children's success in school programs with pride, and they encourage their children to do their best. Nonetheless, a child's failure may be rationalized as inevitable, beyond parental control. In such circumstances, parents believe, they must adjust their demands to the child's innate capacities.

THE LIMITS OF INDIVIDUALITY

Parents' willingness to look to the child and to recognize the child's individual desires and predilections has its limits. As we have seen, parents intervene forcefully in their children's lives when face or family status are at stake. Children who do not behave in a manner that brings their families honor may be dealt with harshly. For some middle-class families or those with middle-class aspirations, this expectation of appropriate behavior extends to academic performance. In such families, children may feel great pressure to achieve academically, and poor grades may provoke strict parental discipline.

What is more, although Khmer commonly refer to destiny and individual predilections to explain the school performance of younger children, such explanations almost disappear from parental discourse as children grow older. Other considerations arise for adolescents, especially questions about sexuality, engagement, and marriage.

Among Khmer, marriage remains the most significant—and expensive—life-cycle celebration. Marriage negotiations are very closely tied to a family's face and standing in the community. As young men approach a marriageable age, they feel more pressure to act responsibly, to study, or to find a job and start saving money. Adolescent girls begin to feel the weight of parental expectations that they avoid all appearance of impropriety and steer clear of the opposite sex.

Role expectations for adolescent sons and daughters have caused serious intergenerational conflicts in Khmer families in the United States. Because of the enduring double standard used to evaluate sexual behavior, the heaviest constraints fall on young women. Since young women are engaged to and marry young men, however, these expectations have had a serious, if uneven, impact on young men's opportunities and comportment, as well.

6

Sexuality and Marriage

In anthropological studies of sexuality and marriage, a central question concerns the nature of the kin groups involved in the establishment of a marital relationship between a man and a woman. Is marriage a matter of alliance, political or otherwise, between kin-based groups? Or, as in the modern West, is it a more individualized affair, determined first and foremost by the personal and perhaps romantic inclinations of a young man and young woman, at best indirectly influenced by parents' expectations or counsel?

In the case of Khmer Americans, the system through which kinship is conceived and practiced is, in anthropological terms, a *cognatic* one. That is, Khmer kinship is based not on the existence of corporately organized descent groups but on a web of relationships emanating from nuclear families to include both maternal and paternal relatives. From this simple organizational perspective, Khmer kinship (like that of many but not all Southeast Asians) resembles the kinship system of most modern Westerners.

Even though Khmer kinship does not involve corporate descent groups, however, marriage and the sexual relations it helps regulate are never entirely a matter of individual choice for a couple. Although Khmer recognize the importance of affective bonds between a husband and wife, the most immediate concern in selection of a spouse is the respective families' interests, particularly the parents' status or face. Even in the United States, a proper Khmer wedding can only be arranged and enacted if the parents consent and marshal the appropriate social and financial resources.

Much of the cultural significance of marriage is visible in the organization and meaning of weddings. They are the most exciting, elaborate, and expensive Khmer life-cycle celebrations. Previously in Cambodia, wedding festivities lasted up to three days and involved lavish feasting and entertainment in the form of dance or theatrical performances (Ebihara 1968:474). Today in the United States, everything may be accomplished in a single day, beginning in the early morning with the ceremony at the bride's home and ending late in the evening with a restaurant reception.

Preparations, however, begin months in advance. New clothes must be bought or rented for the wedding party and family members. Ritual implements, cookware, and serving dishes must be rented or borrowed for the ritual ceremony. The bride's parents' house may also have to be painted, new mats and rugs bought, and curtains sewn. Photographers must be engaged for the ceremony and reception, and a restaurant must be reserved for the wedding banquet. Bands must be hired, including a traditional ensemble for the home ceremony and a modern Khmer rock group for the reception. Several days before the wedding, female friends and family members must begin to prepare the quantities of food required to feed the large number of relatives and guests. Finally, on the wedding day, the monks must be transported to the bride's home, guests must be received, gifts must be dutifully recorded, and a whole array of interactions and exchanges must be carefully performed. In short, though Khmer American wedding ceremonies may last but a single day, the event itself remains one of the most expensive, socially demanding, and status-affirming events in family and individual life.

SETTING THE STAGE

A Khmer wedding ceremony is organized and hosted by the bride's family and takes place at the bridal home. Whereas wedding receptions in rural Cambodia were also held at the bride's home, today in the United States they are almost always held in a restaurant.[1]

Although, as with the home wedding, the bride's parents are primarily responsible for the reception, the groom's family normally shoulders the bulk of the expense by making various payments to the bride's parents. The payments are part of a series of material and symbolic exchanges between the two families that begin with engagement negotiations. By all indications, weddings are many times more expensive today in the United States (in absolute, if not relative, terms) than they were in Cambodia. Even in the years since Khmer have emigrated to the United States, the amount of bride-wealth paid by the groom to the bride and her family has increased considerably.

The groom's parents are said to "pay for the wedding." They

give a large number of gifts consisting of food, alcohol, and clothing to the bride and her family. They also buy the jewelry (a ring, necklace, or bracelet) given to the bride at the engagement (though it is the groom who hands the goods over to his betrothed). Finally, they provide the bride-wealth, a sum negotiated with the bride's parents at the time of engagement. By providing the bride-wealth, the groom's parents indirectly finance the largest portion of the home ceremony and restaurant reception, events otherwise orchestrated by the bridal side.

Both families also draw on relatives, friends, and acquaintances to support the festivities through contributions of labor and cash. Mobilizing such networks in wedding performances is not merely a practical matter; it is also a key index of social status. The number of guests, the value of monetary gifts, the number of relatives and friends who help with cooking and serving—all these are important and much-discussed indicators of a family's standing in the community. In a form of symbolic capital familiar to social anthropologists, a large and successful celebration demonstrates that one's family is secure and intact, one's children are respectful and obedient, and one's social networks are loyal and extensive (see Bourdieu 1977; Ebrey 1991).

Khmer Americans are keenly aware of the status concerns involved in a wedding.

> [Male, age 47] We Cambodians want to keep our culture alive in the United States, and most people want honor. When we see our children get married with a big wedding and we invite the people, our friends, we want to show off, to be proud to say, "Oh, my children are getting married." We feel proud and have honor if it is a big and successful wedding.

> [Widow, age 55] I don't mind about the money. I paid for everything for my son's wedding. The girl's family didn't help at all. I think I paid around $10,000, maybe more than $10,000, because I gave my daughter-in-law a ring and a necklace, too. I wanted to show my son that you only marry one time in your whole life. So I have to consider his wedding like that . . . bigger than the other people's, so that every eye will be looking and people will think, good, you do good, your son's wedding is good.

It is largely because of the status connotations of marriage celebrations—and the potentially problematic relation of female sexuality to family reputation—that weddings have sometimes become a source of conflict in the Khmer American community. When a boy from a "good" (well-established, high-status) family proposes to a girl, she is described as having a "big face" *(mŭk khpŭah)*. The boy's proposal "raises up the face" of the girl and her family. Similarly, the boy's family is raised up if a girl from a family of good standing accepts the proposal.

In contrast, marriages that must be hastily arranged to cover up some wrongdoing or to avert a disaster, such as an out-of-wedlock pregnancy, cause visible grief to the families involved. Such weddings are typically small and somber; relatives, friends, and even members of the immediate families may be conspicuously absent.

Above all, a prestigious wedding requires a virtuous bride. Although the boy's background is important, too, his sexual behavior is viewed far less critically. In fact, it is seen as entirely normal that the groom bring at least some sexual experience to the marriage.

It is another matter entirely for the bride, even though the situation for Khmer women in the United States has changed considerably from what it was in Cambodia. In the United States, Khmer elders acknowledge, it is impossible to shelter girls to the same extent as in Cambodia. Everyone knows that young women interact freely with young men at school. American teachers and friends also encourage young women to join in after-school activities that inevitably include male classmates.

Although most Khmer parents still forbid their daughters to date and even to "hang around" with boys, let alone have boyfriends, parents bemoan their perceived lack of control over their adolescent daughters' behavior. When a young woman becomes involved with a young man, she is immediately regarded as morally compromised, because "good girls" do not go out with young men. If an unmarried girl loses her virginity and the event is made public, it can have disastrous consequences for her whole family's status or face. This is distinctly different from the way Khmer respond to a boy's lost virginity.

The emphasis on women's behavior and demeanor has led observers to posit that conceptions of gender hold a privileged position in Khmer formulations of identity.[2] Certainly, weddings have become an arena in which to express and contest traditional Khmer gender ideals. Here, as elsewhere in Khmer socialization, the tension between the individual's autonomy and the social responsibility to family and community lies at the heart of Khmer Americans' attempts to interpret and adjust to changing cultural realities.

ENGAGEMENT

A child or adolescent has little or no independent face within the community, and that young person's behavior reflects directly on the family, but by marrying and establishing a family, a young person begins to take on an individual and public social identity. For a young man, marriage is an important statement of masculinity; it expresses the central masculine value of being able to support a family. For a young woman, marriage is a public display of the social estimation of her virtue and upbringing. In marrying well and especially in marrying a man her parents deem acceptable, a young woman establishes an independent and approved social identity.

Because young women are not supposed to have boyfriends, a young man must tell his parents of his interest in a particular young woman and ask that they arrange a meeting with her parents. If the boy's parents do not already have a candidate in mind for their son and have no other objections, they will defer responding and inquire in the community about the young woman and her family. In this initial investigation *(soeb suo)*, the parents attempt to confirm that the young woman comes from a good social background, has a virtuous reputation, has never had any boyfriends, and is not already engaged.

If the results of their inquiry are positive, they then enlist a married couple of good standing to act as intermediaries *(něak phlauv)*. The intermediaries' first task is to ask the young woman's family if they would consider a marriage proposal. Often, this is done informally or indirectly, so that if the girl's family rejects the offer, the boy's family does not lose face. If the girl's family is not interested in the boy, they may cite their daughter's youthful age or their desire that she complete high school before marriage. If they are open to the possibility of a proposal, however, they will arrange to meet the young man's family.

Meanwhile, the girl's family begins its own investigation of the prospective groom's background, asking people whether he is from a good family, does not gamble or drink excessively, and is not already married or engaged. In addition, before the prospective in-laws meet (or sometimes shortly thereafter), either the boy's side or the girl's side takes the two candidates' birthdates to a *krou teay*, a traditional astrologer, to determine whether the couple's horoscopes indicate a good match.

The first meeting of the two families, sometimes referred to simply as "the day of chit-chatting" *(thngay dael chaul mok chaechauv)*, takes place at the prospective bride's home. The young man is represented by his parents and accompanied by the *něak phlauv* go-between; he himself is not required to attend. From the young woman's side, the parents and occasionally an uncle or aunt are present. (For this first meeting, the girl's parents may or may not enlist the aid of a go-between.) The bride is never involved at this point and may have no idea that marriage negotiations are taking place.

At this meeting, the young man's side presents itself to the young woman's side, officially expresses the boy's intentions, and answers any questions the girl's parents may have about the boy's background (though usually the girl's side already knows the answers). The young woman's family will often ask for time to consider the proposal and to consult with their daughter. In this case, they will indicate a date by which time they will give their response.

Then the families perform the first of the many exchanges that punctuate social interaction between the groom's and bride's parties. The young man's side presents small gifts of food (typically, fresh fruit) and is offered a simple meal. If the negotiations seem to be going well, the prospective bride may be called on to serve the groom-side guests. Indeed, if senior figures in the groom's party have never met the young woman, they may ask to see her. If the young man's mother likes what she sees, she indicates her approval by handing the prospective bride some money. The exchange that binds marriage ties is thereby deepened.

Parents normally discuss marriage proposals with their daughter and ask her opinion. All parents insist that they would never force their daughter into a marriage to which she did not agree; however, they may apply subtle and even not-so-subtle pressure on a daughter to encourage her to accept a proposal that her family deems especially attractive. If parents consider a particular candidate suitable and continue pressing the girl to agree, the ideal response of the well–reared young woman is to accede with the comment, "*Srach tae mae aeng*" ("It's up to you, Mom"). Such reluctant concessions can lead to unexpected events, though, as we shall see.

If the young woman does agree to the marriage, a meeting is scheduled to discuss the timing and financial arrangements for the wedding. This meeting is called the *pchâb piek,* or "setting the word." By this time, the young woman's parents have usually consulted with relatives to decide what kind of wedding is desirable and how much to request for wedding expenses. To make this assessment, they need to determine how elaborate the wedding will be, how sumptuous the reception, and how many people to invite.

The groom's side is well aware that they are expected to shoulder most of the wedding expenses. Indeed, at this next meeting, they ask directly, "*Damlay samrab tŏek dâh ponman?*" This literally translates as "How much does the milk from your breast cost?" but is understood to mean "How much do you want us to pay you?" There may be some negotiation of the precise amount.

If at all possible, such discussions take place through the families' representatives, who have received instructions beforehand. The negotiations do not involve the families directly, unless the disagreement becomes serious enough to jeopardize the event.

In any case, the *pchâb piek* is less binding than the *ch'noun tŭm* ("the big offering"), which may be combined with the *pchâb piek* or held right before the wedding. Sometimes a family puts on a large *ch'noun tŭm* to mark the engagement and then a smaller *ch'noun* or *saeng* ("offering") just before the wedding. During the *ch'noun tŭm,* the couple's intention to marry is announced to the ancestors. The ceremony gives dramatic form to the theme of interfamilial exchange, which has marked marriage preparations since engagement. Now, however, the ceremony sanctifies the exchange by incorporating it into a ritual exchange with ancestors.

The rite is called "the big offering" because the groom's side brings a large number of beautifully wrapped food gifts and small ritual items to the bride's family. Acting on behalf of the bride's and groom's families, the *achaa* ritual specialist presents the gifts to the ancestors. The gifts are then either used in the ceremony or consumed by the guests.

Everything must be presented in twos. The number invokes the idea of the two sides involved in the ceremony, the two sets of ancestors, the two individuals to be married, and most generally the male and female from whose union life begins. There are two bunches of bananas, two baskets of canned lychees, two trays of betel, two roasted chickens, two bowls of oranges, two packages of candles—two of everything. The offerings are carried into the bride's house by a procession (also arranged in twos) of members of the groom's party, who have been waiting outside the bride's house.

At this time, the bride and groom also exchange gold jewelry and clothing, a symbol of their commitment to one another, and the groom gives the bride's side some or all of the bride-wealth he has promised. Then the bride's parents chew betel with the groom's parents to indicate their acceptance of his intention to marry their daughter.

After the exchange of gifts, the groom's representatives, speaking loudly enough that all the guests can hear, ask the bride's representatives, "If your daughter decides not to marry my son later, what will you do?" The bride's side replies, "If my daughter doesn't marry your son, I will give all the gold and other things back to you." Then the bride's side asks the groom's side, "If your son later doesn't want to marry my daughter, what will you do?" The groom's side replies, "All those things that I gave you, they all belong to you. I don't want them back." The *achaa* ritual specialist then officially informs the ancestors of the couple's intention to wed and begs forgiveness on the part of the future bride and groom should they accidentally offend the ancestors.

> [Wedding *achaa*] We announce to the ancestors that this girl and this boy will be married. We ask them please not to get angry if anything goes wrong later on, like for example if the girl and boy have some physical relations before the wedding. Of course, they are not allowed to do that, but if something bad should happen, we have announced to the ancestors that these two will get married, so they won't be confused about that and so no one will get sick in the family as a result *(méba kăch)*.

The ancestors of both sides are then formally offered food and drink: *"Saum tévoda khang ŏvpŭk, kang mday, kaun srey nĭh, kaun prŏh nĭh."* ("We beseech both ancestral sides [to come and eat the offerings].") Then, all those present are served a traditional Cambodian meal on mats spread on the floor. Through these acts, the engagement has been announced to relatives and sanctified through the ritual invocation of the ancestors.

Now that the engagement has been made official, it is important for the groom to demonstrate a respectful attitude toward his future in-laws. In the past, especially in rural areas, this included actual groom service *(tvoe bǎmraoe)*; the groom would work in his in-laws' fields (Steinberg 1959:85; Ebihara 1974:318). Today, it is still important that the young man address his fiancée's parents with respect, assist them in any ritual endeavors they undertake, bring them small gifts if they or close family members are sick, and offer them food or a small amount of money on important Khmer holidays. Failure to behave properly toward future in-laws can offend the bride's parents greatly; they may even cancel the wedding if the groom proves unworthy.

Once the big offering is completed, the young couple is now formally engaged and can go out together—to the movies, parties, or dinner. However, they must still be accompanied by friends or other family members so that there is no misunderstanding on the part of the ancestors—or living community members, for that matter.

THE WEDDING DAY

On the day of the wedding, the bride's side arises before dawn, cooking for out-of-town family and friends and finishing preparations for the home ceremony. In the early morning, the groom arrives at the bride's house with his attendants, representatives, relatives, and guests, all of whom walk in a procession from the groom's house. The groom is shaded by a umbrella, and the procession is accompanied by a traditional Khmer band. (In the urban United States, the groom's side may arrive by car and merely walk from the parking lot to the bride's apartment.) The groom's side is greeted hospitably at the bride's door and is led into the living area. The groom's relatives and friends are then seated on one side of the room and the bride's on the other.

Even at this late stage, great care is taken to mediate the exchange between the bride's and groom's retinues. Each side has representatives who speak for their families. These are long-married individuals in good standing in the community who also know about Khmer marriage customs. The bride's side has one representative, the *méba*. The groom's side has two representatives, a couple called the *chav moha*. One of the male representatives typically doubles as the *achaa* who orchestrates and officiates at the necessary rites.

After the groom and his retinue have been seated in the living area, the bride is led out of her room to sit next to the groom. The *méba* asks the groom's side loudly enough that everyone can hear, "How much do you give for this girl?" The *chav moha* then announces the amount of money the groom has agreed to pay the bride's family for the home ceremony and the reception.

If the groom has given the bride jewelry, the objects and their value will also be announced. "Do you, the relatives of the bride, all see? The groom has given $6,000 and one necklace worth $200." Here, and in other Khmer ritual, there is little shyness about displaying or referring to money or other valuables exchanged in the rite. (In temple ceremonies, for example, the precise amount that an individual gives the monks may be announced over a loudspeaker. At a wedding, the necklace and an envelope of money may be held up so the guests can see.)

The bride's relatives may examine the jewelry or ask to count the money. The *méba* then asks the bride's side if they accept the payment. The bride's relatives respond loudly, "Yes, yes, we accept!" The *méba* responds, "Then from now on Somalee and Sambo are sworn to become man and wife. May the ancestors receive this information." The *chav moha* and the *méba* of the bride's side end the ceremony by making an offering to both the bride's and groom's ancestors. This is, in effect, another ritual version of the *ch'noun tŭm* described earlier.

The next step is the ritual haircutting of the bride and groom (*kăt sâk*). As is true in other Khmer life-cycle ceremonies (and those of many other Southeast Asian cultures; see Hefner 1985), cutting the hair symbolically chases away evil. The ceremony cleanses and purifies the couple, so that the bride and groom will have good luck and be ready to receive the blessings of their parents, their ancestors, and the monks. Only a small amount of hair, if any, is actually cut, but it is sufficient to prepare the bride and groom for the next ritual, the monks' benediction, or *saut maun*. This ritual is the last of the morning ceremonies.

The *saut maun* is the first occasion in which Buddhist ritual is directly involved in the events that mark the engagement and wedding.

Up to this time, the ceremony has been largely concerned with forging ties between the two families and communicating news of the relationship to the ancestors. The monks' benediction is brief but is nonetheless regarded as critical. It sanctifies the bond between the bride and groom, as well as the bond between their families. The monks intone prayers before the seated bride and groom and sprinkle them with holy water. They then sprinkle the families and the assembled guests in order to "spread the blessing."

The morning ceremonies completed, the monks are escorted home and the guests are served a meal set out on mats on the floor. During the meal, the bride's parents move around the room, anxiously asking friends and relatives, "Is the food good? Are the details of the ritual correct? Has anything been forgotten or left out?"

When the guests have all been fed, the plates have been cleared, and the eating mats rolled up, the afternoon ceremonies begin. The female *méba* leads the bride to the groom to perform the *leang choeung*, the ritual foot washing. She kneels before the groom with a bowl of water and pumice stone. The young man puts his foot on top of the stone, and the bride sprinkles it with water. She bows deeply three times to her betrothed, then wipes his feet and hands him some betel. In return, the groom gives the bride a small sum of money.

In some cases, the bride has her sister or cousin perform the foot washing, because she is "too shy" to do it herself. Some *achaa*, however, recount a cautionary story of a bride whose family hired a woman to wash the groom's feet because they didn't want their daughter to prostrate herself before the groom. He decided to marry the hired woman instead of his betrothed because he suspected that the bride's family looked down on him. (Interestingly, there is some evidence that the foot-washing ceremony was abandoned in many areas of Cambodia before the war, but it has experienced a revival in the Khmer American community, along with some other, more traditional elements of the wedding ceremony.)

After performing the *leang choeung*, the bride is led back to her room to wait nervously until she is called out for the final, most critical ritual of the marriage ceremony, the *sampĕah phtŏem*, or ritual of "paying obeisance as a couple." The obeisance rite begins as the groom is escorted into the living area. He is seated on one of two large decorative pillows laid on the floor, where he faces the guests. In front of the pillows are a sheathed sword and three bunches of areca flowers nestled in a silver urn. Carefully following the *achaa*'s instructions and employing the same gesture of respect impressed on him since his birth, the groom bows in obeisance three times to the assembled relatives and guests. He then bows three times to the bride's father and gives him one bunch of areca flowers. He then bows again three times, this time to the bride's mother, and gives her a second bunch of flowers. He bows and gives a third bunch to an uncle, aunt, or older sibling of the bride. He must then remain seated properly, facing the guests, until the bride comes out of her room.

A percussion band, which has been drinking tea and relaxing since its members accompanied the groom's side to the bride's home, begins to play again. The sounds of a gong indicate that it is time for the bride to emerge. She enters the room with small steps, her head down, her eyes toward the floor. She is led by the female singer and accompanied by several female attendants. With behaviors thought to represent idealized images of wifely femininity, she sits carefully next to the groom, studiously directing her gaze away from him. The *méba*'s wife and the bride's attendants help arrange the folds of her silk *sampôt*.

The *achaa* then says to the young woman, "If you take these three bunches of flowers from this man, it means you are his wife." (These are the same flowers that the groom distributed earlier and that the *achaa* then collected.) The bride takes the flowers and bows her head in obeisance to relatives and guests. The *achaa* then makes offerings to the ancestors, who are invited to recognize and bless the couple as husband and wife.

Bowing in obeisance, the bride and groom prostrate themselves with their elbows on the pillows, the flowers held between their palms. Performing the obeisance at the end of wedding ceremonies graphically illustrates that weddings are the bonds not only between husband and wife but also between parents and children. When the *phtŏem* is accomplished, the couple is considered officially wed.

After the *phtŏem*, the ceremony's mood becomes more playful. The musical ensemble plays loudly, and the female singer dances suggestively while singing in a high-pitched falsetto. Still dancing, she lifts the sword from the floor in front of the couple, and, holding it up so that all can see, she ceremoniously pulls the sword out of its sheath and then replaces it. (Not surprisingly, the sword and sheath are said to symbolize male and female sexuality, respectively.)

The *achaa* brings the groom's and bride's heads together so that they touch, and he declares them to be husband and wife. At this time, each of the newlyweds is supposed to try to hold his or her head higher than the other's. They are typically oblivious, however, to the efforts of relatives and friends who step forward and arrange the pillows so that one will win. Despite any such attempts to assist the bride or groom, the bride's head is usually higher because of her upswept coif. Whereas previous rituals have symbolized feminine subservience, this less "official" gesture is widely said to mean that the woman will not be dominated by her husband.

The couple remains prostrate before the assembled relatives and guests while the *achaa* arranges the offerings to the ancestors. He pours some cognac into a saucer "for the ancestors to enjoy" and begins to cut a piece of a roasted pig's ear to add to it. The *yeichi* seated nearby joke with him, "Hey, don't cut that! The ancestors are eating!" He arranges more food for the ancestors and kneels to set a dish down on the mat as the *méba* quips, "Watch out! You almost stepped on Great-grandfather!"

When the offerings are complete, the *achaa* carefully lights four candles, which are passed around the room seven times for the seven ancestral generations who act as witnesses to the marriage. Each guest waves a hand over the candle flame, chasing dirt and evil from the newlywed couple. When asked about the candle's significance, women guests giggle at the *achaa*'s suggestion that the candle represents Brahma's sexual organ *(lingga)*; the ceremony may only be done if the bride is a virgin.

The final and gayest moment in the marriage ceremony is the *châng dai,* or the "tying of the wrists." First, the newlyweds' parents come forward and tie a white cotton string around the bride's and then the groom's wrists. After them come uncles, aunts, other relatives, and then friends. Each person who ties a string wishes the couple good luck and blesses them *(aoy pau)*.

Wishes conveyed by family and guests to the couple take a ritually conventionalized form. They include such expressions as "May you have two children in the first year" *("Aoy mean kaun pi muoy chnam")*; "May you love each other" *("Aoy chéh srâlăñh knea")*; "May you stick together and earn a living" *("Aoy puot dai knea rok si")*. At this time, some relatives give the couple envelopes of money. A few may put jewelry into the bride's and groom's hands. Unlike contributions given to the couple later at the reception, the money is explicitly for the bride and groom "to begin their life together."

During the *châng dai* at Samnang and Buen's wedding, the female *méba* announces loudly that she has no money to offer but will give her advice to the couple.

> Now you are old, not young anymore—not children, not teenagers, but adults. To the bride I say, "You have to take care of your husband and children. Don't ever look down on your husband! When he is sick, take care of him. Always use soft words and have peace in your family. You owe your parents on both sides a lot. Try to remember, if you have something special, just give it to your parents."

The male representative of the groom's side then steps forward to offer his counsel.

> [Wedding *achaa*] As men, we are very happy to hear the recommendations just given to the bride's side! I only want to say, "You have to stay close together, to cooperate, and to talk things over together." To the groom I say, "You should listen to your wife. Don't make decisions for her. Don't look down on her, either. And be careful not to love any other women. This is now your wife, and everybody is witness to that!"

After all the guests have given their wishes and blessings, the bunches of dried areca flowers are separated, and the seeds are given to the guests to throw. The dried seeds symbolize that the bride and groom have left their youth behind and are now adults. "They are no longer like young, fresh, blooming flowers; now that they are married, the bloom is faded, the perfume is gone," says the *achaa*. His words underscore the couple's newly achieved status in the community's eyes. They also hint at a common metaphor found in Khmer songs and literature that compares sexual allure, particularly that of women, to the fragrance of beautiful flowers; by referring to this metaphor, the *achaa* reminds the newlyweds to remain faithful to one another. The couple then leaves the front room together, the groom following his bride into her bedroom and holding onto the end of her scarf.[3]

Young people follow the newlyweds, crowding into the bedroom, where the two sit self-consciously on the bed. Laughing and joking, individuals ask the bride and groom to perform various feats. Someone gives the bride a piece of a banana to hold in her mouth, and the groom is told to eat it. Someone else puts a cigarette between the bride's lips and tells the groom to try lighting it, even though his friends keep blowing out his lit matches. These antics mark the end of the home ceremony. The guests take their leave to prepare themselves for the wedding banquet.

The details of the wedding ceremony can vary considerably, of course. Some elements depend on the experience of the officiating *achaa;* others on the desires of the families involved, including the amount of money they wish to spend. The American context has also required people to adjust the timing and organization of the festivities. Harsh weather and the short days of winter, for example, prevent early morning and outdoor rites. Similarly, because of the guests' work schedules, celebrations can now be held only on weekends. Many Khmer say the ceremony has changed because of a "loss of culture." In fact, however, the ethnographic literature on Khmer society in Cambodia suggests that there was already considerable variation by region and class in the form of the wedding ceremony.[4]

THE WEDDING BANQUET

The wedding banquet *(nham kăă)* is held either on the evening of the same day or on the day after the home ceremony. Unlike the wedding ceremony, the reception is quite explicitly said to be for the guests' enjoyment; it is considered successful if it is large and happy with abundant food and drink, loud music, and dancing. In metropolitan Boston, Khmer wedding receptions are usually held at a restaurant in Boston's Chinatown, although some young people have recently begun to use larger and less expensive Chinese restaurants outside the city.[5]

When guests arrive at the restaurant, they are greeted by the bride, groom, and their attendants, all of whom have changed into formal, Western-style wedding attire. The newlyweds' parents seat guests at round tables for ten. The wedding meal typically consists of eight or even ten courses. The meal starts with soup, followed by beef, pork, duck, and various kinds of seafood on large platters, one after another. The final course is often fried rice, followed by fresh fruit. The dishes are placed in the center of the table, and guests serve themselves. Bottles of beer and soda are also placed on the table, along with a liter of cognac.

While the guests eat, a Cambodian band plays loud Cambodian pop rock music, making conversation difficult, even with one's neighbors. After several courses have been served, the bridal party and some of the guests begin dancing. Toward the end of the night, the dance floor becomes quite crowded.

Amid the festivities, the newlyweds change into traditional Khmer attire *(sampôt châng kběn)*. They begin to circulate slowly among the guests, followed closely by their attendants. Having expressed their respects to their parents, the bride and groom convey their respects to guests, many of whom, of course, are their parents' friends and relatives. The couple bows in obeisance to each of the guests. In return, each guest offers the couple blessings and good wishes, giving the bride an envelope that is filled with money and clearly labeled with the guest's name and dollar amount of the gift.

The bride graciously receives the offering (which, like the wrist-tying ceremony, is called *châng dai*) and deposits the envelope in a large silver bowl held by one of her attendants. She then offers the guest a cigarette, and the groom follows closely behind the bride with a lighter. The guest is required to take at least one puff. (More health-conscious Khmer and many Christian couples offer their guests a fabric rose or some other small souvenir instead of the cigarette.)

Some of the younger guests, especially the couple's friends, downplay the interaction's serious tone and use the opportunity to tease the couple sexually again. They may, for example, make their offering while standing on a chair, requiring the groom to lift his bride onto his shoulder in order to reach the envelope. Alternatively, before handing over their contributions, the guests may insist that the couple jointly eat a piece of fruit on a wooden skewer.

Many older guests and those with young children leave after the bride and groom have received contributions and the last platter has been served. These guests make take home leftover food and alcohol. Other guests stay late into the night, however, drinking, dancing, and generally enjoying one of the few occasions in which large numbers of Khmer acquaintances can interact in a thoroughly relaxed atmosphere.

Trusted members of the bride's or groom's family open the envelopes and count the contributions inside. Each contributor's name and the amount of the gift are carefully recorded so that the parents can repay it at a later date. Such repayment can be made, however, only in the context of another wedding; the "debt" is ritual-specific, not transferable to other, more mundane situations.

The ritual debt is the responsibility of the parents, not the newlyweds. As recipients of the gift, however, the couple feels indebted to those who have helped sponsor the rite, especially close relatives. In the case of guests who are known only to the bride or groom (such as classmates or workplace colleagues) the debt is understood to be taken on by the young couple themselves.

Most of the contributions are used to defray the costs of the reception and other wedding expenses. In some cases, however, the bride's parents give part or all to the newlyweds, especially when the contributions exceed the expenses. (The money the groom gave the bride's parents as bride-price counts as a contribution.)

WEDDING EXPENSE AND EXCHANGE

The expense of a Khmer wedding and reception is considerable. Together, they can amount to thousands of dollars. Although guests' contributions can cover a substantial portion of the wedding costs and although close family members often contribute large sums of money, it is not uncommon for families to go into long-term debt to finance a wedding (see also Ebihara 1968:485). Therefore, they must carefully calculate the number of guests who can be relied on to attend and to make a significant monetary gift. For this reason, if possible, family members personally deliver invitations to important guests and try to secure a promise of attendance.

Although today in the United States the bride's family may assume some of the wedding expense, as we will see below, Khmer continue to follow a tradition of bride-price or bride-wealth, commonly referred to as the *thlai tŏek dâh mday,* or "the price of the mother's milk." As this idiom illustrates, the groom's payment is regarded as a symbolic reimbursement to the bride's parents, especially the mother, for the young woman's upbringing. A recently married young man explains the payment in just such terms.

> [Male, age 23] The money I give to her mother, the *thlai tŏek dâh mday,* is just to say, "Thank you," for caring for her daughter, because when

a man marries a girl, he will take the girl out of the house and the mother stays alone. The mother loses her daughter when she marries, so the money is something to give back to the mother for all of her care, for taking good care of her.

In some areas of Cambodia, the term *thlai phtĕah*, meaning "price of the house," was more common than *thlai tŏek dâh mday* (Ebihara 1968:472). The amount of *thlai phtĕah* in this case was compared to the cost of a home for the couple and was considered an indication of the groom's ability to support a wife and family.[6] Both in the past and today, the bulk of this payment is put directly toward the expense of the wedding. Today Khmer Americans may still use the term *thlai tŏek dâh mday* to refer to the amount paid by the groom for general wedding costs. Others, however, prefer the more neutral term *prak bandakăă*, or "wedding money."

Khmer insist that when the groom gives money, he is not purchasing the woman, her offspring, or any possessions. Khmer parents say, "We do not sell our daughter like an animal" or "We do not sell our daughter like a pig." Nonetheless, the idioms used in marriage negotiations clearly refer to the groom's "paying" for the bride. The young woman's "value," moreover, is widely believed to depend on her social and sexual reputation. In fact, parents often equate female virtue and bridal "value" quite explicitly.

> [Female, age 47] The girl's value [the amount the groom pays to the bride's family] depends on whether she has had a boyfriend. If she never did any wrong, then she has a high value and she will be very expensive.

> [Female, age 45] The families, when they go to look around for a virgin for their son to marry—a very good girl, no fooling around, stay[s] at home with her parents—that girl will be very rare here and very expensive to marry.

A daughter with a good reputation affords her parents considerable leverage in marital negotiations. If a suitor comes from a low-status or questionable background, the bride's family may ask an excessively large bride-price with the intention of dissuading him. By contrast, if a daughter has a bad reputation, the young woman's family may have to accept a lower amount from the groom's side or forfeit any contribution, paying the full cost of the wedding.[7]

Status distinctions can be blurred by financial wealth, however. Nget Mary's family, for example, asked for a bride-price of eighteen thousand dollars for their daughter Sophal. Whereas the Nget family had been in the United States since 1975 and were recognized as members of the Khmer intelligentsia, the young man's family was from an uneducated, rural background. The young man's side surprised everyone, however, and agreed to the amount. At the *pchâb piek*, when asked, "How much do you give for this girl?" the groom's representative triumphantly placed a plastic bag containing eighteen thousand dollars in cash in the *achaa*'s lap! (The episode only reinforced the perception in the community that important class distinctions are becoming obscured in the United States—much to the distress of previously high-status Khmer.)

The typical home ceremony today involves two hundred guests and costs between $2,000 and $3,000. This includes food, alcohol, flowers, a photographer, the rental of dishes and equipment, and some small home improvements. For a respectable wedding reception for two hundred people, the average cost is between $6,000 and $10,000 for the restaurant alone. (Hence, the deposit is as much as $3,000 to $5,000.) The groom must also pay for the band, the alcohol, and gifts of clothing and jewelry for the bride.

The expense of Khmer weddings has steadily increased over the past ten years in the United States. Today the average wedding costs at least $6,000 to $10,000; larger weddings cost between $20,000 and $30,000. Khmer like to blame the Chinese restaurants, where most receptions are held, for taking advantage of Cambodians and for steadily—and unfairly—increasing their prices. Just five years ago, a good-sized banquet with nine courses cost $25 to $30 per person; today, it costs $40 or even $45 per person. What is clear is that in the same period, the average size of guests' wedding contributions has also increased significantly.

> [Widow, age 52] For regular people who are not dear friends, right now $50 is the usual contribution for one person. Five years ago, it was only $25 or $30. In Cambodia [she laughs], it was maybe the equivalent of $10. That was for an expensive wedding.

Although Khmer insist that guests should give "whatever they feel is appropriate," most try at least to cover the cost of their own "plate" or "seat." That is, guests calculate the amount of their gift roughly on the basis of the cost per person that is paid to the restaurant. If the guest is not close to the wedding couple or to their parents, this may be all that that person pays. Close friends and relatives, however, pay as much as they can afford, depending on the quality of the relationship.

If guests are repaying a contribution made to a wedding they hosted earlier, then the amount is always slightly larger than the original "debt." To "even out" the debt would be considered poor form, implying a closure of the exchange relationship (see Mauss [1925] 1966; Bourdieu 1976; Hefner 1985). One woman explained it this way:

> [Widow, age 52] Everybody understands the way we live here and the way we pay for wedding banquets, so we support each other. If you know a family well, you think, I don't mind [giving] them $100 for the banquet. Those people, your dear friends, when they come to your wedding, they will give at least $110 or $120.

As families become established in the Khmer American community, they are able to draw on wider networks of family, friends, and acquaintances for assistance. Furthermore, as community members become more financially secure, they are able to afford greater contributions. Such social relationships support increasingly large celebrations, allowing Khmer wedding costs to climb steadily in recent years. Anticipating the marriage of a son or daughter in the near future, a woman may easily "invest" $800 to $1,000 in contributions to others' weddings in a single year. Households with larger incomes may spend even more.

Parents insist, however, that to focus on the expense of Khmer weddings is to miss what is of paramount concern for them. They say they are quite happy to pay for a "good marriage" for their children, whatever the cost. That is, if the marriage is appropriately arranged, if the match is between families of good repute, if the bride is virtuous, and if the groom is respectful and compliant, then parents are more than happy to support their children—even if it means going into debt. For years, parents anticipate children's weddings by investing money and labor in the weddings of friends, relatives, and neighbors. They look forward to the day they will be able to call in these debts to support a celebration of their own. Parents feel comfortable doing so, however, only if the occasion is happy. From the parents' perspective, the expense of the wedding is of less concern than that the match is honorable and that the family's face is upheld.

If anything, the concern with publicly and ostentatiously validating one's face and family reputation seems to have increased, not decreased, among Khmer in the United States. The reasons for this are fairly clear, relating as they do to the societal upheaval through which virtually all Khmer have passed. Unlike in prewar Cambodia, it is difficult to determine the status and background of most Khmer American families. The chaos of the war and the fragmentation of Khmer society have caused considerable uncertainty about some individuals' identities. There is endless gossip about where different individuals come from and what they did back in Cambodia. For many people, the only effective measures of status and reputation are people's actions and appearances here in the United States. Weddings have therefore become critical indexes of families' standing and reputations in the community. One young woman put it quite eloquently:

> [Female, age 26] For Cambodians, you have to have a lot of people respecting you. You have to have a good relationship so you can borrow money. You share food, eat food together, give food. If they don't respect you, they won't come to your house. They'll talk behind your back and spread stories, and you can't look at people's faces.

Because the size of a wedding celebration is seen as a direct reflection of a family's standing within the community, there is enormous pressure for families to put on large, elaborate weddings.[8] Status uncertainties have to be neutralized, and doubts about family reputation must be allayed. Once in motion, the cycle of larger and more expensive weddings is difficult to break. Even families who feel that money could be better spent to finance a house or a child's education say they would be much too embarrassed, *kemăh ké*, to host a modest ceremony for their children.

MARRIAGE ARRANGEMENTS AND MORALITY

Khmer parents have deep anxieties about the marriages of their children. To understand these anxieties, one must look closely at the much debated issue of marriage arrangements. Such arrangements highlight important aspects of Khmer cultural change in the United States, especially as regards gender ideology and individuality.

Although their memories are most certainly idealized, Khmer elders insist that before the war and the period of dislocation, parents arranged most Khmer marriages. In extreme cases, the bride and sometimes even the groom had never seen the betrothed before the engagement ceremony. More commonly, he had seen her at a temple ceremony or at the wedding of a relative or he knew of her from school and had asked his parents to make the arrangements with her family.

> [Female, age 50] In Cambodia, I lived with my aunt and took care of my mother; she had a stroke and she couldn't walk or anything. My husband—the one who would be my husband—lived in the same neighborhood. He worked like a blacksmith, something with iron. He saw me at a New Year's celebration and decided to get someone to ask about marrying me. He had an older couple, his relatives I think, come to ask my aunt and my mother if he could marry me.
> My mother came to me and said, "You have to marry him, because I am very old, and I am sick. If you marry him, you will have someone to take care of you when I die."
> I said, "OK, if you want me to marry him, I will listen to you." I agreed even though I hated him *(khnyŏm s'âb kŏat)*. I had never talked to him, but I heard he had a lot of girlfriends—that's why I hated him. But he promised in front of my mother that if he married me, he would stop having girlfriends. He swore he was a good man.[9]

In such discussions of marriage arrangements, the theme of filial piety emerges quite strongly. To convince a child to marry, parents often remind the child that the parents are getting old and might pass away before the child has married. (Particularly during Pol Pot's era, parents justifiably feared that they would not be able to support or protect their children for long, especially daughters, and so pressured them to marry.) Women and men who agreed to an arranged marriage often say that they accepted their parents' decision because they trusted them to make the best choice and because they "owed that to them" for the sacrifices their parents had made over the years.

> [Female, age 45] When my mother asked me, did I want to marry him, I said, "It's up to you, Mom. I am your daughter. I am willing to

do what you say, even if you give me to a blind man." I believed totally in my parents. I trusted them completely.

For their part, parents say that "according to Buddhism," it is the parents' duty to arrange for their children's future before their own deaths. If parents see their children settle happily into a family of their own, parents say, they can die peacefully. Khmer even say that if parents die without fulfilling this duty, their souls will not find release.

> [Male, age 50] Parents want to see their children marry before they die. If the child is not married and the parent dies, their spirit will not rest peacefully. Their eyes will still be open, and the spirit will stay around the house to take care of their children. They say they can't close their eyes because they miss their children.
> Just like my neighbor. She lived two houses away from here. When she died, her spirit stayed around, and one family who lived nearby had a dream about that. In the dream, the soul of the mother said, "Oh, I miss my children so much. I can't go anywhere until my youngest daughter marries." [The daughter's wedding had been arranged before the mother died but had not yet taken place.]
> I was invited to that celebration as a good friend of the family, but the night before the wedding, I was so tired from work and I fell asleep on the couch. At 8:30 the next morning, the spirit of the mother came to wake me up. "Pho, come on, you have to go to my daughter's wedding to witness the ceremony of the ancestors (*phtŏem*)." So I had to hurry and rush over to their house to see that, even though it was already 10:00 by the time I got ready.
> A lot of people had dreams about that woman before her daughter's wedding, but after the wedding, nobody saw the mother anymore. After the wedding, her spirit could rest peacefully.

Beneath the surface of this parental concern lies the conviction that children who are married and comfortably settled are more likely to have the stability and disposition to care for an ailing or elderly parent. Parents hope that if they provide a large and expensive wedding, their children will remember and care for them in their final years. Wedding guests act as witnesses to the union, but they are also expected to ensure that the couple stays together, offering wisdom and advice to the couple if they experience marital difficulties. The larger the wedding, the more guests invited; hence, the more community members who will shoulder this important responsibility.

Weddings, then, are a form of social security and insurance against abandonment in one's old age (see also Hanks 1963:68). Parents often link these two themes quite explicitly. If others point out this connection, however, parents deny that they see the two issues that way. (According to Buddhist doctrine, people should give or make offerings with a pure heart and without any thought of compensation; this includes giving one's children in marriage.)

The following comments, for example, came from a widow whose twenty-year-old son ran away to live with his girlfriend in another state. I asked the woman, "What would you do if your son came to ask you to put on a wedding for him?" Here is her response:

> [Female, age 47] I would ask him, "Where is the money? Do you have the money?" No, I would not pay for that! It used to be that you could depend on your child to think of you, to care for you in your old age. Now they just forget about you like that [like my son did]. In the United States, it's no good. We cannot depend on our children here.

It is this functional logic of intergenerational reciprocity that is under particular strain in the Khmer American community today. Fewer and fewer Khmer marriages are arranged completely by parents; among eastern Massachusetts Khmer, the average appears to have fallen to less than one in five. In an increasingly common pattern, a young man and woman meet at school or at repeated social or religious functions. They fall in love and decide to marry. It is still critical, however, that the couple maintain the appearance of propriety and behave in a way that does not shame their families.

Within these altered circumstances, parents still make formal wedding arrangements, and young people continue to seek their elders' blessings (see also Ledgerwood 1990a:180). Few would attempt to stage a Khmer wedding without their parents' traditional knowledge and expertise—and extended social and financial support.

Considerations of filial piety, face, and status make marriage negotiations a source of significant conflict for Khmer American families. In either accepting the parents' choice of marital partner or in obtaining her parents' blessings for her own choice, the child fulfills her responsibility and indicates that she will continue to remember her parents in their old age and after death. Because unmarried young men are viewed as less responsible with regard to their filial obligations than young women, it is particularly important to ensure that sons marry "good girls," ones who will readily assume this supportive role. In the eyes of Khmer parents, however, "good girls" are in increasingly short supply in the United States. As a result, many, perhaps most, of the disputes that have arisen over marriage arrangements are ostensibly focused on the behavior of young women.

THE DOUBLE STANDARD

A majority of Khmer parents continue to have traditional attitudes about the comportment of young women, particularly where their own sons or daughters are concerned. Because of the prevailing double standard, people commonly blame women in virtually all cases of sexual misconduct, and, in a typically market-charged idiom, say that women "lose their value" when they violate sexual norms. By contrast, Khmer men remain uncompromised in such escapades. This double standard is clear in the well-known Khmer saying *"Satrey tae thlĕak knŏng phok chrŏam sâ'uy brachrăh khâl; ae mnŭh brŏh vĕnh thlĕak knŏng phok chrŏam, dauch mea neov pââ dâdael"* ("A girl who falls in the filth smells against the wind; a boy who falls in the filth is like gold, its color remains").

Many Khmer believe that because of a woman's more passionate nature, she is unable to control herself if she falls in love. One father graphically explained the dangerous potency of a young woman's sexuality by commenting, "An unmarried daughter is like spoiled meat *(săch sâvy)* in the house," attracting men as spoiled meat attracts flies.

> [Female, age 21] Cambodians think women can't control themselves when they are in love. So if they get pregnant, it isn't the man's fault. They blame only the woman, not the man.

> [Female, age 20] Cambodians believe that when a woman falls in love, she loves that guy 100 percent, and nothing else matters. She can't control herself. So if she falls in love, she should marry right away.

In contrast to this view of women, it is accepted that men are promiscuous by nature. A common Khmer proverb states, "Ten rivers can't equal [fill] one ocean." That is, even ten women cannot satisfy one man. Men joke about their sexual infidelities, saying, "A man can't eat *s'lăh mchou* (Cambodian sour soup) every day." Conversely, women are cautioned never to believe the words of a man: "Just as the stream never stops flowing, a man's promises should never be trusted" (see also Ledgerwood 1990a:111). Knowing of men's promiscuous nature, women who let themselves become involved with men are always considered to be at fault.

> [Female, age 50] We believe it's the girl's fault if she behaves inappropriately in front of a man. That's why the man is attracted to her and follows her. We accuse the girl, not the man. It's the girl who shows off her body. It's the girl who has to be firm, [who] has to stay away from men. It's her fault if the man is attracted.

Thus, although women are deemed the more passionate gender by nature, they are always expected to keep their passion under control and to avoid men who would compromise their virtue.

Both ethnographic reports and the memories of contemporary Khmer indicate that, to preserve this virtue, girls in Cambodia were subject to considerably more social supervision than they are in the United States (see chapter 4; see also Steinberg 1959; Ebihara 1974). Women often say of their youth, "We didn't know anything," "We were too shy," and "We didn't say anything." Unmarried women report they were barred even from seeing childbirth. Because of fears that knowledge of sex would encourage female promiscuity, most say they were told nothing about sex before marriage. One woman confided that she assumed that people married because the man needed someone to cook and keep house for him. Another thought that after marriage she would "just sleep next to her husband as she had slept next to her mother." Some said that the *achaa*'s wife or an elder relative "gave them some advice" on their wedding night, but it was not necessarily helpful.

> [Female, age 60] My older aunt said, "You have to respect your husband, the way he does something. You have to accept the way he does it and just keep quiet."
>
> [Female, age 50] The old people just told me, "You have to stay in the room with him. Don't get out from that room, and don't yell or anything to shame your family."

Not all young women were so timid and ignorant, of course. Pregnant brides were not unheard of, and young women sometimes ran away with their lovers or refused to marry the man of their parents' choice. Such themes are common in Khmer folklore and literature, as well as in popular songs and movies. Nevertheless, adults use such idealized memories of life in Cambodia as a standard against which they judge the behavior of Khmer American youth. The ideals sometimes stand in painful contrast with the changing realities that adults and youths now confront.

THE REPERCUSSIONS OF REPUTATION

Young women experience the tension between what Cambodia elders remember and the practical reality of the United States with particular force. There is a clear and often painful contrast between what they are expected to do and what they see their American counterparts doing.

For young women who misbehave, gossip *(ni'yeay daoem)* remains an important and potent sanction within the community. Adults assume that a young man and a young woman left to themselves will have sex ("If you give the ant sugar, he will eat it"). Rumors about a young woman seen with a particular young man are sufficient for community members to conclude that the two are "fooling around." The girl who is seen "hanging out" on the streets is talked about until word of her reputation finally reaches her parents. Teachers complain that female students whom schoolmates merely tease about having a boyfriend may not come to school for a week out of embarrassment.

> [Female, age 21] If people see you, they talk. They say, "I saw this girl at the movies [with a guy]." If they talk like that and the parents hear it, the parents will confront the girl when she comes home. They'll say, "I heard people talk bad about you, that you're going out with some guy and you're not even engaged or married and you let the whole world know! How could you? You're not supposed to do that. In order to go out, you have to be engaged first. You let the whole world see!"

> [Male, age 60] In Cambodia, girls never have boyfriends. Never. If you have a boyfriend *(sângsa)*, nobody will come to ask you to get married. If a girl has a boyfriend, people will spread the word, "This girl has a boyfriend," and then everybody is very afraid. Nobody will talk to her. Nobody will look at her. Sometimes the people will

cross the street so they don't meet her, and everyone talks behind her back, sometimes even to her face. That's why Cambodian parents here can't accept that kind of behavior at all.

Often, the first hint of a daughter's misbehavior results in a desperate parental effort to arrange her marriage. Sometimes the arrangements involve someone other than the (alleged) boyfriend. If parents hear even a rumor of misbehavior on the part of a friend or a relative's daughter, they may try to arrange a wedding for their own daughter "to prevent something ugly from happening."

[Female, age 19] Some parents arrange marriages just to get their daughter away from someone else. They may be afraid the girl will get pregnant because of her carelessness and the family name will be ruined. They are afraid that if the girl has a boyfriend, she will disgrace the family, and their reputation will go down.

Kan Tey's parents, for example, became very concerned about their daughter's behavior when she stopped coming home directly after school and started hanging around with "bad girls." Tey was seventeen at the time and a sophomore in high school. Her parents tried several different measures, including tying Tey to her bed after school. After all else failed, they arranged for her marriage to the son of a close friend from another city. Tey agreed to the engagement.

When the two families met for the *pchâb piek*, Tey's family agreed to pay for the wedding costs—some $6,000. Tey's mother felt that she had to be honest in the marriage negotiations and told the boy's mother that her daughter had already withdrawn from a previous engagement. The prospective groom's parents gave Tey and her family jewelry, food, and money. Tey's parents then charged a $3,000 deposit for the restaurant reception to a credit card, hoping to pay off the debt later with guests' contributions.

Tey soon dropped out of school in order to work and save money toward her wedding. Just two days before the wedding, however, a male classmate called her, urgently begging her to meet with him. She agreed, and he picked her up in a shiny new car near her parents' apartment building. As they drove through the city, he said he loved her and wanted to marry her. (Before this, Tey had no notion that he was even interested in her.) The couple ended up driving all the way to Rhode Island and stayed away for two nights.

When Tey finally called her mother to tell her she was all right, her mother was frantic. "What can we do? We cannot pay [back] the wedding costs! Come home!" Her parents feared that Tey's fiancé would be angry and take revenge on the family.

Fortunately, the family of Tey's new boyfriend was delighted that their son had found a bride; he was extremely shy and had never shown any interest in marrying. They agreed to pay for the cost of a wedding and even assumed the debt owed to the restaurant. The gifts from the *pchâb piek* were returned to the groom's side, and the spurned suitor was convinced not to cause any trouble. Later, at the wedding, members of the community and guests all remarked on how "good" the groom's family was to pay for the wedding under such circumstances.

In the case of Poh Nam, however, the boy's side was much less accommodating. Nam had gone away to college and had lived in the school dormitory, which made many people question her reputation from the start. When it was discovered that she had moved out of the dormitory to live with a boyfriend, people talked about it until the rumor finally reached Nam's parents. Nam's mother and aunt decided to visit the boyfriend's apartment early one morning to see if the rumor was true. When they arrived, they discovered Nam still in bed, though the boyfriend had already left. Confronted by her mother, Nam felt she had to tell the truth.

> [Female, age 23] When my mom confronted me, I couldn't lie to her. I told her the truth about having a boyfriend. Then my mother got really mad and slapped my face really hard. She grabbed one of my boyfriend's exercise weights and was going to hit me with it, but my aunt stopped her. My mom told me that if I hadn't slept with him yet, she wanted me to come home. I told her I already had. She said, "OK, then get married." She cried and cried.

The two families met to arrange the wedding, but a month later, Nam broke off the engagement because her fiancé didn't have a job and kept asking her for money. (He also acted disrespectfully to her parents and other family members, so no one was really unhappy to see him go.) Several months later, Nam met another young man, Buen, and they fell in love. Nam's parents were willing to accept their daughter's choice and were anxious for Nam to marry, but when Buen asked his parents to meet Nam's parents to arrange the wedding, his parents refused because of Nam's sexual history. Nam explained it this way:

> [Female, age 23] My boyfriend's mother is really against me. She pressured my boyfriend to propose to any girl, but not me. He wouldn't do it. He loves me. His mother doesn't like me because I used to have a boyfriend. Cambodians think that if a girl sleeps with a man, that's not a good girl. People say you shouldn't marry that kind of girl because if she agreed to sleep with you, then maybe she will sleep with another man! That's what people try to tell my boyfriend, but he doesn't care about that. He loves me!

Over the next year, in fact, Buen's mother tried to do everything in her power to keep the two apart. She took her son to numerous monk-astrologers *(krou teay)*, hoping they would convince him that marrying Nam was not his destiny and would lead to his unhappiness. When that failed, she tried sending Buen to California for six months to investigate the possibility of opening up a new business there. Nothing could change Buen's mind, though. Nam said that she and Buen rejected the idea of eloping, because "his parents would really lose face if we did that." Eventually, Nam became pregnant and Buen's parents were forced to agree to a wedding.

It is instructive to compare Nam's and Tey's situations. Tey had not yet finished high school; her boyfriend had only completed his general education diploma (GED). Nam, by contrast, had completed several years of college, and Buen was studying engineering on scholarship at a prestigious local university. In neither case was the woman's education (nor for that matter the man's education) an issue in the marriage negotiations, except negatively in Nam's case, because young women who go away to college are automatically suspected of promiscuity. Because of their subsequent pregnancies (Tey became pregnant a few months after her wedding), the women in both cases discontinued their schooling.

When negotiating a daughter's marriage, no parent actually tells her to quit school. In fact, Khmer parents constantly remind children to stay in school and get a good education. When face and family reputation are in jeopardy, though, education quickly becomes a secondary concern—particularly the education of young women. Although some women attend school even after they marry and may participate in special school programs (where available) when they become pregnant, few continue such involvement after a baby is born. Most young couples cannot afford child care, and supporting a family takes precedence over continuing an education.

As a result of social pressures to preserve female virtue, Khmer girls in the United States may actually be marrying at younger ages than girls typically did in Cambodia. Whereas in prewar Cambodia women reportedly married between the ages of eighteen and twenty-one or older (Ebihara 1968:488; Martel 1975:206), in the United States, sixteen- and seventeen-year-old brides are not uncommon.[10] Undoubtedly, pressures to preserve young women's virtue and family names are lowering the marital age, even though contrary pressures (such as the pressure to get an education so as to get a good job) could have elevated it.

Aside from causing young women to miss out on education, there have been numerous, painful examples of even more negative consequences of young women's being pressured into unwanted marriages. Nam, for example, describes what happened to her sister as a consequence of Nam's own behavior.

> [Female, age 23] After my mother found out that I had a boyfriend and had embarrassed the family, [that I had] broken family tradition, my parents convinced my sister to marry some guy. They were afraid that she would do what I did—have a boyfriend, get pregnant. My aunts told her, "His family owns a restaurant and they come legitimately to marry you. *Khpŭah mŭk*, like you are honored by these people to be asked in marriage." So my sister said OK.
>
> But now what kind of life does my sister have? She gets upset every day because my brother-in-law owes a lot of money, like close to ten thousand dollars on his credit card. If he sees something he wants, he just buys it. He gambles, too. And when he loses and needs money, he hits her if she doesn't give him her paycheck!

Pressured by their parents and anxious to conform to filial expectations, many young women agree to the marriages that their parents arrange. Then, feeling desperate, the daughters decide to "do something else."

> [Female, age 19] For Cambodians, if the parents say so, you have to do it. Parents push their daughters to marry. If the girl says no, the parents still push. She doesn't know what to do, so she finally says

yes. But after that, after she says yes, then that girl is really desperate and she has to decide something for herself.

In their desperation, some young women attempt suicide. What most do, however, is run away, either before or after the wedding.

This strategy, too, can incur high costs. If a woman is uncooperative, resists a husband's requests, or flees, the groom is widely regarded to have legitimate grounds for battering her, as he has invested a significant amount of money in bride-wealth and wedding costs. For example, Phat Moem reluctantly agreed to a marriage arranged by her parents to an older, wealthy Chinese Cambodian. After the wedding, however, she refused to have sex with him. He told everyone, "I paid for that," and he beat her so badly that she ended up in the hospital. When she was released, Moem did not return to her husband. She did not even talk it over with her parents. Instead, she ran away with another man.

As the number of such incidents increases, parents are discovering that they are the ones blamed—not only by their own children but also by the wider community—because they "pushed their daughter too hard and against her wishes." As a result, more and more Khmer parents concede that they must allow their children a more active role in marriage negotiations.

> [Female, age 47] In the U.S. now, parents have to listen to their daughters. In our country, the daughter has to listen to the parents. It's different now. If she says, "I love this man," we have to follow her, too. Because if I don't want to follow her, if I don't listen to her, a lot of girls in the U.S. run away from home to join their boyfriend. In the U.S., out of ten girls maybe eight will decide for themselves about the boys. Only two girls will listen to their parents. They don't care about their mother and father. In our country, girls usually have the heart to take care of their parents and siblings. Here, no.

> [Male, age 50] A lot of kids follow Cambodian culture and do what their parents say. Some others want to follow American culture. Their parents don't agree, but the parents have to change because their children have changed. The parents don't want to risk losing contact with their children [if] they decide to run away.

CONTESTED AND HYBRIDIZED IDEALS

It is important to emphasize that the degree to which Khmer women accept gender ideals varies. Some women have, in fact, managed to successfully resist pressures to conform to such ideals in far less dramatic ways.

In women's stories of prewar Cambodia, for example, there is evidence that some were already dissatisfied with and resistant to traditional gender norms. This was especially true of more urban and educated Khmer. Several middle-aged women from Phnom Penh report with some amusement, for example, that when they studied traditional female gender prescriptions *(chbab srey)* in high school, they and other women classmates were vocal in their criticism and enjoyed arguing with the more conservative male students in their classes. Women who had been pressured into unhappy marriages by their parents said they would never do the same to their own daughters. Other women (many of them widows or divorcées) who had fended for themselves against all odds during the Pol Pot era strongly resisted the idea of giving up their hard-won independence for any man.

In the United States, some young women have also managed to avoid or resist the severe constraints of traditional gender ideals. At least some young women have successfully followed their own interests, obtaining higher education, opening a business, or pursuing a career. What is interesting is that they seem to have done so by drawing on a distinctive characteristic of mature Khmer women.

Among older, married Khmer women, there has long been a distinct preoccupation with reestablishing an important measure of personal autonomy once the marriage relationship is secure. As described in earlier chapters, the individual's autonomy is a central theme in Khmer socialization. After several years of marriage, however, women typically begin to distance themselves from the shy restraint thought virtuous in young women. This more independent attitude is especially evident in the behavior of widows, divorceés, or women in second marriages. Whatever the ideals of their adolescence, mature women commonly display a more independent mien and occasionally even express open disregard for men. One long-married woman's comments about her marriage reflect this pattern.

> [Female, age 58] When I got married, the old people said, "You have to put your husband up high like that and always listen and obey him, because he is the head of the family." I was so afraid of him.

I was too shy to talk to him or even to look at him for the first three months of our marriage. We had relations, but I never looked at his face! But after I knew him, after a few years, I would only pretend to listen to him. [Even now,] if he's right, I follow him, but if he's wrong, I have to do what I think is right. I just pretend to listen to him and then do something else.

Khmer involvement with American culture seems to have reinforced this aspiration for personal autonomy among women, especially younger women. Now, they are applying the ideal to new ends. For example, they invoke it to justify personal ambitions.

This change underscores a broader point—what might initially seem like "Americanization" pure and simple is, in fact, a hybrid phenomenon. Khmer women are responding to their situation in the United States and are slowly changing Khmer gender ideals. They are partly doing so, however, by drawing on a subterranean theme in Khmer culture and gender relations.[11]

For example, Kha is just out of high school and is not interested in marriage yet; she wants to get a professional degree first. She saw her older sister, Ratha, give up a scholarship to a prestigious college because her mother insisted that she marry her boyfriend in the summer after her high school graduation. Ratha and her husband fought constantly and separated after only six months of marriage. Once she was divorced and free to lead her own life, though, Ratha went to college and got her bachelor's degree. She is now a high school guidance counselor. Kha says she would never marry before she is ready like Ratha did, but she wants to become a professional like her sister.

[Female, age 19] Ratha led the way for me and my younger sisters. She was the first one in my family to get a college degree and to be successful. I want to be successful like that. Some people called to ask my mother, do I want to marry their son? But when my mother asked me about that, I said, "No, I want to get my career first." I want to have my degree [in nursing] and then maybe get a job for a while. Then I will think about getting married. Then if I have a child or two children, I can take good care of them, help support them. I told my mom that, and she said, "OK, that's OK."

As this example suggests, gender norms and roles for Khmer women in the United States are complex. To an important degree, they are also precariously unstable. The depth and speed of change vary with social class and with people's degree of involvement in the Khmer community.[12]

Nonetheless, two interesting trends are emerging. The first is that some young women have temporarily renounced marriage and romantic involvement with men to pursue educational and career opportunities. Other Khmer view them as anomalous, but they seem to be accepted as long as they are perceived as virtuous and committed to their educational and professional goals. The second trend is that a good number of the young women who drop out of school to marry and have babies are now returning to school as soon as their children are old enough to be taken care of by relatives or friends. These young women say openly that they want their degree so they can help support their families with a better-paying job. Many of these women even insist that they want just one or two children—far fewer than Khmer women have traditionally had. Here indeed is evidence of changing gender roles.

TRADITION AND TRANSFORMATION

Khmer parents tend to view recent changes in young women's behavior, particularly sexual misconduct and intergenerational discord, as evidence of young people's Americanization and parents' loss of control over their children. In seeing events this way, however, parents sometimes forget that the tension evident in gender roles and marriage negotiations plays on familiar and long-existing themes in Khmer socialization and family relations—themes of the individual's autonomy on the one hand and concerns about family, face, and community on the other. Although these themes of autonomy and dependence are in some sense continuous with a prediasporic Khmer culture, they are being reproduced and transformed in a dramatically different social milieu. The environment is one in which Khmer are but one among many minorities in a decidedly different culture. These altered circumstances pose severe problems for the maintenance of Khmer gender ideals.

Khmer Americans have shown great ingenuity in devising arrangements that re-create traditions and relationships functionally equivalent to those that supported marital and gender ideals back in Cambodia. However great their effort, though, the context in which they now live exposes them to social pressures beyond their control.

Whether it is, most banally, their inability to control reception prices in Chinese restaurants, or, more profoundly, the influence of American notions of sexual freedom and romantic love, this effort to preserve traditional gender roles and marital relationships in a radically altered social environment has created as much disruption or destabilization as it has cultural "reproduction."

7

The Search for the Middle Path

Despite the best efforts of its elders, the Khmer community in the United States is beset by powerful centrifugal tensions. However much Khmer might have hoped to re-create a community in the United States that was oriented toward traditional Cambodian values and relationships, most Khmer are daily drawn into the broader and diverse ways of American society. This entirely untraditional situation poses a chronic and profound challenge to Khmer identity and cultural survival.

Khmer family relations particularly feel this tension, as children are pulled into American society faster than their parents and grandparents are. These social involvements have differentially affected community members' moral ideals and their sense of identity as Khmer and Americans. As a result, the older and younger generations espouse increasingly disparate values.

Both groups are aware of this growing gap. Older Khmer respond to this challenge by insisting on traditional morals—often remembering the way things were with a generous dose of romantic nostalgia. They often find, however, that those efforts fail or are simply ignored by their American-raised children.

Most Khmer in the metropolitan Boston area come from rural backgrounds and have little education. Well prepared for Cambodian village life, they have few resources for dealing with the social and economic challenges of urban life in the United States. Their employment opportunities have been limited to unskilled factory jobs, minimum-wage service employment, or piecework with poor benefits and little security. In an era of corporate downsizing and deindustrialization (especially in the Northeast), many have had to work overtime shifts or take multiple jobs to make ends meet.

Equally important, many people are still suffering from the physical and emotional scars of the Pol Pot terror, their flight from Cambodia, and their difficult and uncertain stay in refugee camps. Richard

Mollica and Russell Jalbert cite research indicating that as many as 20 percent of the Khmer who arrived as refugees in this country suffer from serious depression or other mental health problems (Mollica and Jalbert 1989:44); other studies have presented even higher figures (Portes and Rumbaut 1996:168–75). These psychological problems are often exacerbated by physical ailments and social pressures. As state-supported refugee and general assistance programs have been reduced or terminated, the plight of many of these individuals has only worsened.

THE STRUGGLE TO SURVIVE

Not surprisingly, adults who have been physically and psychologically traumatized by wartime and resettlement experiences may also encounter difficulties in parenting. Sam Ny's situation seems typical. She is forty-six years old and has two children, a boy of seventeen and a girl of fourteen. When I first spoke with Ny, she had recently separated from her husband.

Ny suffers from health problems, including liver disease, that leave her unable to work. She supports herself and the children with welfare, food stamps, and an occasional under-the-table job that does not even pay minimum wage. She recently received a notice that the rent on her two-bedroom apartment will increase from $500 a month to $675 at the beginning of the year. She has no idea how she will pay the difference.

Her husband is disabled, having been diagnosed with hepatitis, high cholesterol, and asthma. He cannot help the family financially. Sometimes, he even asks for money from their son, who works part-time as a bagger in a supermarket. He is also severely depressed because of his health and family situation, so he has been seeing a doctor at an outpatient psychiatric clinic. His behavior, Ny says, is antisocial and sometimes violent. She has just received a letter requesting that she appear with him in probate court for "dispute intervention." She is uncertain what the letter means and is afraid she will have to hire a lawyer, something she cannot afford.

In addition to these troubles, Ny worries about her children's education. They go to two schools that are far apart, because the family has had to move several times, and Ny has been unable to arrange for her daughter's transfer. She has received repeated notices from the schools that her children are not attending classes regularly, but she does not know what to do. Her fourteen-year-old daughter must leave home at 5:30 every morning, taking three buses to get to school. When it is cold outside, her mother says, her daughter cuts school and goes to the mall where there are lots of other teens. She and her girlfriends talk, play video games, and "forget about school." Ny explains it like this:

> I don't know what to do. I cannot control my children. When my daughter gets home, I hit her! I hit her because she gets home very late. My son hits his sister too, because he is really worried about her. Like I hit my daughter two days ago because I received the notice that she had not been attending school. I got really angry, and when my son saw that, he got angry too. So after I hit her, he hit her.

There are rumors that Ny's son is involved with a gang, but she denies them. She is happy with his behavior for the moment, because he is working part-time and can pay for some of his own expenses. She is not sure that he always attends school, though. She has tried talking with him about these issues, but she has no idea if he will do what she asks.

> There is nothing I can do. I am afraid my son has bad friends, and they ask him to go somewhere and do something bad, but I can't do anything. I talked with my son after I learned that he was skipping school. When he came home, I talked with him and told him to keep going to school and not get into trouble and don't go with those bad friends. I talked the way that parents talk to their sons, and he listened to me. But whether he will follow that or not, I don't know.

Ny's concern about her son is overshadowed by her distress about her daughter, who seems genuinely adrift. Sam Sarana was involved in a serious incident earlier in the summer, a result of her continued involvement with the "wrong kind of people."

> My daughter knows this girl, *a* Phal, who is now in a juvenile home. That girl dropped out of school; she quit because she was older than all the other students. She was involved in a gang, and she recruited children from the neighborhood to sell marijuana and cocaine. Once, I went to her apartment to look for Sarana, and when I knocked at the door, a child of thirteen or fourteen answered. Inside, I saw lots of children, young children, maybe six, eight, ten years old, but there were no adults there at all.

For children whose parents are demoralized with illness and financial problems, gangs offer an alluring sense of family and community. Khmer gangs organize themselves like extended families (Vigil 1993; see also Hart 1990, 1991). Junior members call senior members *bâng*, or "older sibling," to signal their respect. Younger members may be required to work under-the-table jobs and, as in Khmer families, to give their earnings to gang leaders to help pay for food and rent. Gang houses offer refuge to young runaways.

For the most part, gang membership is loosely structured. There are often only a small number of core members (Conly 1993). Other youth insist they are simply "hanging" together with friends. When disputes arise over territory or when a drug deal goes wrong, however, young people who are merely "hanging out" can find themselves in circumstances beyond their control.

Ny's daughter, Sarana, for example, was good friends with Phal's little sister, Sokha; they often hung around together with Phal. Ny tells us how one night Phal needed drugs, so she "sold" Sokha and Sarana to a man for twenty-five dollars.

> She sold the girls to get the money to buy two cigarettes. Not regular cigarettes—the kind with drugs. Phal told that guy, "I have two girls to stay with you, and you can do whatever you want to do with them!"
>
> When Sarana didn't come home that night and I couldn't find her, I called the police and told them my daughter was missing. They put the story and Sarana's picture on the TV. When Phal saw Sarana's photo, she telephoned the man who kidnapped the girls and told him to let the girls go and quickly run away. The police found the girls in an apartment in the morning. I don't know if the girls stayed the night with that guy or with Phal.
>
> The police took my daughter to a doctor. They told me that the doctor said she had not been raped or anything. When they called me and I went to pick Sarana up at the police station, I was so angry I lost control. I slapped her in front of the policeman and in front of the FBI. My husband's friend was there, and he grabbed me and said, "OK, that's enough. Don't hit her again. Your health is not good. You just got out of the hospital." But I think the police understood [how I felt]. They didn't say anything.
>
> I feel I cannot do anything to control my children. I would like them to go to a juvenile home like Phal. Maybe they would learn what it is like in that kind of prison. I want them to be trained to be good so they know how to behave!

If the reports of community leaders and social service workers are true, gang activity among Khmer youth has increased in recent years. What is most surprising is the increase in young women's participation. Although most young women do not live in gang houses, they signal their allegiance to a particular group by becoming sexually involved with male gang members and by fighting with women in rival gangs. Both behaviors obviously stand in stark contrast to traditional Khmer norms of femininity. This is but one more indication of the strains developing in family and gender roles, as Khmer find the traditional ways of doing things inadequate for the challenges of life in America.

GENERATIONAL DISSONANCE AND SEGMENTED ASSIMILATION

Portes and Rumbaut (1996) have suggested that for some recent immigrant groups, we can no longer assume a linear relationship between time spent in the United States and upward mobility. Portes (1995) coined the term *segmented assimilation* to describe three possible assimilation patterns. The first is the traditional model of upward assimilation; over time, the immigrant group advances economically and is integrated socially and politically into the middle class. The second pattern is one of *downward assimilation* into permanent poverty and the underclass. A third possibility is *selective acculturation* or *selective assimilation,* characterized by a strong ethnic enclave coupled with deliberate preservation of the immigrant culture; this can lead to rapid mobility into the middle class (Portes 1995, cited in Gibson 1997:438).

Portes and Rumbaut (1996) argue further that young people who do not have the support of a strong ethnic community or of parents equally engaged in the acculturation process face the possibility of *generational dissonance.* According to Portes and Rumbaut, "Generational dissonance occurs when second-generation acculturation is neither guided nor accompanied by changes in the first generation. This situation leads directly to role reversal in those instances when first-generation parents lack sufficient education or sufficient integration into the ethnic community to cope with the outside environment and hence must depend on their children's guidance" (241). Children at risk for generational dissonance are those who live in poor, urban neighborhoods; their neighbors and schoolmates are alienated native youth. Generational dissonance does not have to lead to poor school performance and downward assimilation, but it increases the likelihood of those results (Gibson 1997:440). Among Khmer, one sees evidence of such a pattern, but it has an important class dimension.

Although they constitute a minority among Khmer refugees, those from well-educated and middle-class backgrounds have moved into mainstream American culture with relative ease. Some others from less solidly middle-class backgrounds in Cambodia have also joined the ranks of the new immigrant middle class through hard work and education. Most of these individuals arrived as young adults and had at least some schooling in their homeland. They were well positioned to take advantage of ESL classes and job-training programs made available to them in the early years of resettlement. Some eventually managed to obtain a GED or even an associate's or technical degree from a community college. Many of these people now have social service positions within the Khmer American community; they are social workers, teachers, health providers, and job counselors.

The divide between the relatively small number of Khmer who are doing well and the much larger number who are struggling seems only to be growing. Ten years ago, Rumbaut and Ima (1988:78–79) noted an emerging but striking difference between a small group of "haves" and a much larger group of "have-nots" in the Khmer population. They predicted that the gap between the two groups would widen for some time, and they posited that human capital and social class resources would largely determine how well Khmer refugees adapted to American society. My observations of the Khmer population support both of those predictions.

EDUCATION AND UPWARD MOBILITY

Middle-class Khmer and those with middle-class aspirations have urged their children to take advantage of American educational opportunities. For these parents, the expectation of appropriate behavior extends to academic performance, and school failure is linked to the loss of face. Many of their children have gone on to become successful. They are among the Asian "whiz kids" one hears about in the media.

Kim Oeur's son Sonith, for example, has a full scholarship to Harvard University and hopes to become a doctor. His mother is a social worker, his father a plumber. Both parents came from middle-class families in prewar Phnom Penh and managed to finish several years of college before being evacuated to the countryside. Sonith's mother visits his dormitory every few days to give him moral support and home-cooked food and, not insignificantly, to remind him to stay away from young women.

Choen Saray only completed the equivalent of seventh grade in Cambodia. He managed nonetheless to teach himself English in the border camps, and he attended night school when he first arrived in the United States at the age of thirty-four. After only two years, he obtained his GED. He then went on to get a counseling certificate, which allowed him to work in a social service agency. Saray's son Tuen attends a private Christian high school on scholarship and hopes to be accepted next year at Boston College.

The children of Khmer parents who have limited social and economic resources conform less well to the stereotypes of the Asian "model minority" (see Costello 1987). Most of these parents deeply appreciate the importance of education for their children (see also Martin 1994). They just have difficulty translating this idealized appreciation into effective educational support. Other than urging their children to stay in school and to avoid gangs, these Khmer have great trouble providing the persistent parental reinforcement so vital for all children's academic success. The children's difficulties are compounded by a number of factors, including repeated changes of schools. It is not uncommon for Khmer families to move from school district to school district in search of cheaper housing, a better job, or a safer neighborhood. Young people may also be sent to live with relatives temporarily, either to alleviate financial pressures or to separate them from undesirable friends. In the process, children may be removed from a school with a bilingual or ESL program only to be placed in one that has no academic or language support program at all. They may miss weeks of school in the transition. Parents seem unaware of how these changes disrupt their children's education.

Most parents also neglect to provide the necessary resources for their children's school projects or homework; they do not buy books or materials, set aside a space for their children to work, or insist that the television be turned off during specific study hours. When I asked them, "Do you buy your child books?" they most often responded, "I would buy him a book if he asked for one." Most homes show little evidence of reading material in English or Khmer, other than the television guide and church or temple programs. In many homes, the television is left on all day.

In many cases, too, children at home have little or no supervision while parents work. Children left to their own devices or overseen by elder siblings often lack a structured schedule for playing, eating dinner, studying, and sleeping. When school personnel suggest spending more time with their children, these parents respond, "If we don't each work two jobs and overtime, then who will support the family? Who will pay the rent?"

Although parents say that schooling is important, they actually exhibit ambivalence toward their youngsters' academic lives. With young children, one sees evidence of this ambivalence when parents deny their youngsters permission to go on school outings and to do after-school activities, including special remedial programs. Children may not even be allowed to play at the homes of school friends; many young children reported never having been in a non-Khmer home. In both cases, parents stress that their youngsters should stay close to home—and under family control—when not in school. One might say, "The school has my children all day; after the school day is over, I want them close to me in my house." Another will explain, "My children spend all day at school and need time to relax and enjoy themselves at home and on the weekends." Parents expect children to play with their siblings and cousins: "He has his brother, why does he need to play with his friend?"[1]

As school demands increase in middle school and high school, so do parents' ambivalence and their alienation from the educational process and its officials. Whereas grade schools may have some bilingual personnel, such support programs for nonnative speakers become less common at the middle and high school levels.

For parents who speak little English, dealing with secondary school personnel is daunting. Some parents even find high school buildings off-putting, with their large, dispersed layouts. Parents report feeling confused and inadequate when they interact with high school teachers and administrators, so they rarely attend school meetings or conferences.

Subject matter in the upper grades also becomes increasingly remote from what parents perceive as relevant for life and the kind of employment that their children can likely secure. Algebra, biology, and world history, for example, strike most parents as unfamiliar and less critical for their children's future than basic math or English-language literacy.

Parents' lack of academic knowledge is a serious handicap to their children who are in high school. Whereas a young child may receive some assistance from parents or older siblings with simple addition, subtraction, basic reading, or writing, few teens have family members capable of helping them with advanced subject matter. Khmer teenagers fall farther and farther behind in their studies (see also Hopkins 1996).

At the same time, many families want a teenager to earn money, either to contribute to the family's income or to meet the teen's own financial needs. Informed by a view of the individual as having inherent talents and inclinations, many Khmer feel that when adolescents begin to fail in their schoolwork, it is more realistic for them to get a job than to pursue higher education.

The desire to get a job and begin earning money is particularly strong among Khmer young men, as is their alienation from school.

> [Male, age 17] Having money, a car—that's really important for Cambodian guys. And when you have a car, you have to pay for that. My friends, like the guys I know, skip a lot. School is boring for them, not fun. They don't have friends in school, because everybody they hang out with, all of their friends, skip too, so they don't have anyone to talk to in school. They go hang out and play billiards and bowl, drive around, eat at Burger King, spend money. Stuff like that.

Young men in particular report that there is little they can identify with in school. They feel "out of place," unable to keep up, and embarrassed to ask for help. Few are involved in sports. Most prefer to dress in the "gangsta" or "hip-hop" style associated with urban black and Hispanic males; Khmer young men wear baggy pants, hooded sweatshirts, and baseball caps. Some also wear colored bandannas linking them to local gangs. Such identifications obviously do not enhance academic success; rather, gangs' styles explicitly denigrate school achievement. As has been reported for poor and working-class youth in England, this resistance to educational values and school authorities only increases the likelihood that these youth will not acquire the skills with which to escape from the underclass (see Willis 1977).

When conflicts arise between Khmer parents and their Americanized children, few parents are able or willing to negotiate with the children. Their response to what they consider unacceptable behavior can seem unnecessarily harsh. Hamm Chen, a fifty-year-old widow whose only son left college to run away with and eventually marry his Cambodian girlfriend, cut off all communication with her son for months. She refused to accept his calls, changed her phone number to an unlisted exchange, and feigned a total lack of interest in his situation or whereabouts. The young woman her son married was actually a distant relation from a "good" and well-positioned family. She had a university degree and a stable job as a medical researcher. Even after several years passed and a grandchild was born, the grandmother maintained an icy attitude toward her son and his family, insisting that her daughter-in-law was "not a good person" because she had run off with her son. In response to my repeated inquiries about her new granddaughter, Hamm Chen claimed neither to recall the child's name nor to remember her age.

Khmer teenagers and social workers widely agree that families can best avoid major conflicts if the parents are willing to talk to their children and negotiate rather than simply command. Typically, when Khmer parents report that they have "talked with their children," particularly about matters of personal or family import, what they mean is that they lectured and the child listened quietly. For the child to say anything in response or to question a parental decision is considered disrespectful.

Many teens report feeling that in comparison with "American" parents, their own parents do not care about them, or not as much. For example, they point out, their parents do not ask about their school day or about the subjects they are studying. They also perceive that their American friends' parents are more demonstrative than their own; Khmer parents' affective reticence is particularly noticeable in their interactions with older children. Other teens complain that their parents only want them to work for them and do not allow them the freedom to do what they want.

Equally distressing, some parents find that, when they do attempt to talk, their children no longer listen. Khmer youth have caught wind of non-Khmer ways, and many parents are deeply uncertain about how to respond.

In one sense, of course, this generational strain is a familiar and inevitable aspect of newcomers' adaptation to U.S. life. For Khmer "have-nots," though, the situation seems intolerable. Not only are they poor and marginal to the larger society but they are also in danger of losing the most cherished element in their cultural patrimony—their children.

> [Female, age 36] In our culture, when a daughter or son reaches the age of eighteen years old, they have a duty to take care of their parents. But if they're Americanized, they leave the parents in the house without thinking about them at all—how hard they worked to raise them. They just leave their parents, and they don't look back.

It is just this fear that Khmer parents in the United States most commonly voice—that their children will abandon them in a strange land, leaving them to a lonely and destitute old age. Although most parents believe that academic achievement leads to economic success, many also feel that American schools encourage a style of individualism that destroys the family. Through the schools children are exposed to new and competing values—those of independence, self-assertion, competition, material achievement, and challenges to adults and authority in general.

These distinctly untraditional values are evident in the comments of Rem Doul, who has attended school in the United States since age twelve.

> [Female, age 24] In Cambodia, if my parents told me not to have a boyfriend, I would do what they said. There, if you do what your parents say, then everybody will say, "That's a good family, and you are a good girl," no matter how poor your family is. Good behavior, a good reputation, is the most important thing. But here, I don't care what people say. In America, what I like is that you do your thing, I do my thing. I don't care, because you don't give me money, I don't give you money, so we don't depend on each other. That's why I do whatever I feel like doing.

Similar attitudes emerge in the comments of Moem Sopha, a high school student who has been in the United States since age two.

[Female, age 17] My mother worries about my losing my customs or my identity. Anyway, I have! I mean, I didn't lose that much, but it's hard to face the two cultures. Like when I go to school, I have American friends, and I have to join them, to do what they do—go out, have fun, enjoy life.

As far as parents are concerned, the "new individualism" adopted by some Khmer youth is not that of Buddhist modesty and ascetic self-control but of egoistic autonomy and expressive individuality. Parents thus believe that although educational achievement may eventually result in a well-paid job, it also causes children to be concerned for no one but themselves, which is likely to lead to alienation from their families and community.

For the same reasons, community members tend to be suspicious of children who spend a lot of time alone studying. Studying is a solitary and largely invisible activity, unlike doing housework, working at a part-time job to help the family, or providing child care so that a parent can work; these are visible behaviors that win lots of approval. Moreover, the success that comes from studying, in the form of good grades or an eventual job (if it results in success at all), is mainly intangible and long-deferred.

This lack of immediate payoff partly explains why Khmer parents seem to downplay education in choosing a marriage partner for their children. Education is not regarded as an unambiguously positive element in a person. For many parents, higher levels of education increase the all-too-threatening possibility that young people will distance themselves from Khmer values. Education is double-edged indeed.

RELIGION AND CULTURAL ADJUSTMENT

Recent research on Southeast Asian refugees has argued that religion can be and often is an important resource for dealing with past trauma and adapting to a new homeland (Mollica and Jalbert 1989; see also Westermeyer 1973). In her book on Lao Buddhism in North America, Penny Van Esterik (1992) describes how Lao Buddhist ritual helps to affirm, adjust, and reproduce Lao cultural values. She argues that Lao Buddhism aids in cultural adaptation by re-creating the past and legitimating the present. Buddhism provides Lao individuals with social and psychological support and with an important sense of continuity, Van Esterik states; at the same time, it is versatile enough to allow a measure of change.

Most Khmer expect their religion to have capacities similar to those Van Esterik describes for Lao Buddhism. Although the temple has helped many Khmer adults adjust to American society, its ability to help Khmer youth adjust has thus far proved more limited. Many parents and Khmer leaders blame their children's problems on a lack of moral guidance and emotional support—support which they feel (whether justified or not) the temple provided back in Cambodia, where it played a critical role in the moral and intellectual training of Khmer youth.

In the United States, the monk's role as teacher and guardian has almost entirely disappeared, as far as many Khmer are concerned. There are no longer opportunities for young males to work as temple boys *(kaun sĕh vat)*, assisting and learning from the monks. Nor is any provision made now for the temple to receive delinquent youth; back in Cambodia, they would be sent to the monastery to develop discipline and virtue. As we have seen, few men today enter the monkhood even for a short time.

Elders worry—with good reason—that most Khmer American youth receive no formal Buddhist training. Indeed for some, Buddhism seems a foreign religion whose relevance for U.S. life is difficult to see. Elders wonder how Khmer Buddhism will survive in the United States. As they grow old and die, who will be left to recite the prayers and lead the rituals? Moreover, what impact will this development have on the morality and religiosity of Khmer youth?

> [*Achaa,* age 62] I worry about that, about the future of Buddhism here. While I am still alive, I can tell my children to follow Buddhism. But when I die, who will do that? Everybody is very busy here, supporting themselves and their families. I am worried about this. I am alive now, and I can talk to my children to tell them the Buddhist way. But if I die, nobody will talk about that. And my children may be careless about some point, and maybe my grandchildren won't follow Buddhism at all. Nobody will talk with them, nobody will care about Buddhism, and that will be the end of Buddhism here.

Recently, concerns like these have led some members of the metropolitan Boston Buddhist laity to make bitter criticisms of the temple leadership. They have accused certain monks of an inappropriate concern with money and good living and blamed them for the temple's inability to address Khmer youth's problems by introducing social and educational programs. Others, however, have been quick to come to the monks' defense.

> [Male, age 46] How can the monks have the courage and energy to spread Buddhism here? No one supports them! Like one group of *ta chah* (old men) scolded the monks and spread bad rumors. They said one was a former Khmer Rouge and killed somebody in Pol Pot time and has a wife and children in Cambodia. They said he spent money that was supposed to be used to build a temple in Cambodia on his family back home. Another monk, they say he is Vietnamese and not Cambodian at all. Nobody respects the monks! But my family knows their backgrounds. My father, my uncle—they knew them in Cambodia, so I support them.

In eastern Massachusetts, two factions have emerged in the face of this controversy. The first, a more conservative group, primarily consists of older monks and their supporters. This group openly acknowledges that it is more concerned with helping to rebuild Buddhism in Cambodia than with the future of Buddhism in the United States. To justify their resignation in the face of Khmer problems here, the leaders of this group even cite a well-known prophecy of Sammanak Kodam Buddha, to the effect that Buddhism will exist on this earth for just five thousand years.

> [Male, age 46] [In America], we have no money for programs to educate the young people. We can only do for ourselves, focus on ourselves. The young people don't want to come to the temple anyway. Their parents don't want to send them. There is a prophecy saying that Buddhism will die out in five thousand years, and I believe that it will die out like that. We can't do anything about that.

These Khmer insist that Buddhism is not intended to be a proselytizing religion. Indeed, they think it sinful to push religious understanding on a resistant individual.

> [*Achaa*, age 62] Buddha said to all of his followers, "If you want to get other people to understand and escape their suffering, you have to be very careful. If someone doesn't want to listen to you, if they don't have a sense about Buddha, you will never get that person to come close to you, so forget them. If you try to force them to listen, that's a sin (*băb*). Those people will say bad things to you, and you will get angry, and that's a sin."

Members of this conservative faction argue that older monks educated in rural Cambodian monasteries have little experience or religious reason to deal with the problems faced by Khmer American youth. The monks feel that their ability to address young people's problems here—drugs, gangs, illicit sex, and violence—is of little worth, compared with the good they can accomplish in Cambodia. In any case, they argue, such social problems are not temple concerns but are more appropriately handled by American social service agencies.

The second faction in this debate consists of lay leaders on the temple committee and their supporters, including a few younger and better-educated monks. They are particularly concerned with social and educational issues and want to create opportunities so that youth in this country can learn about Buddhism in an innovative and relevant way. They argue that the Khmer community in Massachusetts needs a larger temple to accommodate outreach programs in a safer and more accessible part of the city. They would particularly like to see the temple develop after-school programs for young people and programs that would attract and rehabilitate young gang members.

[*Achaa*, age 62] In Cambodia, the temple is a place for the young people even more than for the older people. The monks have a duty to get the kids to the temple, to teach them about Buddhism.

The influence of American Christian denominationalism on this second faction is obvious here. Indeed, representatives from this group quite openly compare the Buddhist temple to Christian churches, noting that the latter (including some seeking Khmer converts) offer youth fellowship programs and Bible study groups. With this model in mind, these Khmer argue that the temple cannot remain passive in the face of American society but must transform itself into an institution of educational outreach. This, they say, is the key to Khmer Buddhism's survival in the United States.

Struggles over temple finances and programs were not by any means unknown in Cambodia. Nor were debates concerning monks' appropriate role in society (see Lester 1973; Swearer 1981; Sizemore and Swearer 1990). In the United States, however, the stakes are much higher. Among other things, the debate here has now moved to the courts and involves legal procedures; the expense of those proceedings only further depletes temple resources. One recent dispute in a

Boston area temple reportedly cost the Buddhist community nearly twenty thousand dollars in legal fees. (These legal battles are not unique to the Boston community; they have also occurred in Khmer congregations in Pennsylvania, Rhode Island, Texas, Washington, and California.) This controversy has forced community members to reflect deeply on Buddhism's place in their children's education and on general issues of Americanization and adaptation.

The highly segmented quality of American life makes it difficult to sustain institutions that can provide ethical guidance and security throughout a person's life. In a single day in the United States, individuals may be involved with schools, government agencies, stores, public transportation, and medical establishments; all of these contribute to a person's life, but taken as a whole, they do not create an encompassing social affiliation or commonality of moral experience.

Faced with similar challenges, other minority and immigrant communities in the United States have built strong institutions—churches, temples, neighborhood associations, and so forth—that provide a moral anchor. Orthodox Jews, for example, have successfully constructed religious and social institutions that resist mainstream influences; despite the otherwise segmented nature of American life, these institutions provide a secure ground for practicing Jews to maintain a separate identity.

For many other Americans, however, including many immigrants, daily participation in the myriad institutions of American life makes it difficult to maintain such cultural insulation. In a recent study of civil society in America, sociologist Robert Wuthnow (1998) refers to the pervasive "porousness" of minority cultures in American life. By that, he means that community members are deeply involved in mainstream American institutions and only participate intermittently in their own culture. Something of this same quality seems to be developing among Khmer, particularly younger ones.

What we are seeing in the Khmer community is certainly consistent with other immigrants' patterns of religious change. As Jose Casanova (1993) has recently argued, the United States is the birthplace par excellence of religious denominationalism, whereby community and religious ties give way to a more deliberate and voluntaristic style of religious affiliation. Although denominationalism has long been characteristic of American society, it is more typical today, as the sanctioning restraints of "community" have disappeared for some.

It is likely that the association between Khmer identity and Buddhism will remain strong for some time, even as community members' exposure to doctrinal elements of Buddhism declines. Among Khmer adults in particular, the recent past seems to have strengthened the association between being Khmer and being Buddhist. There is evidence even from small, isolated Khmer communities without local temples that Khmer Americans are willing to spend considerable time and energy traveling to distant temples to celebrate important life-cycle celebrations and to attend religious ceremonies (Hopkins 1996).

There are also a host of media now available to community members, enabling new kinds of religious involvements; they can now see Khmer movies on video, listen to audiotapes that friends and relatives have made of religious ceremonies in Cambodia and the United States, and play tape recordings of monks who are reciting prayers and giving sermons. Although these new media have helped to convey information and images across national divides, they have not been able to provide what many Khmer elders feel they most need; more than mere images and information, they want sturdy social ties that constrain and direct their community's daily experiences.

For Khmer, the lack of community is strangely and powerfully disorienting. Although Cambodian villages by no means had the homogeneous and "mechanical" solidarity that Durkheim described, the institutions of *sângha* and neighborhood jointly exercised a profound influence on social interaction and moral discourse.

In America, Khmer encounter a radically different kind of social experience. Drawn out into urban American life, a few find pleasure or release in new freedoms and opportunities. Others, however, lament the fragmentation of their lives and the loss of a (remembered) ethical mutuality. Their uncentered experience tears at their sense of self on community, family, and individual levels.

THE SEARCH FOR THE MIDDLE PATH

The diasporic situation of Khmer in America vividly illustrates general moral processes in a culture. It shows how an individual's affiliation or identity with a community does not flow effortlessly or automatically from the mere fact of community membership. Even in traditional societies or in a relatively integral society such as prewar Cambodia, culture and community are not seamless wholes.

Each community carries with it the seeds of alternative or competing ways of being. In some societies, particularly those that anthropologists view as "traditional," one alternative typically dominates the others so thoroughly that most people can easily identify a "tradition." Even in these circumstances, though, there are glimpses of other ways—individuals who are slightly out of step with established norms or who may even resist them openly.

In a diasporic setting, such rival ways of being often explode on the scene with a visibility and force unseen in the "traditional" order. They do so because, as in the Khmer American community, the institutions and socialization that led most people to identify with the dominant cultural style are no longer intact. They now coexist with a plethora of institutions and alternative ways of being. This sort of situation has long characterized plural societies, particularly in times of change, but circumstances have made it far more widespread in our postmodern world.

The effects of such pluralization are felt most poignantly by parents watching their children grow and adapt to the larger society. Childhood and adolescence are when identity formation and moral education occur and when changes in identity and morality may be registered with greatest force. Elders and youths drift farther and farther apart across a generational divide. Many Khmer Americans now find themselves in just such a cultural drift.

The pull of American society on Khmer children and the lure of American styles and materialism are inevitable aspects of Khmer accommodation to the United States. American schools have exposed Khmer youth to new values, new choices, and new ways of being. The result is a clash of values and generations that most likely will irreversibly change the balance between karmic individualism and sociomoral relationalism—a balance that undergirded Khmer socialization for so long. The balance of autonomy and honor so central to Khmer ways has been thrown into disequilibrium.

The themes of autonomy and honor that lie at the heart of Khmer social ethics entail a morality that is both individual and relational. It is individual in that Khmer view the most essential qualities of a human "being" as uniquely individual, premised as they are on karma and rebirth. If this aspect of Khmer social ethics is individual, though, it is not individualistic in the Western, liberal sense of the term. In particular, it is not invoked as an ethical and ideological premise on which society and politics are thought to be ultimately founded.

On the contrary, social and political order for ordinary Khmer is based on a social ethics that is highly relational. The system is not merely hierarchical, as in some characterizations of traditional Indian caste ideologies, for example (Dumont 1970). Instead, it integrates elements of individual responsibility, mutual obligation, and status into a broader whole. In this sense, the Khmer system of social ethics more closely resembles that described by S. J. Tambiah in his pathbreaking study of Buddhism and ancestral belief in northeast Thailand (Tambiah 1970; see also Keyes 1977).

The broader political and societal institutions that once reinforced the Khmer social ethics system no longer survive in the United States. The Khmer genocide was so inhumane as to destroy the major social institutions of Khmer society, especially those premised on ideas of hierarchy. In the United States, Khmer now encounter powerful social institutions and a pervasive cultural ethic, neither of which is conducive to re-creating a Khmer community, religion, and ethical system.

The one exception to the disintegration of the Khmer social hierarchy has been the family. Even here, though, refugees have experienced serious difficulties. The larger society in which they now live is quite happy to support the institution of the family. Its primary political and educational institutions, however, do not endorse all features of the Khmer family. Thus, Khmer ideas of socialization, physical discipline, face-based obligation, and gender roles find only partial sanction in American society. The Khmer pattern of placing the family's interest and collective welfare above those of the individual is particularly problematic for Americans and for American schools. Khmer ideas and practices relating to female sexuality likewise clash with the more individualistic and permissive values of contemporary American society.

This conflict of values emerges with particular poignancy at Khmer American weddings, which otherwise provide the most elaborate and expansive expression of Khmer gender ideals. Here again, in improvising and relying on new social arrangements—Chinese restaurants, as well as American styles, services, and consumer goods—Khmer have exposed themselves to new social influences and, inevitably, to values that subvert tradition. Rather than merely reproducing marriage arrangements and notions of female virtue, Khmer have opened themselves to moral pressures quite different from those of the Cambodia they remember.

The disjuncture between Khmer ideals and the practical realities of American society has led some young people to question the expense of extravagant weddings. They complain that weddings are more about their parents' social standing than about the newlyweds' individual or shared welfare. In addition, some young people, particularly women, have begun to question the link between female virtue and family reputation. Finally, at least some parents have begun to realize that rising divorce rates and male desertion make extravagant marriages an expensive and unreliable guarantee of status and social security.

In these and other ways, Khmer community and elders are slowly relinquishing control over Khmer youth. The same process is giving rise, at times painfully, to more individualized and less honor-bound notions of sexuality, love, and virtue. At this point, the long-term implications of this development seem unclear.

At the very least, parents' all-consuming preoccupation with female virtue may well give way somewhat to arrangements in which young women have more lifestyle options. In pushing for such changes, many Khmer women may invoke American ideals of romantic love and freedom. Some may also look to their own history and culture, albeit perhaps with nontraditional interests. As they do so, they will find a heritage of female dignity and autonomy that can have new relevance for their lives in the United States. Here, as in so many spheres of Khmer American life, what may look like simple Americanization in fact entails a more complex dialectic between American horizons and Khmer ideals.

It seems likely that the relational, status-bound dimensions of Khmer social ethics will continue to encounter more severe problems in the United States than the individually grounded ethics of personal and karmic development. Even those elements of the latter perspective that are explicitly linked to Buddhist ideas will face problems, however, especially because Khmer Buddhist institutions are in jeopardy in the United States.

We are now witnessing a difficult and unfinished effort on the part of Khmer parents and youth to find a middle path *(phlauv kandal)* between the old and new: between the culture of American individualism and material success, on one hand, and Khmer Buddhism and filial responsibility on the other. This process of transposing and re-creating a culture is arduous. Under stressful circumstances, Khmer Americans must decide what is essential to their identity and what they can forsake. Such decisions are tough, and consensus is even harder to achieve. The outcome of the effort, however, will determine just what it means to be Khmer and American in years to come.

Even under the most favorable circumstances, it would be challenging for a migrant population to survive and thrive in a new homeland, particularly a population with a tradition as different from mainstream American culture as that of Khmer Buddhism. The challenge has been all the more daunting for a people shattered by warfare, genocide, famine, and flight. In light of all that the Khmer have suffered, the outside observer can only marvel at how much Khmer Americans have accomplished as individuals and as a community.

Notes

PREFACE

1. During the fifty or so interviews that specifically addressed issues of child socialization, I requested that the children be present during our meetings so that I could observe and note family interactions. In addition, I followed five families with children of various ages more intensively over a three-year period, observing their home life and interviewing parents and children at intervals of several months.

2. In a number of extremely moving personal accounts, Cambodians have documented their experiences under Pol Pot and the details of their escape to the Thai border (see Sheehy 1987; Criddle and Mam 1987; Pin 1987; Szymusiak 1986). See also several collections of oral histories of Khmer survivors (Nguyen-Hong-Nhiem and Halpern 1989; Welaratna 1993; Dith and DePaul 1997). In some cases, these accounts include descriptions of individual struggles to adapt to life in the United States. They typically supply little sociocultural analysis or ethnographic context, however.

A NOTE ON TRANSLITERATION

1. *Khmer* is an approximation of what Cambodians call their language and themselves, *khmae*. The overwhelming majority of people from Cambodia are ethnic Khmer. Individuals who are members of ethnic minorities from Cambodia also refer to themselves as *khmae*. Only when necessary do they specify their identity as, for example, *khmae cham* (Muslim Cambodian), *khmae chen* (Chinese Cambodian), or *khmae kraom* (ethnic Cambodian from South Vietnam). In this book, I use the terms *Khmer* and *Cambodian* to refer to both the people and the language of Cambodia.

CHAPTER 1

1. For a discussion of the internal politics of the Khmer Rouge, see Kiernan 1980; Vickery 1984; Chandler 1991.

2. Ablin and Hood (1987) attribute the small numbers of initial refugees to the feeling of many Khmer that their traditional peaceableness would prevail, but see Vickery 1984 for an alternative explanation.

3. See, for example, Vlahou 1988; Costello 1989; Coakley 1989.

4. Community leaders argue that census figures underestimate the num-

bers of secondary migrants to the area, as well as the numbers of illiterate Khmer who did not respond to the census.

5. These figures are based on 1990 federal census results (U.S. Bureau of the Census 1990) and the reports of community leaders.

6. This process of modernization has continued in Cambodia, as well (Kate Frieson, personal letter, spring 1996). In fact, some cultural developments in Cambodia may parallel those taking place in the United States. Khmer in the United States nevertheless look back to an idealized prewar Cambodia, comparing that (rather than the current situation in Cambodia) with their current American situation.

7. In a cognatic, or bilateral, kinship system, the individual recognizes kin relations on both the mother's and the father's sides, and both sides are treated equally.

8. See, however, Judy Ledgerwood's groundbreaking dissertation (1990a) on Khmer refugee women and representations of gender in traditional Khmer literature. See also the recent work by MaryCarol Hopkins (1996) on Khmer Americans in a midwestern city.

CHAPTER 2

1. Pali terms for Khmer religious concepts are more familiar to religious scholars than are their Khmer equivalents; both are provided where relevant.

2. Milada Kalab (1976:167) reported that during the Lon Nol period, some parents encouraged their sons to join monasteries in order to avoid being drawn into the fighting; however, this option was relatively short-lived.

3. Penny Van Esterik cites figures from the Committee for the Coordination of Services to Displaced Persons in Thailand, which identified forty member groups working in Thai refugee camps in 1988. Of the forty, twenty-one had a Christian affiliation, and one was Zen Buddhist. The Christian groups ranged from those like the Young Women's Christian Association, whose activities are not primarily religious, to groups like Youth with a Mission, whose activities are strongly evangelical and geared toward conversion. The religious groups' influence outweighed their relative numbers, however. Van Esterik writes, "The dominant Christian presence is very obvious to refugees, and the Christian groups have the most extensive resources and services" (Van Esterik 1992:21).

4. The Washington, D.C., temple is actually located in Silver Spring, Maryland, but community members always identify it as the "Washington, D.C., temple."

5. In fact, there was a hierarchy for each of the two orders of Buddhists in Cambodia: the smaller, more urban Thammayut and the larger, more populous Mohanikay order (Ebihara 1966:175; Kalab 1994:61).

6. There is also a "diasporic" council of monks that includes *bhikkhu* from countries with significant numbers of Khmer refugees: France, Australia, New Zealand, the United States, and Canada. In terms of enforcing particular rulings, however, this diasporic council faces even greater difficulties

than the North American council does. Peter Gyallay-Pap describes the diasporic council as "a vehicle for the exchange of views and to promote peace in Kampuchea" (Gyallay-Pap 1990:17). See also Milada Kalab (1994) for an interesting comparison of developing and administering Khmer Buddhist temples in France versus in North America.

7. This attendance pattern is not unlike that of Buddhists from other parts of Southeast Asia. In a Buddhist village in northeast Thailand, Tambiah found that 60 percent of male household heads and 48 percent of their spouses reported attending the temple only on major Buddhist holy days (1970:146). May Ebihara (1966) described a similar pattern among village Khmer in prewar Cambodia.

8. See Keyes and Daniel 1983 for an extended discussion of the concept of karma in Theravada Buddhist societies.

9. See Tambiah 1970 for parallels with ordination in northeast Thailand.

10. I was struck by the resemblance between this ceremony and the Hindu Javanese purification rites *(ĕntas-ĕntas)* that my husband and I had witnessed in the highlands of East Java (see Hefner 1985; Smith-Hefner 1990b).

11. In the U.S. community, the temple also facilitates such heterodox beliefs and practices by allowing them to be performed in the *wat*. Later in my fieldwork, I learned that a monk from a local temple had undergone a similar purification rite *(p'dâh kruoh)* in order to prepare his body for a serious operation.

12. Ghost stories, the subject of many of the films that Khmer enjoy, remain a favorite topic of conversation among young children, as well as adults. I first encountered them when I had just begun fieldwork at an elementary school. The children there asked me excitedly if I knew about "Bloody Mary." When I said no, they proceeded to tell me in hushed tones about a woman who died after an evening ESL class she attended at the school. The woman was ill from some mysterious disease and asked her teacher if she could be excused. The teacher thought she just wanted to leave early and pressed her to wait until the end of class. Mary dutifully waited. At the end of the class, she staggered into the girls' restroom and collapsed in a pool of blood. Now, the children told me, nobody wants to go into the girls' bathroom, because Bloody Mary's spirit is waiting there. In fact, one girl saw Mary's bloody face in the bathroom mirror.

13. A *krou* (related to the Indic term *guru*) is a specialist in a particular field of knowledge. Schoolteachers are *krou*, as are medical doctors and astrologers.

14. Mom Davy told the following story of her mother-in-law's attempts to change her son's feelings for Davy.

> [Female, age 45] My future husband was my classmate. He saw me in school and asked his mother to ask my parents about marrying me. (I never thought about him at that time. In fact, I really hated him, because he always spoke French to show off.) But his mother already had someone in mind as a daughter-in-law—her niece. He tried to argue with his mother, saying that

he loved his cousin as a relative, not as a wife. He asked her again and again, Would she go to speak with my parents?

His mother began to take him to different temples to try to get him to forget me. She took him to seven temples! Finally, at the seventh temple, there was a famous meditation monk who was also a *krou*. That monk could see into the past and the future. He gave the mother some kind of magic blessing water to take home to sprinkle on her son to make him forget his feelings for me. But it didn't work at all. He told his mother, "If I please you and marry my cousin, I will die." At that time, he stopped eating. After a week of fasting, he ended up in the hospital. On the fifteenth day, his mother came to see my parents to arrange the wedding.

15. Many Southeast Asians believe in the individual's susceptibility to soul loss and in ceremonies to recall the soul. See, for example, Hanks (1963) and Keyes (1977) on Thai; Laderman (1983) on Malays; Van Esterik (1992) on Lao.

16. Khmer are inconsistent in their translation of *vĕ'nhean* and *prâlŏeng;* they informally refer to both to mean "soul" or "spirit." Historically, the terms probably both referred to similar concepts; one *(prâlŏeng)* was an original Khmer term and the other *(vĕ'nhean)* came from Pali; see Keyes 1977:116.

17. Some Khmer even include Christ as an inhabitant of one of these lower levels of heaven. He, like other gods, has not yet achieved a Buddha's level of enlightenment.

18. The *Tripitaka* contains three books, each consisting of several volumes: the *Sutta,* which are "sermons and discourses of the Buddha"; the *Vinaya,* which are "rules for religious life"; and the *Abdhidhamma,* which is "commentary on the teachings of the Buddha" (Tambiah 1970:33; Lester 1973:12). These are considered the most authentic records of Buddha's teachings that his followers have collected and preserved.

19. One case that has created significant controversy in the Khmer American community is that of Băng Ousath, a man who entered the monkhood when he was in his late thirties, leaving behind his young wife and three small children. The case is controversial because Băng Ousath's wife, who married before completing high school, has been unable to work, and the family has subsequently gone on welfare. Many community members say that in this situation, it is inappropriate for a man to become a monk, because his first responsibility is to support his family.

20. Some young men, however, shave their heads, don monks' robes, and sleep at the temple for short periods (typically a day or two) when a close relative dies, as a means of making merit for the deceased's soul.

21. It is taboo, however, for a funeral *achaa (achaa yŏki)* to be involved in rituals other than funerals.

22. There are also monk-*krou*—usually monks with special healing powers. A small number of these monk-*krou*, however, become involved in black magic *(baek chvéng)*. Community members report that some monks become so powerful that other members of the order fear their abilities and do not dare to challenge them.

23. In contrast, *yeichi samatĕk* (meditation *yeichi*, or those who study and practice meditation) tend to be more middle-class and to have more education. Unlike the temple *yeichi*, the *yeichi samatĕk* are considered exemplary in their focus on preparing themselves for their next life through good actions and right thinking. In addition, they do not live at the temple with the monks, thereby avoiding any suspicion of sexual impropriety.

24. See Van Esterik's description of *Wan Sin*, the Lao Precept Day (1992:62–66).

CHAPTER 3

1. Childbirth itself is referred to as "crossing the Tonle Sap," Cambodia's "Great Lake" (Steinberg 1959:81).

2. Although a belief in the *mday daoem* is most widespread among rural Khmer, even educated, urban Khmer worry about "invisible spirits." The wife of a Phnom Penh engineer told the following story about her husband's anxieties regarding the *mday daoem* and his newborn son.

> [Female, age 40] When our first son was born, my husband, who was university educated and widely read in French, said it was not good for the baby to breathe in the carbon dioxide of his sleeping parents. He thought the baby should have fresh air to make him healthy. This was maybe the influence of French custom on his thinking. So for only two or maybe three months, my son slept next to me, and then we put him in a crib in a separate room. A maid slept near him on the floor, and a lamp was kept lit all night long. But my husband still worried about invisible spirits, and every night at 12:00, he would go into the room to check on his son, because he worried about the *mday daoem.*

3. *Kaun preah* ("angel children" or "Buddha children") are often particularly sensitive to spiritual imbalance and are said to be closely watched over by protector spirits. These children are born as a result of special offerings and prayers to the Buddha (typically because the mother has had trouble conceiving, has experienced a series of miscarriages, or has had several children die in infancy).

4. Khmer women friends urged me to take this precaution when I told them about my three-year-old daughter's make-believe friends, Sini and Chakra. Because my daughter had come up with what sounded like Southeast Asian names for her invisible playmates these women were convinced that she had been Southeast Asian in her previous life; after all, I had lived for an extended period in Southeast Asia. To be safe, they insisted, I should at least place a knife on the shelf above her bed.

5. *Prâkăk*, which means something like "apologize," actually refers to the apology made to the midwife.

6. A *m'kuob* ceremony can take place anytime in the first year.

7. The dual offerings symbolize the bond between the husband's and wife's families that the newborn represents.

8. For descriptions of similar ceremonies among the Thai, see Hanks 1963 and Van Esterik 1992.

9. Most Khmer children continue to sleep with their parents up to the age of five. Although parents' bedrooms often contain cribs, babies rarely sleep in them except for very short periods.

10. See Schieffelin and Ochs 1986 for an interesting cross-cultural comparison of dyadic and multiparty patterns in child socialization.

11. The Khmer Issarak, or "Free Khmer," were groups of armed guerrillas who sprang up across the Khmer countryside in the 1940s to fight for independence from the French (Shawcross 1979:47; Chandler 1983:176).

12. In a description of a Malay pregnancy ritual, Carol Laderman writes that hard-boiled eggs, "symbolic of birth," are used to denote a change in status (1983:89).

13. In the *prâkăk kaun* ceremony, the new baby may also be placed in a rice-winnowing basket. Hanks reports that in Thai birth rituals, the rice-winnowing basket is a central element, as well (1963:66).

14. This parental focus on "observing the child" should not be confused with an interest in internal psychological states. I agree with Marie Martin: "Psychology is nonexistent among the Cambodians. A mother does not try to understand the internal problems that motivate her infant's act, but rather the external reasons that might have provoked it" (1994:14). Nonetheless, parents are interested in what the child's behavior indicates about the child's previous-life status and, by extension, their own.

15. Hanks reports that in Northern Thailand, children born with some kind of defect cause embarrassment to their parents, because the defect is understood to be a sign of demerit. As a result, such children may be suffocated if born alive (1963:35). In the United States, for the same reason, Cambodian children born with birth defects may be abandoned or given up for adoption at the hospital. Those who are taken home are reported to be particularly susceptible to abuse.

16. For a discussion of cross-cultural modeling as a strategy in caregivers' interactions with young children, see Schieffelin and Ochs 1986.

17. Today in the United States, many Khmer wives continue to call their husbands "older brother" *(bâng)* and in return are called "younger sister" *(aun),* regardless of their relative ages. To some degree, a wife's behavior toward her husband is supposed to be modeled on that of a youth toward an elder, the younger deferring to the greater wisdom and authority of the one who "saw the sun rise first." The socialization practice in which the mother or caretaker adopts the child's point of view (e.g., using *pa* instead of *bâng*) in order to teach the child proper terms of address and respectful vocabulary is also prevalent among Javanese caretakers of young children (see Smith-Hefner 1988a, 1988b).

18. Even twins are differentiated in this way in Cambodia, with the one who was born first considered the elder.

19. In Java, for example, parents say that the ideal treatment of all children is continued indulgence. They insist that they "do not have the heart" to be harsh with or to deny their offspring (Geertz 1961).

CHAPTER 4

1. A similar contrast between reason and passion in conceptions of male and female exists in many areas of Southeast Asia (see, for example, Peletz 1996).

2. These asymmetrical conceptions of Khmer gender roles, however, coexist with others that emphasize the complementarity of male and female roles and even female power (see "The Moral Significance of Menarche" in this chapter; see also Ledgerwood 1990a).

3. See also Hanks 1963:68–70 on "binding rituals" and their significance.

4. It should be pointed out, however, that Khmer American parents do not always handle their children's exposure to sexual information consistently. For example, children's television viewing is often not well regulated if parents work long hours. Young people may therefore watch sexually explicit shows without their parents' knowledge. In other instances, children may be exposed to sexually explicit movies or videos that parents or older siblings view—under the assumption that children don't understand what's happening. The result is that young people may know quite a bit about sex but still be ignorant of basic physiological facts.

5. Hanks writes, "Contact with a woman's skirt, undergarments or menstrual blood completely negated any of a man's protective amulets" (1963:79).

6. Many elder Khmer still feel that it is extremely dangerous for a man to have sex with a menstruating woman; see also Ledgerwood 1990a.

7. Not only would it be unseemly for a young woman to have a birthday party and invite young men to "see her," but adolescent girls should also not allow their birthdates to be widely known. A prelude to marriage negotiations requires that the young woman's birthdate be taken to a fortune-teller to see whether it is compatible with the man's. Birthdates are also an essential ingredient in "love magic" *(tvoe senae)*.

8. Ortner (1974) and, more recently, Gilmore (1990) note the widespread nature of this pattern cross-culturally.

9. The concern with physical and mental strength among Khmer in this country is evidenced in the widespread popularity among men, particularly young men, of special tonics and herbal drinks *(tenam khmae)* reported to augment male powers *(kamlăng)*. A drink made of flavored soda and raw egg is especially popular and is widely available in Khmer American restaurants that young Khmer men frequent.

10. This focus on employability extends to participation in sports. Khmer parents see little obvious connection between sports and future employment possibilities and so discourage participation.

11. The contradictions inherent in Khmer conceptions of gender are not lost on Khmer youth; see chapter 6.

12. Even men who left the monastery late in life were considered desirable spouses. Whenever I found an older man married to a significantly

younger woman, the man usually turned out to have been a monk for some years before marrying.

13. "He who stole would be born and die 500 times before he could even grow up" (Hanks 1963:28).

CHAPTER 5

1. See Gibson 1988 and Gibson and Bhachu 1991 for a discussion of "noninterventionist educational strategies" among immigrant minorities.

2. Following the French system, Cambodian secondary school includes middle school *(collège)* and high school *(lycée)*.

3. See Mortland and Ledgerwood 1985 and Ledgerwood 1990b for more about Khmer patterns of patron-clientism.

4. Teachers complain that when youths become involved in gang activities in California or Hawaii, their parents routinely send them to live with relatives in Boston. The parents hope that their children will change their ways once they leave their delinquent friends. More often, say the teachers, they just become involved in Boston gangs.

5. Ouk, Huffman, and Lewis (1988:61) make a similar observation.

6. Political events in the summer of 1997, however, have once again delayed many individuals' plans to return to Cambodia.

7. See Jim Cummins's discussion (1979) of the transferability of skills from a first language into a second. In general, Cambodian parents believe that bilingual education will make their children literate in Khmer, as well as in English.

8. These were the grade point averages for the Southeast Asian students in Rumbaut's study (1989:169): Vietnamese, 2.97; Sino-Vietnamese, 2.88; Hmong, 2.78; Khmer, 2.64; and Lao, 2.57. Portes and Rumbaut (1996) report lower figures but do not include a breakdown comparing all five groups. In the same study, they report a dropout rate of 12.8 percent among Cambodian students in San Diego. This rate exceeds that of Mexican-origin students "who, along with Pacific Islanders, have the highest [dropout] rate in the school district" (205–6). Ethnographic studies conducted in the Northeast and Midwest (Smith-Hefner 1993; Hopkins 1996) support these findings, indicating that by middle school, many Khmer children begin experiencing serious academic difficulties; in high school, many drop out.

CHAPTER 6

1. The small number of Christian Cambodians and those who marry non-Khmer Christians hold their weddings and sometimes even their receptions at Christian churches.

2. See Nepote 1986; Ledgerwood 1990a. See also Watson (1991:259): "The use of women to represent cultural values and tensions is a common phenomenon in many societies."

3. "In the same manner, the first prince of Cambodia followed the daugh-

ter of the king of the Nagas who had given him his kingdom" (my translation from the French; Porée and Maspero 1938:214). Chandler (1983:13) also discusses the folk myth that explains the meaning of this gesture.

4. The ceremony described here is based on my ethnographic observation of eight Khmer American weddings. For earlier descriptions of Khmer weddings in Cambodia, see Aymonnier 1900; Porée and Maspero 1938; Ebihara 1968.

5. Most Khmer American restaurants are not large enough to accommodate the number of guests at a typical Khmer wedding reception. The Chinese restaurants that Khmer use for their receptions adapt their menus to Khmer tastes.

6. It seems unlikely, however, that the money was actually used to build the newlyweds a house, because previously in Cambodia and in the Khmer American community today, the couple typically moves in for a while with the bride's or groom's parents. As Ebihara (1968) described in her study of a Khmer village in 1959–60, there is an expressed preference for living with the bride's family, but factors such as space, the need for assistance, or simple economics may be the deciding issue in the end.

7. No matter which side actually pays, in order to maintain the appearance of propriety, the groom's side is always given credit for all the wedding costs whenever the *tlai tŏek dâh mday* is announced during public ceremonies.

8. Marie Martin notes a similar phenomenon in Phnom Penh before the war and among Khmer who have resettled in Paris: "Before 1975 feasts given at home or in restaurants were on such a grand scale as to shock people of modest means. Today, this practice continues in Paris, where weddings are sometimes celebrated with lavish displays that shock non-Khmers who are aware of the great difficulties inside Cambodia and in the border settlements controlled by the opponents. . . . The same hierarchy, based on external signs of wealth, remains" (1994:16).

9. In this and other engagement stories that older women tell, the woman often insists that she "hated" her fiancé before the wedding. Such claims seem to allow a woman to emphasize that she had an appropriate distance from the engagement process.

10. Judy Ledgerwood's study (1990a:267) of Khmer refugee women in six states notes a similar pattern. The tendency to marry younger may be exacerbated by a lower age of menarche for Khmer women in the United States.

11. Arguing along similar lines, in a recent volume on gender and development in Southeast Asia, Karim (1995) emphasizes the resilience and adaptability of Southeast Asian women in the face of modern economic development. Seeing the "inherently bilateral" nature of Southeast Asian gender roles as offering women strength and flexibility, she defines bilateralism as "the composite meanings of ideas of complementarity unaccompanied by statements of differential value, and the egocentricity of behavior allowing status differences to be reduced within and without local groupings" (37). Karim invites us to consider whether apparent inequalities in Southeast

Asian gender relations that seem concomitant with modern economic development are temporary or actually indicate serious, structural changes in male-female relations.

12. Although they were a distinct minority among the women I interviewed, the middle-class Khmer women I met were generally well educated and independent. These included several Khmer bilingual teachers, the head of a Khmer community organization, the organizer of a widows' group, a Christian minister, and a woman who obtained her master's degree in education from Harvard. Some of these women have managed to distance themselves from the social constraints of the Khmer community and subscribe to a distinctly untraditional lifestyle. A number have even married Chinese Americans or European Americans.

CHAPTER 7

1. In parents' defense, it should be noted that this intense concern with keeping children at home also results from well-founded fears. Khmer parents who live in poor, urban neighborhoods justifiably worry that their children's friends may be "bad influences," introducing their offspring to crime and drugs.

References

Ablin, David A., and Marlowe Hood.
    1987.   "The Path to Cambodia's Present." In *The Cambodian Agony*, edited by David A. Ablin and Marlowe Hood. Armonk, N.Y.: Sharpe.

Ang Choulean.
    1986.   *Les Êtres surnaturels dans la religion populaire Khmère.* Collection Bibliothèque Khmère, Série Travaux et Recherches. Paris: Cedoreck.

Atkinson, Jane, and Shelly Errington, eds.
    1990.   *Power and Difference: Gender in Island Southeast Asia.* Stanford, Calif.: Stanford University Press.

Aymonnier, Étienne.
    1900.   *Le Cambodge.* Vol. 1, *Le Royaume actuel.* Paris: Leroux.

Baker, Reginald P., and David S. North.
    1984.   *The 1975 Refugees: Their First Five Years in America.* Washington, D.C.: New TransCentury Foundation.

Banister, Judith, and Paige Johnson.
    1993.   "After the Nightmare: The Population of Cambodia." In *Genocide and Democracy in Cambodia: The Khmer Rouge, the United Nations and the International Community,* edited by Ben Kiernan. New Haven, Conn.: Southeast Asia Studies, Yale University.

Barth, Fredrik.
    1969.   Introduction to *Ethnic Groups and Boundaries: The Social Organization of Cultural Difference.* Boston: Little, Brown.

Beck, Ulrich, Anthony Giddens, and Scott Lash.
    1994.   *Reflexive Modernization: Politics, Tradition, and Aesthetics in the Modern Social Order.* Stanford, Calif.: Stanford University Press.

Bloch, Maurice.
    1989.   "From Cognition to Ideology." In *Ritual History and Power: Selected Papers in Anthropology.* London School of Economics Monographs on Social Anthropology, no. 58. London: Athlone.

Bourdieu, Pierre.
    1976.   "Marriage Strategies as Strategies of Social Reproduction." In *Family and Society: Selections from the Annales, Economies, Societies, Civilisations,* edited by Robert Forster and Orest Ranum. Baltimore: Johns Hopkins University Press.

1977. *Outline of a Theory of Practice.* Cambridge, Eng.: Cambridge University Press.

Caplan, Nathan, John K. Whitmore, and Marcella H. Choy.
1989. *The Boat People and Achievement in America: A Study of Family Life, Hard Work and Cultural Values.* Ann Arbor: University of Michigan Press.

Casanova, Jose.
1993. *Public Religions in the Modern World.* Chicago: University of Chicago Press.

Center for Applied Linguistics.
1981. *Teaching English to Cambodian Students.* Washington, D.C.: Center for Applied Linguistics.

Chandler, David P.
1983. *A History of Cambodia.* Boulder, Colo.: Westview.
1984. "Normative Poems *(Chbap)* and Pre-Colonial Cambodian Society." *Journal of Southeast Asian Studies* 15(2):271–79.
1991. *The Tragedy of Cambodian History: Politics, War and Revolution since 1945.* New Haven, Conn.: Yale University Press.

Coakley, Tom.
1989. "Burden of Arrival Felt by All." *Boston Sunday Globe,* January 22.

Conly, Catherine H.
1993. *Street Gangs: Current Knowledge and Strategies.* Issues and Practices in Criminal Justice Series. Washington, D.C.: National Institute of Justice.

Costello, Nancy.
1987. "Whiz Kids? Myth and Reality of Asian Students." *Lowell (Mass.) Sun,* September 9.
1989. "Refugee Wave Swells City's Asian Population." *Lowell (Mass.) Sun,* August 14.

Crawford, James.
1989. *Bilingual Education: History, Politics, Theory, and Practice.* Trenton, N.J.: Crane.

Criddle, Joan D., and Teeda Butt Mam.
1987. *To Destroy You Is No Loss: The Odyssey of a Cambodian Family.* New York: Anchor Books.

Cummins, Jim.
1979. "Linguistic Interdependence and the Educational Development of Bilingual Children." *Review of Educational Research* 49(2): 222–51.

DeVos, George.
1975. "Ethnic Pluralism: Conflict and Accommodation." In *Ethnic Identity: Cultural Continuities and Change,* edited by George DeVos and Lola Romanucci-Ross. Palo Alto, Calif.: Mayfield.

Dith Pran, and Kim DePaul.
1997. *Children of Cambodia's Killing Fields.* New Haven, Conn.: Yale University Press.

Dumont, Louis.
    1970.   *Homo Hierarchicus.* Chicago: University of Chicago Press.
Dunnigan, Timothy.
    1986.   "Processes of Identity Maintenance in Hmong Society." In *The Hmong in Transition,* edited by Glenn L. Hendricks, Bruce T. Downing, and Amos S. Deinard. New York: Center for Migration Studies.
Ebihara, May M.
    1966.   "Interrelations between Buddhism and Social Systems in Cambodian Peasant Culture." In *Anthropological Studies in Theravada Buddhism,* edited by Manning Nash. Cultural Report Series, no. 13. New Haven, Conn.: Southeast Asia Studies, Yale University.
    1968.   *Svay: A Khmer Village in Cambodia.* Ph.D. diss., Columbia University. Ann Arbor, Mich.: University Microfilms.
    1974.   "Khmer Village Women in Cambodia." In *Many Sisters: Women in Cross-Cultural Perspective,* edited by Carol Matthaisson. New York: Free Press.
    1985.   "Khmer." In *Refugees in the United States: A Reference Handbook,* edited by David W. Haines. Westport, Conn.: Greenwood.
    1987.   "Revolution and Reformulation in Kampuchean Village Culture." In *The Cambodian Agony,* edited by David A. Ablin and Marlowe Hood. Armonk, N.Y.: Sharpe.
Ebihara, May M., Carol A. Mortland, and Judy L. Ledgerwood, eds.
    1994.   *Cambodian Culture since 1975: Homeland and Exile.* Ithaca, N.Y.: Cornell University Press.
Ebrey, Patricia B.
    1991.   Introduction to *Marriage and Inequality in Chinese Society,* edited by Rubie S. Watson and Patricia B. Ebrey. Berkeley: University of California Press.
Ehrman, Madeline E.
    1972.   *Contemporary Cambodian: A Grammatical Sketch.* Washington, D.C.: Foreign Service Institute.
French, Lindsay C.
    1994.   *Enduring Holocaust, Surviving History: Displaced Cambodians on the Thai-Cambodian Border, 1989–1991.* Ph.D. diss., Harvard University. Ann Arbor, Mich.: University Microfilms.
Geertz, Clifford.
    1960.   *The Religion of Java.* New York: Free Press.
Geertz, Hildred.
    1961.   *The Javanese Family.* Glencoe, Ill.: Free Press.
Gibson, Margaret A.
    1988.   *Accommodation without Assimilation: Sikh Immigrants in an American High School.* Ithaca, N.Y.: Cornell University Press.
    1997.   "Conclusion: Complicating the Immigrant/Involuntary Minority Typology." In *Ethnicity and School Performance: Complicating the*

Immigrant/Involuntary Minority Typology. Theme Issue, *Anthropology and Education Quarterly.* 28(3):431–37.

Gibson, Margaret A., and Parminder K. Bhachu.
    1991. "The Dynamics of Educational Decision Making: A Comparative Study of Sikhs in Britain and the United States." In *Minority Status and Schooling: A Comparative Study of Immigrant and Involuntary Minorities.* New York: Garland Publishing.

Giddens, Anthony.
    1991. *Modernity and Self-Identity: Self and Society in the Late Modern Age.* Stanford, Calif.: Stanford University Press.

Gilmore, David D.
    1990. *Manhood in the Making: Cultural Concepts of Masculinity.* New Haven, Conn.: Yale University Press.

Glendon, Mary Ann, and David Blankenhorn, eds.
    1995. *Seedbeds of Virtue: Sources of Competence, Character and Citizenship in American Society.* Lanham, Md.: Madison Books.

Gombrich, Richard F.
    1988. *Theravada Buddhism: A Social History from Ancient Benares to Modern Colombo.* New York: Routledge.

Gombrich, Richard F., and Gananath Obeyesekere.
    1988. *Buddhism Transformed: Religious Change in Sri Lanka.* Princeton, N.J.: Princeton University Press.

Gordon, Linda W.
    1987. "Southeast Asian Refugee Migration to the United States." In *Pacific Bridges: The New Immigration from Asia and the Pacific Islands,* edited by James T. Fawcett and Benjamin V. Carino. New York: Center for Migration Studies.

Gorgoniyev, Iuri A.
    1966. *The Khmer Language.* Moscow: Nauka.

Gosling, David L.
    1984. "Buddhism for Peace." *Southeast Asian Journal of Social Science* 12:59–70.

Gyallay-Pap, Peter.
    1990. *Khmer Monk Education in the Thai Border Camps (A Situation Report, Program Report, and Background Article and Bibliography on Khmer Buddhism).* Amherst, Mass.: Khmer-Buddhist Educational Assistance Project.

Hanks, Jane R.
    1963. *Maternity and Its Rituals in Bang Chan.* Ithaca, N.Y.: Southeast Asia Project, Cornell University.

Hansen, Anne R.
    1988. "Crossing the River: The Secularization of the Khmer Religious World View." Master's thesis, Harvard Divinity School.

Hart, Jordana.
    1990. "Cambodian Refugees Preyed on by Gangs." *Boston Sunday Globe,* July 15.

1991. "Lowell Takes on Cambodian Gangs: Community Musters to Root Out Violence." *Boston Globe*, October 29.

Hawk, David R.
    1987. "International Human Rights Law and Democratic Kampuchea." In *The Cambodian Agony*, edited by David A. Ablin and Marlowe Hood. Armonk, N.Y.: Sharpe.

Hefner, Robert W.
    1985. *Hindu Javanese: Tengger Tradition and Islam*. Princeton, N.J.: Princeton University Press.
    1990. *The Political Economy of Mountain Java: An Interpretive History*. Berkeley: University of California Press.

Hopkins, MaryCarol.
    1996. *Braving a New World: Cambodian (Khmer) Refugees in an American City*. Westport, Conn.: Bergin and Garvey.

Huffman, Franklin E.
    1970a. *Cambodian System of Writing and Beginning Reader*. New Haven, Conn.: Yale University Press.
    1970b. *Modern Spoken Cambodian*. New Haven, Conn.: Yale University Press.

Indra, Doreen M.
    1987. "Social Science Research on Indochinese Refugees in Canada." In *Uprooting, Loss, and Adaptation: The Resettlement of Indochinese Refugees in Canada*, edited by Kwok B. Chan and Doreen M. Indra. Ottawa: Canadian Public Health Association.

Kalab, Milada.
    1976. "Monastic Education, Social Mobility, and Village Structure in Cambodia." In *Changing Identities in Southeast Asia*, edited by David Banks. The Hague: Mouton.
    1994. "Cambodian Buddhist Monasteries in Paris." In *Cambodian Culture since 1975: Homeland and Exile*, edited by May M. Ebihara, Carol A. Mortland, and Judy L. Ledgerwood. Ithaca, N.Y.: Cornell University Press.

Kammerer, Cornelia A.
    1990. "Customs and Christian Conversion among Akha Highlanders of Burma and Thailand." *American Ethnologist* 17(2):277–91.

Karim, Wazir Jahan.
    1995. "Bilateralism and Gender in Southeast Asia." In *'Male' and 'Female' in Developing Southeast Asia*, edited by Wazir Jahan Karim. Oxford: Berg.

Kelley, Barbara R.
    1991. *Cambodian Childrearing Practices and Beliefs*. Ph.D. diss., Boston University. Ann Arbor, Mich.: University Microfilms.

Kelly, Gail P.
    1986. "Southeast Asians in the United States." In *Dictionary of Asian-American History*. New York: Greenwood.

Keyes, Charles.
- 1977. *The Golden Peninsula: Culture and Adaptation in Mainland Southeast Asia.* New York: Macmillan.
- 1984. "Mother or Mistress but Never a Monk: Buddhist Notions of Female Gender in Rural Thailand." *American Ethnologist* 11(2):223–41.
- 1990a. "Buddhism and Revolution in Cambodia." *Cultural Survival Quarterly* 14(3):60–63.
- 1990b. "Buddhist Practical Morality in a Changing Agrarian World: A Case from Northeastern Thailand." In *Ethics, Wealth, and Salvation: A Study in Buddhist Social Ethics,* edited by Russell F. Sizemore and Donald K. Swearer. Columbia: University of South Carolina Press.

Keyes, Charles F., and E. Valentine Daniel.
- 1983. *Karma: An Anthropological Inquiry.* Berkeley: University of California Press.

Kiernan, Ben.
- 1980. "Conflict in the Kampuchean Communist Movement." *Journal of Contemporary Asia* 10:75–118.
- 1986. *Cambodia: The Eastern Zone Massacres.* Documentation Series, no. 1. New York: Center for the Study of Human Rights, Columbia University.
- 1990. "The Genocide in Cambodia, 1975–1979." *Bulletin of Concerned Asian Scholars* 22(3):35–40.

Kinsey, J. David.
- 1987. "The 'Concentration Camp Syndrome' among Cambodian Refugees." In *The Cambodian Agony,* edited by David A. Ablin and Marlowe Hood. Armonk, N.Y.: Sharpe.

Kleinman, Arthur.
- 1988. *Rethinking Psychiatry: From Cultural Category to Personal Experience.* New York: Free Press.

Knoll, Tricia.
- 1982. *Becoming Americans: Asian Sojourners, Immigrants, and Refugees in the Western United States.* Portland, Oreg.: Coast to Coast Books.

Laderman, Carol.
- 1983. *Wives and Midwives: Childbirth and Nutrition in Rural Malaysia.* Berkeley: University of California Press.

Lambeck, Michael J.
- 1993. *Knowledge and Practice in Mayotte: Local Discourses of Islam, Sorcery, and Spirit Possession.* Toronto: University of Toronto Press.

LeBar, Frank M., Gerald Hickey, and John K. Musgrave.
- 1964. *Ethnic Groups of Mainland Southeast Asia.* New Haven, Conn.: Human Relations Area Files Press.

Leclère, Adhémard.
- [1899] 1975. *Le Buddhisme au Cambodge.* New York: AMS Press.

Ledgerwood, Judy L.
- 1990a. *Changing Khmer Conceptions of Gender: Women, Stories, and the Social Order.* Ph.D. diss., Cornell University. Ann Arbor, Mich.: University Microfilms.
- 1990b. "Portrait of a Conflict: Exploring Changing Khmer-American Social and Political Relationships." *Journal of Refugee Studies* 3(2):277–91.

Lester, Robert C.
- 1973. *Theravada Buddhism in Southeast Asia.* Ann Arbor: University of Michigan Press.

Mabbett, Ian, and David Chandler.
- 1995. *The Khmers.* Cambridge, Mass.: Blackwell.

Marcucci, John L.
- 1986. *Khmer Refugees in Dallas: Medical Decisions in the Context of Pluralism.* Ph.D. diss., Southern Methodist University. Ann Arbor, Mich.: University Microfilms.

Martel, Gabrielle.
- 1975. *Lovea: Village des environs d'Angkor—aspects démographiques, économiques, et sociologiques du monde rural Cambodgien dans la province de Siem-Réap.* Paris: Publication de l'École Française d'Extrême-Orient.

Martin, Marie Alexandrine.
- 1994. *Cambodia: A Shattered Society.* Berkeley: University of California Press.

Massachusetts Department of Education (MDE).
- 1976. *Two Way.* Boston: Bureau of Transitional Bilingual Education and the Bureau of Educational Information Services, Commonwealth of Massachusetts.
- 1987. *The Condition of Massachusetts Transitional Bilingual Education Programs: Annual Report.* Boston: Bureau of Transitional Bilingual Education, Commonwealth of Massachusetts.
- 1988. *October 1 Report.* Boston: Bureau of Data Collection, Commonwealth of Massachusetts.

Massachusetts Office for Refugees and Immigrants (MORI).
- 1988. *Refugees and Immigrants in Massachusetts: A Demographic Report.* Boston: Executive Office of Human Services, Commonwealth of Massachusetts.

Mauss, Marcel.
- [1925] 1966. *The Gift: Forms and Functions of Exchange in Archaic Societies.* New York: Norton.

Ministry of Education.
- 1965. *La Femme Cambodgiènne.* Phnom Penh: Ministry of Education.

Mollica, Richard F., and Russell R. Jalbert.
- 1989. *Community of Confinement: The Mental Health Crisis in Site Two (Displaced Persons Camps) on the Thai-Kampuchean Border.* Alexan-

dria, Va.: Committee on Refugees and Immigrants, World Federation for Mental Health.

Mollica, Richard F., Grace Wyshak, and James Lavelle.
    1987. "The Psychosocial Impact of War Trauma and Torture on Southeast Asian Refugees." *American Journal of Psychiatry* 144(12):1567–72.

Mortland, Carol A.
    1994. "Khmer Buddhists in the United States: Ultimate Questions." In *Cambodian Culture since 1975: Homeland and Exile*, edited by May M. Ebihara, Carol A. Mortland, and Judy L. Ledgerwood. Ithaca, N.Y.: Cornell University Press.

Mortland, Carol A., and Judy L. Ledgerwood.
    1985. "Refugee Resource Acquisition: The Invisible Communication System." In *Cross Cultural Adaptation: Current Approaches*, edited by Young Tun Kim and W. B. Gudykunst. Newbury Park, Calif.: Sage.

Narada, Thera.
    1990. *Buddhism for Beginners: The Life of the Buddha.* 3 pts. Hampton, Minn.: Minnesota Cambodian Buddhist Society.

Nepote, Jacques.
    1986. "La Place ambigue du genre dans la société Cambodgiènne." Paper presented at the Social Science Workshop on Kinship and Gender in Cambodia, Laos, and Vietnam, De Kalb, Ill., July.

Nguyen-Hong-Nhiem, Lucy, and Joel M. Halpern, eds.
    1989. *The Far East Comes Near: Autobiographical Accounts of Southeast Asian Students in America.* Amherst: University of Massachusetts Press.

Ortner, Sherry.
    1974. "Is Female to Male as Nature Is to Culture?" In *Woman, Culture, and Society*, edited by Michelle Rosaldo and Louise Lamphere. Stanford, Calif.: Stanford University Press.
    1989. *High Religion: A Cultural and Political History of Sherpa Buddhism.* Princeton, N.J.: Princeton University Press.

Ouk, Mory, Franklin E. Huffman, and Judy Lewis.
    1988. *Handbook for Teaching Khmer-Speaking Students.* Folsom, Calif.: Folsom Cordova Unified School District, Southeast Asia Community Resource Center.

Peak, Lois.
    1991. *Learning to Go to School in Japan: The Transition from Home to Preschool Life.* Berkeley: University of California Press.

Peletz, Michael G.
    1996. *Reason and Passion: Representations of Gender in Malay Society.* Berkeley: University of California Press.

Phillips, Herbert P.
    1965. *Thai Peasant Personality: The Patterning of Interpersonal Behavior in the Village of Bang Chan.* Berkeley: University of California Press.

1969. "The Scope and Limits of the 'Loose Structure' Concept." In *Loosely Structured Social Systems: Thailand in Comparative Perspective*, edited by Hans-Dieter Evers. Cultural Report Series, no. 17. New Haven, Conn.: Southeast Asia Studies, Yale University.

Piker, Steven.
    1975. "Changing Child Rearing Practices in Central Thailand." *Contributions to Asian Studies* 8:90–108.

Pin Yathay.
    1987. *Stay Alive, My Son.* New York: Free Press.

Ponchaud, François.
    1977a. *Approaches to Khmer Mentality.* Washington, D.C.: Cambodian Apostolate, Pastoral Care of Migrants and Refugees, National Conference of Catholic Bishops.
    1977b. *Cambodia: Year Zero.* New York: Holt, Rinehart and Winston.

Porée, Guy, and Evéline Maspero.
    1938. *Moeurs et coutumes des Khmèrs.* Paris: Payot.

Portes, Alejandro.
    1995. "Segmented Assimilation among New Immigrant Youth: A Conceptual Framework." In *California's Immigrant Children: Theory, Research, and Implications for Educational Policy*, edited by Rubén G. Rumbaut and Wayne A. Cornelius. San Diego: Center for U.S.-Mexican Studies, University of California.

Portes, Alejandro, and Rubén G. Rumbaut.
    1996. *Immigrant America: A Portrait.* 2d ed. Berkeley: University of California Press.

Refugee Resource Center of the Committee on Migration and Refugee Affairs. October 1981–March 1982. *Cambodian Cluster Project: Final Report.* Report prepared for the Office of Refugee Resettlement, Department of Health and Human Services. Washington, D.C.: Government Printing Office.

Rumbaut, Rubén G.
    1989. "Portraits, Patterns, and Predictors of the Refugee Adaptation Process: Results and Reflections from the IHARP Panel Study." In *Refugees as Immigrants: Cambodians, Laotians, and Vietnamese in America*, edited by David W. Haines. Westport, Conn.: Greenwood.

Rumbaut, Rubén G., and Kenji Ima.
    1988. *The Adaptation of Southeast Asian Youth: A Comparative Study.* Report prepared for the Office of Refugee Resettlement, Department of Health and Human Services, by the Southeast Asian Refugee Youth Study, Department of Sociology, San Diego State University. Washington D.C.: Government Printing Office.

Schieffelin, Bambi, and Elinor Ochs, eds.
    1986. *Language Socialization across Cultures.* New York: Cambridge University Press.

Schwartz, Theodore.
    1978. "Where Is the Culture? Personality as the Distributive Locus

of Culture." In *The Making of Psychological Anthropology*, edited by George D. Spindler. Berkeley: University of California Press.

Scott, George M., Jr.
  1987. "The Lao Hmong Refugees in San Diego: Their Religious Transformation and Its Implications for Geertz' Thesis." *Ethnic Studies Report* 5:32–46.

Shawcross, William.
  1979. *Sideshow: Kissinger, Nixon and the Destruction of Cambodia*. New York: Simon and Schuster.

Sheehy, Gail.
  1987. *Spirit of Survival*. Toronto: Bantam.

Shweder, Richard A.
  1991. *Thinking through Cultures: Expeditions in Cultural Psychology*. Cambridge, Mass.: Harvard University Press.

Shweder, Richard A., Manomohan Mahapatra, and Joan C. Miller.
  1987. "Culture and Moral Development." In *The Emergence of Morality in Young Children*, edited by Jerome Kagan and Sharon Lamb. Chicago: University of Chicago Press.

Sizemore, Russell F., and Donald K. Swearer, eds.
  1990. *Ethics, Wealth, and Salvation: A Study in Buddhist Social Ethics*. Columbia: University of South Carolina Press.

Smith-Hefner, Nancy J.
  1988a. "The Linguistic Socialization of Javanese Children in Two Communities." *Anthropological Linguistics* 30(2):166–98.
  1988b. "Women and Politeness: The Javanese Example." *Language in Society* 17(4):535–54.
  1990a. "Language and Identity in the Education of Boston-Area Khmer." *Anthropology and Education Quarterly* 21(3):250–68.
  1990b. "The Litany of 'The World's Beginning': A Hindu-Javanese Purification Text." *Journal of Southeast Asian Studies* 21(2):287–328.
  1993. "Education, Gender, and Generational Conflict among Khmer Refugees." *Anthropology and Education Quarterly* 24:135–58.
  1994. "Ethnicity and the Force of Faith: Christian Conversion among Khmer Refugees." *Anthropological Quarterly* 67(1):24–37.
  1995. "The Culture of Entrepreneurship among Khmer Refugees." In *New Immigrants in the Marketplace: Boston's Ethnic Entrepreneurs*, edited by Marilyn Halter. Amherst: University of Massachusetts Press.

Spiro, Melford E.
  1967. *Burmese Supernaturalism: A Study in the Explanation and Reduction of Suffering*. Englewood Cliffs, N.J.: Prentice Hall.

Stafford, Charles.
  1995. *The Roads of Chinese Childhood: Learning and Identification in Angang*. Cambridge, Eng.: Cambridge University Press.

Steinberg, David J.
- 1959. *Cambodia: Its People, Its Society, Its Culture.* New Haven, Conn.: Human Relations Area Files Press.

Strand, Paul J., and Woodrow Jones, Jr.
- 1985. *Indochinese Refugees in America: Problems of Adaptation and Assimilation.* Durham, N.C.: Duke University Press.

Swearer, Donald K.
- 1981. *Buddhism and Society in Southeast Asia.* Chambersburg, Pa.: Anima Books.

Szymusiak, Molyda.
- 1986. *The Stones Cry Out: A Cambodian Childhood, 1975–1980.* New York: Hill and Wang.

Tambiah, Stanley J.
- 1970. *Buddhism and the Spirit Cults of Northeast Thailand.* Cambridge, Eng.: Cambridge University Press.

Tapp, Nicholas.
- 1989. "The Impact of Missionary Christianity upon Marginalized Ethnic Minorities: The Case of the Hmong." *Journal of Southeast Asian Studies* 20:70–95.

U.S. Bureau of the Census.
- 1990. *Census of Population and Housing, 1990.* Prepared by the State Data Center, Massachusetts Institute for Social and Economic Research. Amherst: University of Massachusetts.

Van Esterik, Penny.
- 1982. "Laywomen in Theravada Buddhism." In *Women of Southeast Asia,* edited by Penny Van Esterik. De Kalb: Center for Southeast Asian Studies, Northern Illinois University.
- 1992. *Taking Refuge: Lao Buddhists in North America.* Tempe: Program for Southeast Asian Studies, Arizona State University.

Vickery, Michael.
- 1984. *Cambodia: 1975–1982.* Boston: South End.
- 1990. "Cultural Survival in Cambodian Language and Literature." *Cultural Survival Quarterly* 14(3):49–52.

Vigil, James Diego.
- 1993. "Gangs, Social Control, and Ethnicity: Ways to Redirect." In *Identity and Inner-City Youth: Beyond Ethnicity and Gender,* edited by Shirley Brice Heath and Milbrey W. McLaughlin. New York: Teachers College Press.

Vlahou, Toula.
- 1988. "A New Wave of Immigrants: Cambodian Influx Threatens to Overwhelm Services." *Lowell (Mass.) Sun,* March 6.

Watson, Rubie S.
- 1991. "Afterword." In *Marriage and Inequality in Chinese Society,* edited by Rubie S. Watson and Patricia B. Ebrey. Berkeley: University of California Press.

Welaratna, Usha.
- 1993. *Beyond the Killing Fields: Voices of Nine Cambodian Survivors in America.* Stanford, Calif.: Stanford University Press.

Westermeyer, Joseph.
- 1973. "Lao Buddhism, Mental Health, and Contemporary Implications." *Journal of Religion and Health* 12:181–88.

Whitaker, Donald P., ed.
- 1973. *Area Handbook for the Khmer Republic (Cambodia).* Washington, D.C.: American University.

Whiting, Beatrice, and Carolyn Pope Edwards.
- 1988. *Children of Different Worlds: The Formation of Social Behavior.* Cambridge, Mass.: Harvard University Press.

Whitmore, John K., Marcella Trautmann, and Nathan Caplan.
- 1989. "The Socio-cultural Basis for the Economic and Educational Success of Southeast Asian Refugees (1978–1982 Arrivals)." In *Refugees as Immigrants: Cambodians, Laotians, and Vietnamese in America,* edited by David W. Haines. Westport, Conn.: Greenwood.

Willis, Paul.
- 1977. *Learning to Labor: How Working Class Kids Get Working Class Jobs.* Westmead, Eng.: Saxon House Press.

Wood, Susan P.
- 1983. *Cambodian Families in a Refugee Processing Center: Parental Attitudes and Childrearing Practices.* Providence: Rhode Island Group Health Association.

Wuthnow, Robert.
- 1998. *Loose Connections: Civic Involvement in America's Fragmented Communities.* Cambridge, Mass.: Harvard University Press.

Yang Sam.
- 1987. *Khmer Buddhism and Politics from 1954 to 1984.* Newington, Conn.: Khmer Studies Institute.

Index

abandonment, parental fear of, 79–80, 81, 91, 96
Ablin, David A., and Marlowe Hood, 2, 3, 6, 8, 209n2
achaa (ritual specialist), 51–53, 212nn21, 22; and meditation, 31; role at *bâng-skaul*, 61; role at exorcisms, 38; role on Precept Day, 56–57; role at *sâng khåtean*, 60; role at weddings, xi, 159–65 (*see also* weddings)
achievement, educational, 18. *See also* education, and performance of Khmer youth
adaptation, 19
address, norms of, x, 84–86, 87–88, 94, 130, 139–41; under Khmer Rouge, 2, 140. *See also* respect
adolescence, x–xi, 94, 100–106, 109–11, 195. *See also* puberty
altar, 31, 68
Americanization, 96, 184, 185, 202, 206
ancestors, 161, 163; wrath of (*méba kåch*), 72, 158, 163. *See also* spirits, ancestral
Ang Choulean, 38
ângkǎǎ (the organization), 2
areca flowers (*pka slaa*): symbolism of, 164; use in wedding ceremony, xi, 161–62
Asian-American experience, xvi
Atkinson, Jane, and Shelly Errington, 18
autonomy: of the child, 77, 84; theme of, in Khmer Buddhism, 19; theme of, in Khmer socialization, 154–55, 204; of women, 183, 206
Aymonnier, Étienne, 217n4

Baker, Reginald P., and David S. North, 9
Banister, Judith, and Paige Johnson, 5, 8, 134
Barth, Fredrik, 33
base people, 2
Beck, Ulrich, Anthony Giddens, and Scott Lash, 15

bilingual education, 133–34, 193; parental attitudes toward, 18, 135–38, 142–46
birth, 64, 68; customs, 72–73; premonitions of, 66; of sons and daughters, 96–97, 106
birth control. *See* sex education
birthdays: first, 72–74, 89, 214n13; sixteenth, 104–5, 215n7
"Blessings of Ordination," 112–13
Bloch, Maurice, 13
Boston / Suffolk County, 9
Bourdieu, Pierre, 13, 15, 153, 170
boys: breast-feeding of, 97; and dating, 110; and education, 108–9, 195–96; and puberty, 109–11; raising of, 107–9; and rationality, 110; rules for (*chbab proh*), 106–7. *See also* sons
Brahma, 163
breast-feeding, 97–98
bride-wealth, 19, 152–53, 157, 167–71
Buddha, 30, 43–44, 56; life story of, 44–45; prophecy of, 200; teachings of (*dhamma*), 45–46
Buddhism (Theravada): and Cambodian identity, 16, 32–33, 199, 203; core beliefs, 34–41; doctrine of, 13, 19; and education, 123, 201; and gender, 111–13; official national religion of Cambodia, 21, 28; during Pol Pot era, 2; "practical," 13, 37, 62; as practiced by Khmer, 16; and proselytization, 100; and socialization, 65, 111–15; and spirit beliefs, 37–38 (*see also* spirit beliefs; spirits)
Buddhist University, Phnom Penh, 27, 28

Cambodia, 5
Cambodian Buddhist Association of Massachusetts, 25
Cambodians in eastern Massachusetts, 10–11
Caplan, Nathan, John K. Whitmore, and Marcella H. Choy, 12, 144, 149

Casanova, Jose, 202
ceremonies, home, 52, 101, 114. *See also* weddings, description of home ceremony
Chandler, David P., 1, 4, 5, 99, 126, 209n, 214n11, 216n3
chbab proh. *See* rules for boys
chbab srey. *See* rules for girls
Chinese: cultural influences, 12; tradition, 13
ch'noun tŭm (big offering). *See* engagement
Christianity, 16, 216n1; conversion to, 23, 32–33
Church, Christian: influence of, 201; and refugee camps, 23, 210n3; and resettlement, 24
cluster communities, 9. *See also* community
community, 20, 26, 187, 202, 203–7; Boston Khmer, 10, 11–12; and socialization, 65, 87. *See also* secondary migration
Costello, Nancy, 209n3, 193
council of monks (*kanak sâng*), 27–29, 210n6
Crawford, James, 133
Criddle, Joan D., and Teeda Butt Mam, 209n2
cultural discontinuity, 16, 18
culture: and adaptation, 16; and ambivalence, 19; and identity, 132
Cummins, Jim, 216n7

dating, 110, 154, 177–78
daughters, 106, 110, 121; ritual responsibilities of, 111. *See also* girls
death, 35–36, 78, 80, 112; *bângskaul* ceremony for the dead, 60–61; preparations for, 46–47, 173. *See also* reincarnation
deference: to elders 85; to monks 85. *See also* respect
Democratic Kampuchea (D.K.), 2
destiny, 78, 82–83, 180; and schooling, 146–47, 149. *See also* fate
DeVos, George, 33
dhamma, 45–46. *See also* Buddha, teachings of
discipline, 18, 70, 89–91, 95, 115–20; and education, 123, 144–45; and face, 119–20
Dith Pran, and Kim DePaul, 209n2
dreams, 173; and childbirth, 66; and reincarnation, 80
dropping out of school, 178, 180–81, 216n8

Dumont, Louis, 205
Dunnigan, Timothy, 32

Ebihara, May M., 2, 6, 12, 22; on Buddhism, 21, 29, 31, 32, 34, 48, 49, 62, 109, 210n5, 211n7; on education, 123, 127; on family relations, 89, 90; on gender 96, 100, 101, 111, 176, 181; on Khmer refugees, 8, 9; on spirits, 58, 72; on weddings, 151, 159, 168, 217nn4,6
Ebihara, May M., Carol A. Mortland, and Judy L. Ledgerwood, xix
Ebrey, Patricia B., 153
education: and ambivalence, 193–98, 141; and destiny, 147–49; and discipline, 144–45; and economic advancement, 124; and gender ideology in Cambodia, 124–28; 192–93; of Khmer elders, 11, 129; and performance of Khmer youth, 144, 216n8, 147–49. *See also* schooling
Ehrman, Madeline E., 138, 139
elders, 31, 46–47, 55, 84, 95, 187
employment: of parents, xiii; and resettlement, 10, 135, 187; socialization of boys for, 108–9, 150
engagement, 155–59; *ch'noun tŭm* (big offering), 157–59; intermediaries, 155–56; *pchâb piek* (setting the word), 157; representatives, 158. *See also* marriage, arrangements
English: in Cambodian schools, 126; lessons for adults, xiii; use in interviews, xii; use among Khmer Americans, 135, 141, 194
ESL (English as a Second Language), xiii, 24, 193; in Boston schools, 133–34
ethnographic methods: participant observation, xiv; use in research, xii; and reflexivity, xiv
exorcism. *See* purification ceremony

face (*mŭk môt*), 17, 65, 86, 192; and adolescence, 94; and marriage, 155, 180, 181; and morality, 92–93; and physical punishment, 119–20. *See also* reputation
family, 12, 86, 92, 96, 120, 205; under Khmer Rouge, 2; reputation, 120–22
fate (*veasna*), 37, 40–41. *See also* destiny
father-child relationship, 77, 90–91
filial responsibility, 17, 18, 95–96, 114–16; and marriage, 172, 174, 181

Four Noble Truths, 46
French: colonialism and Khmer education, 125; independence from, 126; language, 126
French, Lindsay C., 7
"French schools," 125
Frieson, Kate, 210n6

gangs, 216n4, 189–91, 195, 201
Geertz, Clifford, 98
Geertz, Hildred, 75, 214n19
gender: ideals, 98, 154, 175–77, 182–86, 217n11, 218n12; relations, 18; and religious roles, 35; and ritual responsibilities, 97–98, 111, 215nn2,9. *See also* education, and gender ideology in Cambodia
generational dissonance, 187, 191–92
generational reciprocity, 62
ghosts (*khmaoch*), 37, 40, 211n12. *See also* spirits
Gibson, Margaret A., 216n1, 191, 192
Gibson, Margaret A., and Parminder K. Bhachu, 216n1
Giddens, Anthony, 15
gifts, 115; engagement, 156, 157–58; wedding, 166–67, 169–70
Gilmore, David D., 215n8
girls: breast-feeding of, 97–98; socialization of, 96–106; and virtue, 105. *See also* rules for girls
Glendon, Mary Ann, and David Blankenhorn, 14
Gombrich, Richard F., and Gananath Obeyesekere, 31, 60
Gordon, Linda W., 8, 9
Gorgoniyev, Iuri A., 138, 139
Gosling, David L., 23
gossip, 88, 177–78
groom service, 159
Gyallay-Pap, Peter, 22, 24, 210n6

haircutting, 160
Hanks, Jane R.: on beliefs surrounding childbirth, 66, 213n8, 214nn13,15; on gender, 111, 215nn3,5; on parent-child relationship, 79, 83, 174
Hansen, Anne R., 64, 73, 103, 104
Hart, Jordana, 190
Hawk, David R., 22
health, 188
heaven (*thansuo*), 43, 44, 212n17
Hefner, Robert W., 16, 211n10, 160, 170
hell, 30, 36, 42–43, 44, 83, 112

Hindu gods, 44. *See also* Brahma
Hinduism, 34
Hmong, refugees, 8, 12; educational attitudes of, 149; educational performance of, 144. *See also* Christianity, conversion to
Hopkins, MaryCarol, 195, 203, 210n8, 216n8
Huffman, Franklin E., xix, 138, 139
husband-wife relationship, 214n17, 163, 164, 176, 183–84

identification, moral, 14–16
identity, 12–14, 19, 154, 198, 203; and reflexivity, 15; and tension, 65
Indian influence, 12
individualism: and adaptation, 198, 204–6; within Buddhism, 13, 19–20, 61–62, 65, 205; and educational attitudes, 149–51, 198, 204–5; of Khmer, 13, 17, 94. *See also* autonomy
Indra, Doreen, 16
indulgence: and discipline, 117; in socialization, 17, 64, 75, 77; withdrawal of, 82, 89–91, 92
infants: care of, 67–77; differences between male and female, 97–98
in-laws, 159
intergenerational conflict, 150, 187, 197, 204
intergenerational reciprocity, 94, 174. *See also* filial responsibility
investigation of marriage partners (*soeb suo*), 155–56
invisible mother (*mday daoem*), 69–70, 71, 74, 213n2
Issarak, 78, 214n11

Judgment, Day of, 30, 42. *See also* hell

Kalab, Milada, 21, 57, 109, 125, 210nn2,5,6
Kammerer, Cornelia A., 33
Karim, Wazir Jahan, 217n11
karma (*kam*), 13, 34–35, 41, 42; and retribution, 36, 83; and social inequalities, 35; and socialization, 77; and suffering, 36–37
kǎthěn (ceremony to give new robes to the monks), 35
Kelley, Barbara R., 17, 64, 75
Kelly, Gail P., 9
Keyes, Charles F., 12; on Buddhism, 20, 32, 35, 37, 55, 62, 205; on the concept

Keyes, Charles F., (continued)
of the soul, 42, 212nn15,16; on karma, 13, 37; on the monkhood, 109, 112; on the Sangha, 28, 50
Keyes, Charles F., and E. Valentine Daniel, 211n8
Khmer Rouge: accusations of being, 25; destruction of the sângha, 22; factions in, 3, 209n; takeover of Phnom Penh, 1–3; treatment of Khmer, 3–5, 7
Kiernan, Ben, 3, 5, 209n1
kinship, 151, 210n7; and descent, 12–13
Kleinman, Arthur, 14
Knoll, Tricia, 5, 8
krou (teacher/specialist), 41, 53–54, 70, 81; *krou teay* (astrological specialist), 40, 156, 180; teacher spirit, 68–69. See also teachers

Laderman, Carol, 212n15, 71, 214n12, 98
Lambeck, Michael J., 16
language, Khmer: and hierarchy, 138–41; and identity, 137–38, 141; literacy, 129, 136–38, 143; policy under Pol Pot, 2; and social status, 84–86; socialization, 84–86; transcription of, xvii, xix–xx; use in interviews, xii; writing, 139
Lao: Buddhism and adaptation, 198–99; educational performance, 144; refugees, 12
LeBar, Frank M., Gerald Hickey, and John K. Musgrave, 12
Leclère, Adhémard, 12, 83
Ledgerwood, Judy L., 210n8; on discipline, 117; on education, 127, 128; on gender, 99, 100, 104, 176, 215n2, 216n2; on Khmer weddings, 174, 217n10; on patron-clientism, 216n3
Lester, Robert C., 29, 44, 47, 201, 212n18
literature, Khmer, 138
Lon Nol, 3; government, 1
love, 174, 175, 186, 206; magic (*twee snae*), 40, 103, 211n14

Mabbett, Ian, and David P. Chandler, 12
Marcucci, John L., 53
marriage: age for women, 181, 217n10; arrangements, 171–75, 178, 179; parental responsibility for, 173
Martel, Gabrielle, 181
Martin, Marie Alexandrine, 4, 17, 86, 95, 99, 123, 139, 193, 214n14, 217n8
Mauss, Marcel, 107
mday daoem. See invisible mother

meditation, 26, 31, 41, 46, 213n23
medium, 40, 67
menstruation, 103; first (menarche), 100–105; and ritual seclusion (*chaul mbŭb*), 101, 104
mental health, 188
merit (*bŏn*), 34, 57, 92, 96; to make (*twee bŏn*), 47, 111–13; and rebirth, 66; to spread, 57–58, 161; to transfer, 58–61
middle class (*nĕak mean*), 11, 192–93, 218n12
middle path, 46, 48, 187–207
midwife (*chmâb*), 73
migration. See refugees, Khmer, migration to the United States
Mollica, Richard F., and Russell R. Jalbert, 188, 198
monastic rules (*vinaya*), 51
monks, 21, 26, 34, 48; daily activities of, 51; and education, 123, 124–25, 199, 201; as merit conduits, 47; as moral mentors, 125, 159; role on Precept Day, 56–58; and spirit beliefs, 37, 38; in the United States, 25–26, 28, 49, 50–51. See also Khmer Rouge, destruction of the *sângha*; ordination
moral education, 16, 92–93, 94–122; concept of, 14–15
moral identification, 14
Mortland, Carol A., 24, 36
Mortland, Carol A., and Judy L. Ledgerwood, 216n3
mother-child relationship, 69, 75–76, 80, 90–91
music, 162

names, use of, 85, 94. See also address, norms of
naming the child, 73
Narada, Thera, 56
Nepote, Jacques, 216n2
new people, 2
New Year (*Chaul Chnăm*), 31, 59, 113, 116
Nguyen-Hong-Nhiem, Lucy, and Joel M. Halpern, 209n2
nirvana (*nĕ' pean*), 43, 45, 47
non-governmental organizations (NGOs), 23

observing the child, 64, 65–66, 82–83, 214n14
offerings: at *Chaul Chnăm*, 59, 113; at *kåthĕn* (ceremony to give monks new robes), 35; to monks, 57 (*see also sâng*

khåtean); at Phchŭm Bĕn, 113; to spirits, 58, 70, 74, 163
ordination (buoh), 21, 35; in Cambodia, 48–49; conditions on, 47–48; and education, 26, 49; and merit, 48, 112–13; in the United States, 25, 26, 49, 50–51, 109. See also "Blessings of Ordination"; monks
Ortner, Sherry, 18, 65, 215n8
Ouk, Mory, Franklin E. Huffman, and Judy Lewis, 125, 126, 128, 130, 132, 138, 216n5

Pali language, 21, 25, 56, 138; borrowings in Khmer, 138–39. See also literature, Khmer
parent-child relationship, 95, 113–19, 187; during Pol Pot era, 2
patron-client relationship, 132, 216n3
pchâb piek (setting the word). See engagement
Peak, Lois, 13
Peletz, Michael G., 18, 19, 98, 215n1
People's Republic of Kampuchea, 6, 28
Phchum Bĕn (Souls' Day), 58, 59, 113, 116
Phillips, Herbert P., 62
Phnom Penh, evacuation of, 1
Piker, Steven, 81, 89, 96, 124
Pin Yathay, 209n2
Pol Pot, xi, 1, 2, 12, 36; "Brother Number One," 3. See also Khmer Rouge
politeness, 84, 86, 94. See also address, norms of
Ponchaud, François, 17, 86
Porée, Guy, and Evéline Maspero, 12, 216n3, 217n4
Portes, Alejandro, 191
Portes, Alejandro, and Ruben G. Rumbaut, 144, 188, 191, 216n8
praise, 90
Precept Day (Thngay Sĕl), 55–58
precepts, 35, 55, 57. See also Precept Day
pregnancy, 42, 62; and marriage, 180–81, 185. See also soul, and rebirth
puberty, 94, 95; for boys, 109–11; for girls, 100–106, 127. See also adolescence
purification ceremony (p'dâh kruoh), 37–38, 72

reflexivity. See identity, and reflexivity
Refugee Act of 1980, 8
refugee camps, 6–7, 23
refugees, Khmer: and adaptation, 16; migration to the United States, 8–9; population in greater metropolitan Boston, 11–12; resettlement in the United States, 9–10
reincarnation, 34, 43, 46; children's stories of, 78–81
release ceremony. See purification ceremony
religion: and cultural adjustment, 198–203; and education, 31. See also Buddhism
representatives: of the bride's family (méba), 160, 162, 164; of the groom's family (chav moha), 160, 162, 163, 164
reputation, 153–54, 155, 177; of the bride, 168–69. See also family, reputation
research: background, xii–xvi; interviews, xii, 209n1; methods, xii–xiii
resettlement. See secondary migration; United States, law and resettlement policy
residence patterns, 11. See also secondary migration
respect, 92–93; for monks, x; for parents, 14, 95; for teachers, 130–31. See also address, norms of
ritual, 58. See also achaa; menstruation, and ritual seclusion; soul, ritual to recall; weddings, ritual foot washing and ritual of obeisance
rules for boys (chbab proh), 106–7
rules for girls (chbab srey), 99–100, 105, 183
Rumbaut, Ruben G., 144, 149, 216n8
Rumbaut, Ruben G., and Kenji Ima, 149, 192
runaways, 182, 190, 192, 196

safekeeping the child (pǐ' thy prâkåk kaun), 72–74
såmdach sâng (supreme patriarch), 27, 28
sângha (monastic order): in Cambodia, 21, 28; destruction of, 21. See also council of monks; temple
sâng khåtean (feeding the monks), 35, 38, 59–60, 114–15
Schieffelin, Bambi, and Elinor Ochs, 13, 214nn10,16
schooling: of boys in Cambodia, 124–29; of elders in Cambodia, 129–32; of girls in Cambodia, 125–29; in the United States, 132–35 (see also bilingual education)
schools: in Cambodia, 130; in the United States, 133–35

Schwartz, Theodore, 13
Scott, George M., Jr., 32
secondary migration, 9, 10
segmented assimilation, 191
sex education, 102, 215n4
sexual double standard, 175. *See also* sexuality
sexuality, 18, 97, 104, 154, 164–65, 166
Shawcross, William, 1, 214n11
Sheehy, Gail, 209n2
sheltering of young women, 100, 154, 176. *See also* menstruation, and ritual seclusion
Shweder, Richard A., Manomohan Mahapatra, and Joan C. Miller, 13, 14, 18, 120
siblings, 78, 85, 89, 214n18
sin (*băb*), 42–43, 69, 82–83, 112. *See also* reincarnation
Sino-Vietnamese, 12, 144, 149
Sizemore, Russell F., and Donald K. Swearer, 201
social order, 84, 85, 139. *See also* language, Khmer, and social status
socialization, 13–14; and gender, 17–18, 97–98 (*see also* gender); inherent tension in, 121–22; and Khmer Buddhism, 64–65, 77, 78; of young children, 121–22
sons: discipline of, 107; duties of, 107–9, 121; ritual responsibilities, 111; upbringing of, 106–11. *See also* boys
soul (*prâlŏeng*), 41–42, 212n15; loss, 41, 74–75, 101–2, 212n16; and rebirth, 42, 66–67; ritual to recall, 41
Souls' Day (*Phchŭm Bĕn*), 31, 113
spirit beliefs, 37, 101–2; and children, 68–72; and exorcism, 38; and the Khmer psyche, 37; and socialization, 64
spirits: ancestral (*méba*), 38–39, 40, 74 (*see also* ancestors); hungry (*prĕay*), 39, 40, 73, 211n12 (*see also* ghosts); and socialization, 64; territorial (*nĕak taa*), 38, 39–40; world of (*assaurâkkay*), 42. *See also* soul, and rebirth
Spiro, Melford E., 37
Stafford, Charles, 13
Steinberg, David J., 132, 139, 159, 176; on address, terms of, 84, 94; on Buddhism, 65; on childbirth, 213n1; on the monkhood, 21, 112, 124
Strand, Paul J., and Woodrow Jones, Jr., 8, 9, 126
students, in Boston schools, 9. *See also* education; schooling

suffering, 36, 43, 44, 45, 46. *See also* karma, and suffering
Swearer, Donald K., 201
Szymusiak, Molyda, 4, 209n2

Tambiah, Stanley J.: on Buddhism, 20, 37, 55, 205, 211nn7,9, 212n18; on merit, 13, 36, 47, 62; on the *sângha*, 27; on the soul, 42
Tapp, Nicholas, 32, 33
teachers, 123; as patrons, 132; role in Cambodia, 129–32. *See also krou*
teenagers, 196. *See also* adolescence; puberty
temple (*wat*): administration of, 27 (*see also* council of monks); attendance, 31; boys (*kaun sĕh lŏk*), 124; establishment in United States, 24, 25–27; under Khmer Rouge, 4, 21; role in Cambodia, 21, 29; role in the United States, 29–31, 34; schools, 125–26
Thai Sangha, 28
The Three Refuges, 56–57
toddlers, 89–90, 96, 98
toilet training, 76

United Nations High Commission for Refugees, 6, 23
United States: census, 10; law and resettlement policy, 9

values, 197, 198; of Khmer parents, 11–12, 15
Van Esterik, Penny, 16, 23, 54, 198, 199, 210n3, 212n15, 213nn24,8
vĕ' nhean (vital essence), 42. *See also* soul, and rebirth
Vickery, Michael, 24, 123, 126, 209nn1,2
Vietnamese: educational attitudes, 149; educational performance, 144; invasion of Cambodia, 4–5, 6; refugees, 8, 12; religion, 33; withdrawal from Cambodia, 28
Vigil, James Diego, 190
virginity, 19, 154
Vlahou, Toula, 209n3

wages, 96
wat. See temple
Watson, Rubie S., 216n2
weddings, 151–54; description of home

ceremony, ix–xii, 159–65; expense of, 152, 166–71, 206; monks' benediction (*saut maun*), 160–61; reception and banquet, 165–67; ritual foot washing (*leang choeung*), 161; ritual of obeisance (*phtoĕm*), 162; and status, 153; tying the wrists (*châng dai*), 163–64
Welaratna, Usha, 209n2
Westermeyer, Joseph, 198
Whitaker, Donald P., 125, 127, 134

Whiting, Beatrice, and Carolyn Pope Edwards, 14
Whitmore, John K., Marcella Trautmann, and Nathan Caplan, 144, 149
Willis, Paul, 196
Wood, Susan P., 17, 64, 107, 125
Wuthnow, Robert, 202

Yang Sam, 27
yeichi, x, 54–55, 113, 213n23

Compositor: Integrated Composition Systems, Inc.
Text: 10/13 Palatino
Display: Palatino